CSET Social Science

114
115
116

Teacher Certification Exam

By: Sharon A. Wynne, M.S.

XAMonline, INC.
Boston

To obtain permission(s) to use the material from this work for any purpose including workshops or seminars, please submit a written request to:

XAMonline, Inc.
21 Orient Avenue
Melrose, MA 02176
Toll Free 1-800-301-4647
Email: info@xamonline.com
Web: www.xamonline.com

Library of Congress Cataloging-in-Publication Data

Wynne, Sharon A.
    CSET Social Science 114, 115, 116/ Sharon A. Wynne.
    ISBN 978-1-64239-053-7

1. Social Science 114, 115, 116   2. Study Guides.   3. CSET
4. Teachers' Certification & Licensure.   5. Careers

Disclaimer:
The opinions expressed in this publication are the sole works of XAMonline and were created independently from the National Education Association, Educational Testing Service, or any State Department of Education, National Evaluation Systems or other testing affiliates.

Between the time of publication and printing, state specific standards as well as testing formats and website information may change that is not included in part or in whole within this product. Sample test questions are developed by XAMonline and reflect similar content as on real tests; however, they are not former tests. XAMonline assembles content that aligns with state standards but makes no claims nor guarantees teacher candidates a passing score. Numerical scores are determined by testing companies such as NES or ETS and then are compared with individual state standards. A passing score varies from state to state.

Printed in the United States of America   œ-1

CSET Social Science 114, 115, 116
ISBN: 978-1-64239-053-7

TABLE OF CONTENTS

Study and Testing Tips

In the preface, emphasis was placed upon the idea of focusing on the right material, in other words, *what* to study in order to prepare for the subject assessments. But equally important is *how* you study.

learning (lurn'ing) n. 1. the acquiring of knowledge of or skill in (a subject, trade, art, etc.) by study; experience, etc. 2. to come to know (of or about) 3. acquired knowledge or skill. *(Definition courtesy of Webster's New World Dictionary of the American Language, 1987)*

What we call "learning" is actually a very complicated process built around multi-faceted layers of sensory input and reinforcement.

When you were a child, learning largely consisted of trial and error experimentation, (i.e. don't touch that, it's *hot*! Or this tastes *good*!). But as we grow older and the neurotransmitters within our brain develop, learning takes on deeper, subtler levels. As adults the neural pathways are fully in place, allowing us to make abstract connections, synthesizing all of our previous experiences (which is essentially what knowledge is), into tremendously complicated, cohesive thoughts.

However, you can increase your chances of truly mastering the information by taking some simple, but effective steps.

Study Tips:

1. Some foods aid the learning process. Foods such as milk, nuts, seeds, rice, and oats help your study efforts by releasing natural memory enhancers called CCKs (*cholecystokinin*) composed of *tryptophan*, *choline*, and *phenylalanine*. All of these chemicals enhance the neurotransmitters associated with memory. Before studying, try a light, protein-rich meal of eggs, turkey, and fish. All of these foods release the memory enhancing chemicals. The better the c connections, the more you comprehend.

Likewise, before you take a test, stick to a light snack of energy boosting and relaxing foods. A glass of milk, a piece of fruit, or some peanuts all release various memory-boosting chemicals and help you to relax and focus on the subject at hand.

2. Learn to take great notes. A by-product of our modern culture is that we have grown accustomed to getting our information in short doses (i.e. TV news sound bites or USA Today style newspaper articles.)

Consequently, we've subconsciously trained ourselves to assimilate information better in neat little packages. If your notes are scrawled all over the paper, it fragments the flow of the information. Strive for clarity. Newspapers use a standard format to achieve clarity. Your notes can be much clearer through use of proper formatting. A very effective format is called the **Cornell Method:**

> Take a sheet of loose-leaf lined notebook paper and draw a line all the way down the paper about 1-2" from the left-hand edge.

> Draw another line across the width of the paper about 1-2" up from the bottom. Repeat this process on the reverse side of the page.

Look at the highly effective result. You have ample room for notes, a left hand margin for special emphasis items or inserting supplementary data from the textbook, a large area at the bottom for a brief summary, and a little rectangular space for just about anything you want.

3. **Dissect the material.** Too often we focus on the details and don't gather an understanding of the concept. However, if you simply memorize only dates, places, or names, you may well miss the whole point of the subject.

A key way to understand things is to put them in your own words. If you are working from a textbook, automatically summarize each paragraph in your mind. If you are outlining text, don't simply copy the author's words, **rephrase** them in your own words. You remember your own thoughts and words much better than someone else's, and subconsciously tend to associate the important details to the core concepts.

4. **Turn every heading and caption into a question.** Pull apart written material paragraph by paragraph and don't forget the captions under the illustrations.

Example: If the heading is "Stream Erosion," flip it around to read: "Why do streams erode?" Then answer the questions.

If you train your mind to think in a series of questions and answers, not only will you learn more, but it also helps to lessen the test anxiety because you are used to answering questions.

5. **Read, Read, Read.** Even if you only have 10 minutes, put your notes or a book in your hand. Your mind is similar to a computer; you have to input data in order to have it processed. *By reading, you are storing data for future retrieval.* The more times you read something, the more you reinforce the storage of data. Even if you don't fully understand something on the first pass, *your mind stores much of the material for later recall.*

6. **Create the right study atmosphere.** Our bodies respond to an inner clock called biorhythms. Burning the midnight oil works well for some people, but not everyone. If possible, set aside a particular place to study that is free of

distractions. Shut off the television, cell phone, pager and exile your friends and family during your study period.

If you really are bothered by silence, try background music. Not rock, not hip-hop, not country, but classical. Light classical music at a low volume has been shown to aid in concentration. Don't pick anything with lyrics; you end up singing along. Try just about anything by Mozart, generally light and airy, it subconsciously evokes pleasant emotions and helps relax you.

7. <u>**Limit the use of highlighters.**</u> At best, it's difficult to read a page full of yellow, pink, blue, and green streaks. Try staring at a neon sign for a while and you'll soon see my point; the horde of colors obscure the message. A quick note, a brief dash of color, an underline, and an arrow pointing to a particular passage is much clearer than a horde of highlighted words.

8. <u>**Budget your study time.**</u> Although you shouldn't ignore any of the material, *allocate your available study time in the same ratio that topics may appear on the test.*

Testing Tips:

1. <u>**Don't outsmart yourself. Don't read anything into the question.**</u> Don't make an assumption that the test writer is looking for something else than what is asked. Stick to the question as written and don't read extra things into it.

2. <u>**Read the question and all the choices *twice* before answering the question.**</u> You may miss something by not carefully reading, and then re-reading both the question and the answers.

If you really don't have a clue as to the right answer, leave it blank on the first time through. Go on to the other questions as they may provide a clue as to how to answer the skipped questions. If later on, you still can't answer the skipped ones . . . *Guess.* The only penalty for guessing is that you *might* get it wrong. Only one thing is certain; if you don't put anything down, you will get it wrong!

3. <u>**Turn the question into a statement.**</u> Look at the way the questions are worded. The syntax of the question usually provides a clue. Does it seem more familiar as a statement rather than as a question? Does it sound strange?

By turning a question into a statement, you may be able to spot if an answer sounds right, and it may also trigger memories of material you have read.

4. <u>**Look for hidden clues.**</u> It's actually very difficult to compose multiple-foil (choice) questions without giving away part of the answer in the options presented. In most multiple-choice questions you can often readily eliminate one

or two of the potential answers. This leaves you with only two real possibilities and automatically your odds go to fifty-fifty for very little work.

5. Trust your instincts. For every fact that you have read, you subconsciously retain something of that knowledge. On questions that you aren't really certain about, go with your basic instincts. **Your first impression on how to answer a question is usually correct.**

6. Mark your answers directly on the test booklet. Don't bother trying to fill in the optical scan sheet on the first pass through the test.

Just be very careful not to miss-mark your answers when you eventually transcribe them to the scan sheet.

7. Watch the clock! You have a set amount of time to answer the questions. Don't get bogged down trying to answer a single question at the expense of 10 questions you can more readily answer.

Are these tips foolproof? *No.* The Educational Testing Service (ETS) test writers are well versed in the "art" of writing assessments, and very seldom present "flawed" (read very easy to dissect) questions.

However, by applying these tips, you can generally improve your odds of making the right choices.

DOMAIN 1   WORLD HISTORY

COMPETENCY 1.1   ANCIENT CIVILIZATIONS

Skill 1.1a   Describe what is known of the early physical and cultural development of humankind from the Paleolithic era to the agricultural revolution, explaining how the methods of archeology and anthropology contribute to the understanding of prehistory.

Prehistory is the earliest time of human existence. Human ancestors are believed to have developed 4-6 million years ago, yet the earliest written records only go back about 4,500 years ago. How do you we know about the time in between? We have some knowledge about prehistory from anthropology and archeology.

ANTHROPOLOGY is the scientific study of human culture and humanity. Anthropologists study different groups and how they relate to other cultures. Through cross-cultural and comparative research, anthropologists can find patterns of behavior, similarities, and differences. While anthropologists often study and learn about people and cultures by living among them and observing, paleo-anthropologists look at artifacts to understand early human culture.

ARCHAEOLOGY is the scientific study of past human cultures by studying the remains they left behind—objects such as pottery, bones, buildings, tools, and artwork. Archaeologists locate and examine evidence to help explain the way people lived in past times. They use special equipment and techniques to gather evidence.

Archaeologists survey sites and make a detailed description of the site with notes, maps, photographs, and artifacts from the surface. Excavation is used to find physical evidence below the surface. Evidence is preserved for eventual classification, dating, and evaluating.

Sources of knowledge about early humans come from

- Bones from burial pits
- Fossils found in rock deposits
- Artifacts, such as tools, pottery, and cave paintings
- Studies of living primates

Archaeological and anthropological research tells us that the earliest humans developed in Africa between 2 to 6 million years ago. **Homo sapiens** evolved from these early humans around 2 millions years ago. Some migrated first into

Asia and later into Europe. Further understanding of prehistory is helpful by classifying it into archaeological periods.

Paleolithic Age (early human history to 10,000 BCE)
The earliest period of human history is the Old Stone Age or **Paleolithic** Age. It is known as the Stone Age because tools were made from chipped stone. They used hatchets, awls, needles, and cutting tools.

Paleolithic humans demonstrated great adaptability living in nomadic hunter-gatherer societies. It's not clear when language began to develop, but there was likely communication even before language as we know it developed.. They left behind cave paintings, but the purpose of those paintings isn't known.

Neolithic Age (10,000 BCE – 3,000 BCE)
Artifacts of the New Stone Age, or **Neolithic Age** included polished stone tools, domesticated animals, the wheel, and the first appearance of agriculture. Pottery and textiles have been found dating to the end of the New Stone Age. These artifacts suggest that humans of this age had begun to form small communities with dwellings.

Bronze Age (3300 BCE-1,300 BCE)
The **Bronze Age** is identified by the first uses of metal to make tools and weapons. It is also concurrent with the establishment of what are believed to be the first civilizations.

By 4000 BCE, humans lived in villages, engaged in animal husbandry, grew grains, sailed in boats, and practiced religions. Earliest civilizations arose in the fertile river valleys of the Nile, Mesopotamia, the Indus, and the Hwang Ho.

Iron Age (1,300 BCE- 900 BCE)
The Iron Age, followed quickly on the heels of the Bronze Age and was characterized by the use and working of iron for various applications.

It is generally believed that prerequisites of civilization include the following

- Use of metals rather than stone for tools and weapons
- A system of writing
- Agriculture
- Shared religions or philosophies
- Labor or social class divisions
- Political organizations
- Pursuit of knowledge and artistic expression

Skill 1.1b **Describe and analyze the impact of human interaction with the physical environment (e.g., climate, landforms, soils, water) on the development of the ancient cultures of the Fertile Crescent (e.g., Sumerian, Babylonian, Hebrew), Persia, Egypt, Kush, Greece, India, China, Rome, and pre-Columbian America.**

Many of the earliest known civilizations were river-valley civilizations and are known as **fluvial civilizations**. Geography and the physical environment played a critical role in the rise and the survival of both of these civilizations.

Rivers provided a source of water that would sustain both human and animal life. Hunters had access to a variety of animals, initially to provide food. Parts of the animals: hides, bones, antler could be used for clothing, tools and art. Some animals began to be herded and husbanded to provide a stable supply of food and animal products.

Rivers in these regions overflowed their banks each year, leaving behind a deposit of very rich soil. Early people in these areas began to experiment with growing crops rather than gathering food because of the fertile soil and available water. They developed systems of irrigation that channeled water to the crops without significant human effort on a continuing basis.

Asia

One of the earliest civilizations developed in the **Tigris-Euphrates Valley** of Mesopotamia (mainly modern Iraq) between 4000 BCE and 3000 BCE. Mesopotamia, located between the Tigris and Euphrates, meant "land between the rivers."

Mesopotamia was bounded on the West by the Mediterranean Sea, on the South by the Arabian Desert, on the north by the Taurus Mountains, and on the east by the Zagros Mountains.

Mesopotamia had a nickname, the Fertile Crescent from the fertile soil and its crescent shape. The designation "Fertile Crescent" was applied by the famous historian and Egyptologist James Breasted to the part of the Near East that extended from the Persian Gulf to the Sinai Peninsula.

East of the Zagros Mountains, another culture developed in what would later become Iran. This civilization was called Persia or the Achaemenid Empire. The Caspian Sea was to the north and the Persian Gulf to the South. It was also a fertile land. The many tribes of Persia were semi-nomadic and may have herded livestock. They eventually built homes, first from available mud and later stone.

Also between 4000 BCE and 3000 BCE, another civilization began around the Indus River of today's northern India. Farming settlements began in the Indus Valley.

Many of the earliest known civilizations were river-valley civilizations and are known as **fluvial civilizations**. Geography and the physical environment played a critical role in the rise and the survival of both of these civilizations.

Chinese culture developed around the same time. The first people settled around the Yellow River. Villages were created. The culture was successful in agriculture. They raised silkworms, which allowed them to produce silk for clothing. The use of crop rotation and terrace farming proved useful and they became proficient in the growing of rice. This early culture made tools and weapons from copper.

Africa

Another ancient culture was Egypt, which developed south of the Mediterranean Sea. This North African culture is dominated by the largest hot desert in the world, the Sahara. People settled around the Nile, one of the largest rivers in the world. The Nile River would flood the valley from July to September, leaving behind a layer of alluvial soil good for agriculture. Due to limited rainfall, they developed irrigation techniques that allowed them to grow food like barley, lentils, and figs. Other important crops were papyrus for making paper, ropes, and sandals and flax for making linen for clothing. Animals were also domesticated

South of Egypt was the Kush culture, also known as Nubia (northern Sudan). This early culture also settled around the Nile and grew barley, fruits, and vegetables. Date palms were an important crop for trade as well.

Europe

The earliest cultures in Europe were the Greek, Roman, and Macedonian cultures. In Greece, settlement is believed to have started on Crete, the largest of the Greek Islands. Surrounded by mountains, inland rivers provided water needed for agriculture around 2500 BCE. Other groups developed, most notabiliy the Minoans and Mycenaean.

The Macedonian culture began in river valleys near the Balkan Mountains around 700 BCE. Roman culture started around the same time near the Tiber River.

Mesoamerica

Mesoamerica was a region in the Americas including the southern half of Mexico and Central America. This is where pre-Columbian cultures began around 2500 BCE. Unlike the other ancient civilizations, this area didn't originate in river valleys. This is most likely due to the region's moderate rainfall. There were highlands and lowlands bordered by the Pacific Ocean to the west and the Atlantic Ocean (Gulf of Mexico) to the east. Development began in the lowlands where the soil was most fertile. Around 500 BCE, corn or maize was domesticated.

Skill 1.1c   **Describe and analyze the religious, social, economic, and political structures of the ancient cultures of Mesopotamia, Persia, Egypt, Kush, Greece, India, China, Rome, and pre-Columbian America, and describe and analyze their intellectual, ethical, scientific, and artistic accomplishments and values.**

Ancient civilizations began from cultures that developed to a greater degree and were considered advanced. Each had its own major accomplishments. Trade was important to these civilizations.

Asia

The Sumerian, Amorite, Hittite, Assyrian, Chaldean, and Persian civilizations controlled various areas of Mesopotamia at different times. Mesopotamia was arranged as city-states. Each Sumerian city-state had its own god. The city-state's leader doubled as the high priest. Subsequent cultures also had a handful of gods but they had more of a national worship structure, with high priests centered in the capital city who advised the supreme leader, usually a king. One of those city-states was Babylon. The Babylonians devised the famous **Code of Hammurabi**, the first written code of laws that would later form the basis for our modern laws.

In addition to the Code of Hammurabi, other important things from these cultures include

- The first known use of writing called cuneiform writing
- Development of , the wheel and banking (Sumeria)
- The first written set of laws (Code of Hammurabi)
- The first epic story (*Gilgamesh*)
- The first library dedicated to preserving knowledge (instituted by the Assyrian leader Ashurbanipal)
- The Hanging Gardens of Babylon (built by the Chaldean Nebuchadnezzar)

The **Phoenicians** were sea traders, but were best known for creating purple dye. They were proficient sailors who could navigate by the stars. They devised the first known alphabet using symbols to represent single sounds. The Phoenicians were later assimilated into the Greek civilization.

Ancient **Assyrians** were warlike and aggressive, had a highly organized military, and used horse drawn chariots.

The **Hebrew** civilization was ruled by king. Also known as the ancient Israelites, this civilization instituted **monotheism**, the worship of one God. The Old Testament and Judaism derive from this civilization.

The social and political conditions of the Indus Valley civilization is believed to have been similar to Mesopotamia and Persia. There were kings, and a caste system would develop. Indus Valley cities were advanced with underground drainage and homes with wells and bathrooms. The major religions of Hinduism and Buddhism both are believed to have developed in the Indus Valley.

In **India**, industry and commerce developed along with extensive trading with the Near East. Indian goods found their way to western ports through trade with the ancient Mediterranean civilizations, including Rome. Outstanding advances in the fields of science and medicine were made. This civilization also developed the decimal system of the numbers 1-10.

Early Chinese civilizations were organized into dynasties. The first three of these were the Zia, Shank and Zhou dynasties. Rulers may have been called kings in the beginning, but were later referred to as emperors. A class system developed.

The Chinese studied nature and weather, stressed the importance of education, family, and a strong central government. The religions and philosophies of Confucianism and Taoism came from Chinese culture. Inventions include gunpowder, paper, printing, currency, and the magnetic compass.

China built the **Great Wall** and developed caravan routes across Central Asia for extensive trade. These routes are known as the **Silk Road**. They became proficient at producing beautiful artworks and exporting them, along with silk, to the rest of the world along the Silk Road. They developed a written language based on more than 3,000 symbols.

Africa
Egyptian and Phoenician cities were powerful and regular trading partners of the various Mesopotamian cultures.

Egypt's significant contributions include the **Great Pyramids at Giza**, hieroglyphic writing, preservation of bodies after death, making paper from papyrus, creating a solar calendar; and laying the foundation for science and astronomy.

The earliest historical record of **Kush** is from Egyptian sources. The region upstream from the first cataract of the Nile is described as wretched and characterized by life in fortified mud-brick villages that subsisted on hunting and fishing, herding cattle, and gathering grain. The Kush civilization appears to be the second-oldest in Africa after Egypt. They appear to have spoken Nilo-Saharan languages in the area called Nubia. The capital city was Kerma, a major trading center between the northern and southern parts of Africa.

Kushite society was organized on the Egyptian model. The Kushites adopted Egyptian royal titles and Egyptian architecture, but with smaller and steeper pyramids.

In a magnificent irony of history the Kushites conquered Egypt in the eighth century, creating the twenty-fifth dynasty. The dynasty ended in the seventh century when Egypt was defeated by the Assyrians.

The Kushite ruler was a **female monarch** elected from the royal family and ruled through a law of custom that was interpreted by priests. Descent was determined through the mother's line (as in Egypt). Their religion was polytheistic, including all of the primary Egyptian gods and regional gods derived from other African cultures. This civilization was strong through the first millennium BC, but it suffered about 300 years of gradual decline until it was conquered by the Nuba people.

The civilizations in **Africa** south of the Sahara developed the refining and use of iron, especially for farm implements and later for weapons. Trading was overland, using camels who traveled to important seaports. Later on the Arab influence was extremely important, as was their later contact with Indians, Christian Nubians, and Persians.

Europe
The classical civilization of **Greece** was based on the foundations already laid by such ancient groups as the Egyptians, Phoenicians, Minoans, and Mycenaeans. Extensive trading and colonization resulted in the spread of the Greek civilization.

The **Minoans** had a system of writing using symbols to represent syllables in words. They built palaces with multiple levels containing many rooms, water and sewage systems with flush toilets, bathtubs, hot and cold running water, and bright paintings on the walls. The **Mycenaeans** changed the Minoan writing system to aid their own language and used symbols to represent syllables.

The modern **Olympic Games** came from the ancient Greek civilization. Greek mythology, centered around a pantheon of gods and the mortals they interacted with, has been the source of inspiration for literature. The Greek alphabet, derived from the Phoenicians, formed the basis for the Roman alphabet and our present-day alphabet.

Greeks influenced drama, epic and lyric poetry, fables, myths centered on the many gods and goddesses, science, astronomy, medicine, mathematics, philosophy, art, architecture, and recording historical events. The works of the Greek epic poet **Homer** are considered the earliest in western literature. The tradition of the theater was born in Greece, with the plays of **Aristophanes** and others. **Pythagoras** and **Euclid** laid the foundation of geometry and Archimedes calculated the value of pi. **Herodotus** and **Thucydides** were the first to apply research and interpretation to written history. The Greeks were also noted for the arts and sculpture.

Alexander the Great was the Macedonian king. He spent much of his rule conquering Europe, the Middle East, and Egypt. He spread Greek/Macedonian ideas to the areas he conquered and shared Asian philosophies and ideas from the countries he conquered.

The ancient civilization of **Rome** lasted approximately 1,000 years, including the periods of Republic and Empire, but its lasting influence was much longer. The Romans spread and preserved the ideas of ancient Greece and other culture groups. Their contributions and accomplishments are numerous but their greatest included language, engineering, building, law, government, roads, trade, and the **Pax Romana.** The Pax Romana was the long period of peace enabling free travel and trade, spreading people, cultures, goods, and ideas all over a vast area of the known world.

Mesoamerica

The people who lived in the Americas before Columbus arrived had a thriving, connected society. Civilizations formed as knowledge and capabilities with agriculture grew. Religion was an important part of life with religious leaders having a great deal of power. In some civilizations, human sacrifice was part of the beliefs. Mesoamerican civilizations tended to evolve into empires, with the strongest city or tribe assuming control of the lives and resources of the rest of the nearby peoples.

The most well-known empires of the Americas were the Aztec, Inca, and Maya. Each had a central capital with an emperor. The empires traded among each other when they weren't at war. The **Aztecs** had access to large numbers of metals and jewels and created weapons and artwork. The **Inca Empire** stretched across the western coast of South America and was connected by a series of roads. A series of messengers ran along these roads, carrying news and instructions from the capital, Cusco. The **Mayas** are known for their famous pyramids, calendars, and their language.

In what would become the Southwest United States, ancient Pueblo people settled, building homes on the mesas and the cliffs. They practiced agriculture and engaged in trade. Some of their cities, such as Chaco, became quite large.

Skill 1.1d   **Describe and analyze the foundations of western political and philosophical thought in ancient Greek, Roman, and Judeo-Christian traditions.**

Ancient Greece is often called the "**Cradle of Western Civilization**" because of its enormous influence on the Roman civilization and later all of Western culture. Rome contributed a republican form of government that it established in 509 BCE to limit how much power one person could have.

Greece is often called the birthplace of democracy because the **Athenian form of democracy** with each citizen having an equal vote in his own government is a philosophy upon which all modern democracies are based. This is why many U.S. government buildings are built in the Greek architectural style.

In philosophy, **Aristotle** developed an approach to learning that emphasized observation and thought, and **Socrates** and **Plato** contemplated the nature of being and the origins and ideals of government and political relations.

Judaism and **Christianity** are two **monotheistic** religions that grew during the time of ancient civilizations. Along with Islam, these religions promoted the worship of one god.

Judeo-Christian traditions created a powerful legacy of political and philosophical traditions, much of which survives to this day.

The Israelites was not the first ancient civilization to have a series of laws for its people, but their **Ten Commandments** were revolutionary because they applied to everyone. Similar to the Code of Hammurabi and Rome's Twelve Tables, the Ten Commandments provided a written record of laws, so all knew what was prohibited.   **(See also Skill 1.1c)**

Skill 1.1e   **Describe and analyze the foundations of Asian political and philosophical thought found in ancient Chinese and Indian traditions (e.g., Legalism, Taoism, Confucianism, Hinduism, Buddhism).**

The Indus Valley civilization (India and Pakistan) is where Hinduism developed.

It was begun by people known as Aryans (not related to the 20th century Aryans) who migrated into the Indus Valley around 1500 BCE. The Aryans blended their culture with the culture of the Dravidians, the natives they conquered. Today, Hinduism continues to be a polytheistic religion with many sects and promotes the belief in reincarnation. Though forbidden today by law, a prominent feature of Hinduism in the past was a rigid adherence to a caste system.

Buddhism developed in India from the teachings of Siddhartha Gautama around 500 BCE. Spreading throughout Asia, Buddhism stressed being free of attachment to all things worldly and devoting of self to finding release from life's suffering. This religion opposed the worship of numerous deities, the Hindu caste system, and the supernatural.

Other important religions originated in China,

Confucianism is based on the teachings of the Chinese philosopher Confucius. There is no clergy, no organization, and no belief in a deity or in life after death. Confucianism is a social and political philosophy more than a religion. It emphasizes political and moral ideas with respect for authority and ancestors. Rulers were expected to govern according to high moral standards.

Taoism is a native Chinese philosophy that combined with traditional folk religion. And as such, it has more deities than almost any other religion. It teaches all followers to make the effort to achieve the two goals of happiness and immortality. Practices and ceremonies include meditation, prayer, magic, reciting scriptures, special diets, breath control, beliefs in witchcraft, fortune telling, astrology, and communicating with the spirits of the dead.

Legalism was a classical school of thought in Chinese philosophy during the Warring States (5th–3rd century BCE) period. It was based on the need for political reform, and its principles were used by China's first emperor. It focused on achieving order and remains influential today.

Shinto is the native religion of Japan based on both good and bad spirits living in animals, trees, and mountains. According to its mythology, deities created Japan and its people. The first emperor was believed to be the grandson of the sun goddess. Shinto was strongly influenced by Buddhism, which became the state religion around 580 CE.

Skill 1.1f	**Describe and analyze the importance and patterns of expansion and contraction of empires, religions, and trade that influenced various regional cultures through the decline of the Roman Empire.**

The first empire in history is believed to be Mesopotamia, started by the Akkadians, led by Sargon, conqueror of Sumeria. He was succeeded by other leaders of other sects, such as the Amorite leader Hammurabi, for whom the famous Code is named. Another leader was Nebuchadnezzar, leader of the Chaldeans, who built the Hanging Gardens of Babylon. He is also known for the capture of and transport of the ancient Israelites, known as the Babylonian captivity. Other rulers of the Fertile Crescent include the warrior-tribes the Hittites and the Assyrians. The Middle East empire-building phase didn't really begin until Darius the Great came onto the scene.

The Persian Empire began under the rule of Cyrus the Great, who began conquering other lands. A later emperor, **Darius** expanded the Persian Empire, until it stretched from Egypt to the boundaries of India.

The Egyptian empire covered north Africa. Because of Egyptian goods and trade centers, other rulers often tried to take over Egypt.

As the Persian Empire grew, it set Greece as a goal. The Greeks referred to these battles as the Persian Wars. Specific battles were at Marathon, which the Greeks won despite being vastly outnumbered. Thermopylae, where a valiant group of Spartans held off thousands of Persian warriors for several days. Salamis, a naval battle that the Greeks won despite being outnumbered, and Plataea, where the Greeks sealed the deal by finally outnumbering the Persians. These victories convinced the Persians not to attempt another invasion of Greece, but it didn't mean the end of the Persian Empire. **(See Skill 1.1c).**

No one could match the Macedonian general and leader known as **Alexander the Great,** who conquered both Greece and Persia, eventually adding Egypt, Phoenicia, and part of India to his empire. This empire more than any other resulted in cultural exchange that was known as **Hellenization.** It brought the Greek enlightened way of life to the Eastern civilizations while also bringing the exotic goods and customs of the East to Greece.

Rome was a later, but perhaps the most successful of the ancient empires, building itself from the western coast of Italy to a worldwide empire stretching from Scotland to the Middle East.

Building on the principles of Hellenization, Rome imported and exported goods and customs, melding the production capabilities and the belief systems of all it conquered into a heterogeneous yet distinctly Roman civilization. Trade, religion, science, political structure all expanded in the Roman Empire. **(See Skill 1.1d)**

The official end of the **Roman Empire** came when Germanic tribes conquered most of Europe. The five major tribes were the Visigoths, Ostrogoths, Vandals, Saxons, and the Franks. In later years, the Franks successfully stopped the Muslim invasion of southern Europe by defeating them under the leadership of Charles Martel at the Battle of Tours in 732 CE. Thirty-six years later in 768 CE, his grandson, **Charlemagne,** became King of the Franks. Charlemagne was a man of war, yet respected and encouraged learning. He made great efforts to rule fairly and ensure just treatment for his people.

COMPETENCY 1.2   MEDIEVAL AND EARLY MODERN TIMES

Skill 1.2a   **Analyze the impact of geography, including both human and physical features, on the development of medieval and early-modern Asian, African (including sub-Saharan), Middle Eastern, pre-Columbian American, and European civilizations.**

As civilizations developed through the Middle Ages and early-modern times, changes occurred in communication, exploration, politics, and business. Mountains and rivers had formed formidable boundaries for ancient civilizations. But when transportation began to expand it opened up the world.

Especially in the deserts of northern Africa and the jungles of South America, people depended on rivers and lakes for their very survival, both for drinking water and for growing crops. People also lived near waterways because they depended on those waterways for trade. The larger the boats, the more they could carry, which increased the efficiency of trade. Bigger and faster ships and advances in navigation allowed people to explore, trade, and conquer new lands across oceans. Foods and spices that previously were nonexistent in the markets of Europe, because they would spoil before they ever reached their destination, were increasingly for sale.

Following the success of roads in the Roman Empire, more and more people built serviceable roads, making land-based trade easier and an alternative to water trading. In the Americas, some canoes were used along coastlines, but some empires were landlocked, so roads were necessary for trade.

People began to move around more. And with the moving came the spreading of diseases such as the **Black Plague.**

In Europe during this period, the **castle** was a dominant feature on the landscape throughout the country. Castles housed kings, soldiers, retinues, and peasants. They also served as watchtowers, guardhouses, and barracks. In a way, the castle was the new high ground. In battles of old, the army that held the high ground held the advantage because its opponents would have to tire themselves out running uphill just to engage, while the high ground holders could pepper them with rocks, arrows, and other airborne weapons.

Walled cities were popular as defensible positions throughout history, but they weren't as easy to create as castles were and they couldn't be as easily defended. By building castles, the people of these periods changed their landscape to create an advantage.

The landscapes of the world changed because people changed them. Where broad plains had been before, towns and villages, castles and fortifications, ports and trade centers dotted the landscape. The populations of the world continued to expand, with people always seeking to expand their living spaces and the demand for basic and exotic goods. As civilization spread outward from its beginnings in the Fertile Crescent, ancient Africa, and along the rivers Indus and Yangtze, the needs of mankind spread out with it.

Skill 1.2b **Trace the decline of the Western Roman Empire and the development of the Byzantine Empire, and analyze the emergence of these two distinct European civilizations and their views on religion, culture, society, and politics.**

Byzantine Empire

The Roman Empire split in the early fourth century. The Eastern Roman empire was closer to Asia, farther away from Germany, and easier to defend. It assimilated many religions and traditions from the Middle East.

The early religion of the Empire was one of many gods, representing the various parts of Nature and the skies. As Rome conquered various peoples with varied religions, the Empire assimilated the religions of those peoples. By the time that the Eastern Empire was created, it was a melting pot of faiths. Christianity began its dominance when Emperor Constantine made it the state religion in 312 CE.

The more centralized Eastern Empire became the **Byzantine Empire.** Uniquely situated at the gateway to both West and East, Byzantium could control trade going in both directions. The Byzantines were more rigid in enforcing policies.

The **Byzantine** and **Saracenic** (or Islamic) civilizations were both dominated by religion. The major contributions of the Saracens were in the areas of science and philosophy, including accomplishments in astronomy, mathematics, physics, chemistry, medicine, literature, art, trade and manufacturing, agriculture, and a marked influence on the Renaissance. The Byzantines (Christians) made important contributions in art and the preservation of Greek and Roman achievements including architecture, the Code of Justinian, and Roman law.

Western Roman Empire

The Western Roman Empire was based more on ancient Greece. Its decline resulted from a variety of factors, including the increasing sprawl of the Empire, Germanic and other "barbarian" foes, and dissatisfaction among the non-ruling classes.

Skill 1.2c **Describe the role and expansion of Christianity in medieval and early modern Europe and the Middle East.**

Early modern Europe became a Christian continent with the fall of Rome. Christianity unified Europe, and the Church became very powerful. Roman Catholicism had the Pope as the leader. Other leaders within the Church, such as bishops, also retained a great degree of power. At times the Church battled for power with kings.

The church was the only place where people could be educated. The Bible and other books were hand-copied by monks in the monasteries. Cathedrals were built and were decorated with religious art.

Christianity also encouraged knights to travel to the Holy Land (present day Israel) and battle Muslims for control of Jerusalem. These battles were known as the Crusades. On the march to Jerusalem, the Crusaders would massacre the inhabitants of Jewish villages they passed through. Large slaughters occurred in Speyer and Worms and other Rhineland towns. Violent conflicts took place, but it also exposed the Crusaders to other religions, cultures, and new ideas.

Skill 1.2d   Identify the basic tenets of Islam, and describe Islamic society and culture between the beginning of the 7th century and the end of the 18th century.

The prophet **Mohammed** was born in 570 CE in a small Arabian town called Mecca near the Red Sea. Arabia was a vast desert of rock and sand, except the coastal areas on the Red Sea. It had been populated by nomadic wanderers called **Bedouins**, who lived in scattered tribes near oases where they watered their herds. The family or tribe was the social and political unit under the authority of the head of the family.

Religion was mainly superstitious paganism and idolatry. There was regular contact with Christians and Jews through trade interactions but the idea of monotheism was foreign. The most important of these was a small square temple called the **Kaaba** (cube), located in the town of **Mecca**. Arabs made annual pilgrimages to Mecca during the sacred months when warfare was prohibited. For this reason, Mecca was considered the center of Arab religion.

In 610, **Mohammed** began teaching and speaking publicly about the word of God, heard from the angel Gabriel. Mohammed called his new religion **Islam** (submission to the will of God) and his followers were called **Muslims** (those who submit). When Muslims began to make their faith public, they met with opposition and persecution from the pagan Arabians.

Islam slowly gained ground, and the persecutions became more severe around Mecca. In 622, Mohammed and his close followers fled the city and found refuge in **Medina** to the North. His flight is called the **Hegira**. This event marks the beginning of the Muslim calendar. Mohammed took advantage of the ongoing feuds between Jews and Arabs in the city and became a leader in Medina.

In the early years of Islam, religious leaders worked closely together. As time passed, their roles became more separate. Followers of Islam grew, and in 630, they followed Mohammed to Mecca. Mecca was made the religious center of Islam, toward which all Muslims turn to pray. Medina remained the political capital.

Islam after Mohammed
After Mohammed's death in 632, his followers gathered all writings based on his divine revelations (**surahs**) delivered by the angel Gabriel. These were published

in a book called the **Qur'an** (also sometimes spelled as Koran). This is considered the holy scripture of Islam.

Islam has five basic principles, known as the **Pillars of Islam**

- The oneness and omnipotence of God—**Allah**
  - Mohammed is the prophet of Allah to whom all truth has been revealed by God
  - To each of the previous prophets (Adam, Noah, Abraham, Moses and Jesus) a part of the truth was revealed
- One should **pray five times a day** at prescribed intervals, facing Mecca,
- **Charity**—for the welfare of the community
- **Fasting** from sunrise to sunset every day during the holy month of Ramadan to cleanse the spirit
- **Pilgrimage to Mecca** should be made if possible and if no one suffers thereby

Mohammed drew upon Christianity, Judaism, and Arab paganism. The resulting doctrine was a mixture of ideas that is original when taken as a whole. It appealed to both the simple Arab of the prophet's day and to the faith of more civilized people. Mohammed died without either a political or a religious succession plan. His successor took the title of **Caliph**. The title was retained throughout the duration of the Muslim Empire.

Muslim Conquests
The Muslim-Arabians launched a series of conquests which, in time, extended the empire from the Indus River Valley to Spain. An aristocratic family of Mecca called the **Umayyad** later became caliphs, and the family ruled for nearly a century. Their strongest support was in Syria, and the capital was moved from Medina to Damascus.

The Umayyads had always represented Arabia rather than broader Muslim interests. More devout Muslims, especially in Persia, were unhappy with their rule. They turned to the **Abbasid** family who were descended from Mohammed's uncle. The Abbasid dynasty overthrew the Umayyad family in 750, although an Umayyad emir continued to rule in Spain. This group then became separated from the rest of the empire. Persia replaced Syria as the center of the empire, and the capital was moved from Damascus to Baghdad.

The Arab aristocracy was succeeded by a mixed official aristocracy drawn from all of the Muslim nations. The caliphs modeled themselves after the Persian kings. Muslim civilization became a composite of Arabs, Persians and Greeks who were united by the teachings of Islam and the Arabic language. The Abbasid dynasty ushered in a period of great prosperity and absolute power that lasted for about 75 years. It was during the reign of Haroun al Rashid (786–809) that the caliphate reached its greatest power. Baghdad was one of the richest cities in the world. The center of an empire that reached from central Asia to the Atlantic. But the empire was too large and its people too diverse to be held together by a single individual for very long. Shortly after Haroun's reign, the caliph began to lose power and the empire began to disintegrate. This continued through the tenth century.

In Egypt, a descendant of Mohammed's daughter (Fatima) founded the caliphate of Cairo. From 945 to1055 the caliphs of Baghdad were completely dominated by a Persian dynasty of emirs until they were conquered by the Seljuk Turks who had come from central Asia and adopted Islam with fanatical zeal. The Turkish emirs and sultans ruled for 200 years, reviving the political strength of the empire for a time. It was the Turkish emirs who dealt with the crusaders. Finally, in the middle of the thirteenth century they were overcome by a fresh invasion from Asia—the Mongols.

In less than 100 years, Islam had spread across the whole of northern Africa and into Spain.

Despite these political divisions, the Muslim world maintained strong economic, religious and cultural unity throughout this period. This blending of cultures, facilitated by a common language, a common religion, and a strong economy created learning, literature, science, technology, and art that surpassed the Western Christian world during the Early Middle Ages.

Schools were attached to the mosques and mosques offered advanced education in literature, logic, philosophy, law, algebra, astronomy, medicine, science, theology and the tradition of Islam. Books were produced for the reading public. The wealthy collected private libraries, and public libraries arose in large cities.

Muslim armies repeatedly marched north in an effort to spread their religion and influence into Europe. The only reached as far as Spain, however they controlled Palestine and Jerusalem, considered by Christians as the **Holy Land**. In a series of campaigns and battles that have been collectively called the **Crusades**, European armies sailed and marched to the Holy Land in attempts to return the Holy Land to European hands.

Skill 1.2e **Analyze the religious and secular contributions of Islam to European, African and Asian civilizations and the impact of medieval Muslim civilization on Asia, Africa, and Europe between the beginning of the 7th century and the end of the 18th century.**

Islam's religious, economic, and cultural contributions to Europe, Africa, and Asia are many and varied.

Theology, philosophy, and the law were important subjects in Islam. The works of the Greek and Hellenistic philosophers were translated into Arabic and interpreted with commentaries. These were later passed on to Christian societies and schools in the twelfth and thirteenth centuries. The basis of Muslim philosophy was Aristotelian and Neo-platonic ideas, which were essentially transmitted without creative modification.

The Muslim world was also interested in natural science. The works of Galen and Hippocrates were translated into Arabic and they adopted the work of the Greeks in the other sciences and modified and supplemented them with their own discoveries. The Muslim doctor **Al-Razi** was one of the most well-known physicians in the world and was the author of a medical encyclopedia and a handbook for smallpox and measles.

The Muslims adopted the heritage of Greek mathematics and borrowed a system of numerals from India, laying a foundation for modern arithmetic, geometry, trigonometry and algebra.

Their art and architecture tended to be mostly uniform in style, allowing for some regional modification. They borrowed from Byzantine, Persian and other sources. The floor plan of the mosques was generally based on Mohammed's house at Medina. The notable unique element was the tall **minaret** from which the faithful were called to prayer. Interior decoration was in the style now called **arabesque**. Mohammed banned paintings or other images of living creatures. These continued to be absent from mosques, although they occasionally appeared in book illustration and secular contexts. Their skilled craftsmen produced the finest art in jewelry, ceramics, carpets, and carved ivory.

The Muslims produced sophisticated literature in prose and poetry. Little of their poetry or prose, however, was carried down by Western culture. The best-known works of this period are the short stories known as the **Arabian Nights** and the poems of **Omar Khayyam**.

The Muslim religion was important to the poor residents of Arabia and northern Africa, who were starving and had little hope of a better life.

One major contribution from Muslim culture was to improve methods of **irrigation**. As a result, more food became available. The existing canals of the Middle East were extended, bringing much-needed resources to people living in the arid areas of the Arabian Peninsula.

Muslim trade centers and goods became known in other parts of the world. Goods were distributed by boats, Arabian horses, and camels, the **ships of the desert**.

Muslim merchants made a name for themselves with their shrewd business practices. They were some of the first businessmen to take checks and give receipts. We can trace the terms *bazaar, tariff*, and *caravan* to them.

Skill 1.2f Analyze and compare and contrast the development of feudalism as a social, political, and economic system in Europe and Japan.

Europe

During the Middle Ages, **feudalism** dominated the economic and social system in Europe. Feudalism began as a way to ensure that nobility could raise an army when needed. In exchange for the promise of loyalty and military service, **lords** would grant a section of land, called a **fief,** to a **vassal**, who took an oath of loyalty. The vassal was then entitled to work the land and benefit from its proceeds or to grant it in turn as a fief to another. At the bottom of this ladder were **peasants** or **serfs** who actually worked the land. At the top was the king to whom all lands legally belonged. The king or ruler ensured loyalty among his advisers by giving them use of large sections of land which they in turn could grant as fiefs.

Feudalism was a system of loyalty and protection. The strong protected the weak who returned the service with farm labor, military service, and loyalty. Improved tools and farming methods made life more bearable although most serfs never left the manor or traveled from their village during their lifetime. The lord or noble, in return for the serfs' loyalty, offered them his protection. The serf was considered property owned by his lord with little or no rights at all. The lord's sole obligation to the serfs was to protect them so they could continue to work for him. This system would last for many centuries in Europe and Japan. In Russia, feudalism lasted until the 1860s.

Manorialism, which also arose during the Middle Ages, overlapped with feudalism. It was a system of economic, social, and political organization for a rural economy. Manors usually consisted of a large house for the lord and his family, surrounded by fields and a small village that supported the activities of the manor. The lord of the manor enjoyed rights over the peasants through serfdom. And the peasants were dependent upon the lord and manor.

Because land is a finite resource, and the population continued to grow, the manorial/feudal system became less effective as a system of economic organization. The end of the feudal manorial system was sealed by the outbreak and spread of the infamous **Black Death**, which killed over one-third of the total population of Europe. Those who survived and had skills in demand found freedom and an improved standard of living.

With the increase in trade and travel, cities sprang up and began to grow. Craft workers in the cities developed their skills to a high degree, eventually organizing

guilds to protect the quality of the work and to regulate the buying and selling of their products. City government developed and flourished, centered around strong town councils. Wealthy businessmen who made up the rising middle class were active in city government and the town councils. Strong nation-states became powerful and people developed a renewed interest in life and learning.

Japan

Feudalism developed in Japan at the same time but independent of Europe. In the twelfth century, Mongol invasions in Japan were thwarted by typhoons called **kamikaze** or divine winds. Japan refrained from interacting with the West. This isolation, and thus the feudal system, lasted until the nineteenth century.

From its beginnings, Japan had an imperial form of government with an emperor serving for life. Yet the emperor held little real power. Instead, the most powerful person was the chief general or **shogun** of the emperor. **Kyoto**, the capital, became one of the largest and most powerful cities in the world. Slowly, the rich landowners, the nobles, grew powerful. Eventually, they had more power than the emperor.

Nobles who owned large amounts of land were called **daimyos**. They were of the highest social class and had peasants working for them.

Daimyos developed their own armies, who battled the armies of other daimyo. A warrior class developed, and the warriors were known as **samurai**. The samurai code of honor was an exemplification of the overall Japanese belief that every man was a soldier and a gentleman. Peasants served the samurai class.

The main economic difference between imperial and feudal Japan was that the money that continued to flow into the country from trade with China, Korea, and other Asian countries went into the pockets of the daimyos.

Skill 1.2g   Compare and contrast the geographic, political, economic, religious, and social structures of pre-Columbian American civilizations in North and South America between 500 and the end of the 18th century.

The indigenous people of the Americas shared some ways of life like living off the lands, deep spiritual practices, and a respect for nature. In general, North American tribes were distinct units with various political, social, and economic structures that depended upon geography and the number and origin of visitors from overseas.

North America

The North American landscape was hospitable to settlement and exploration. The North American continent, especially in what is now the United States, had a few mountain ranges and a handful of wide rivers but nothing like South

America's dense jungles or the high mountains of the Andes. The area that is now Canada was cold but otherwise conducive to settlement. As a result, the Native Americans in the northern areas of the Americas were more spread out and their cultures more diverse than their South American counterparts.

In North America, the Ancestral **Pueblo** dominated the American Southwest (from 100 CE-1600 CE). The Puebloans lived in distinct communities, each with its own ruler, often a priest of some kind. Each community contained many clans or family groups. Lineage was often matrilineal. In some civilizations like those at Chaco and Mesa Verde, cities and trade routes. Pueblo descendants continue living today, primarily in New Mexico and Arizona.

One of the oldest representative governments in the world is the **Iroquois Confederacy,** also known as the League of Five Nations. Around 1450, five Native American tribes of the Northeast (Cayuga, Mohawk, Oneida, Onondaga, and Seneca) decided to join together to establish peace and cooperation. A council of 50 chiefs was elected by the clan mothers. This group agreed on laws and customs of the Confederacy, called the Book of the Great Law. They also made decisions on how to deal with outside tribes or European groups who came to America. Each year, the tribal representatives met to restate laws and to settle differences. In the early 18th century, a sixth tribe, the Tuscarora, joined the confederacy. Some historians believed the Iroquois Confederacy was a model when the new government of the United States formed in the late 18th century.

For the North Americans, life was about finding food. People were first hunters and gatherers. Depending on the geographical location, native people hunted buffalo, deer, and smaller mammals for food and often clothing, tools, or shelters.

Some tribes began growing food and established semi-permanent communities. They grew such crops as **maize** or corn, plus squash, pumpkins, and beans. The only domesticated animal in early years were dogs. After the Spanish brought horses to the Americas, Plains people began to domesticate horses.

Native Americans who lived in the wilds of Canada and along the Pacific coast lived off the land and the nearby water. Fishing was a source of food and trade.

Religion or a strong spiritual life was common for most tribes. Many tribes had legends and myths that explained the creation of the world. But unlike Europe and Asia, religion was rarely used as a reason to go to war.

The native people north of Mexico varied widely in customs, housing, dress, and religion. Among the native peoples of North America there were at least 200 languages and 1500 dialects. Communication was achieved through similarities in dialects and non-verbal communication.

Mexico

The earliest known civilizations in the Americas existed in Mexico and Central America. The earliest known culture was the **Olmecs** (1200 BCE – 400 BCE) in what is now Mexico. We know little of their existence except a series of huge carved figures. It's believed that civilizations of the southern half of Mexico and Central American came from the Olmecs.

The largest and most successful civilization in Mexico were the **Aztecs.** The Aztecs had access to large amounts of metals and jewels, which they used to make weapons and jewelry. They also traded with other groups. When they weren't trading, they conquered neighboring tribes, which increased the size and riches of the civilization.

Aztecs were a polytheistic group who believed that the gods demanded human sacrifice in order to continue to smile on the Aztecs. The center of Aztec society was the great city-state of **Tenochtitlan**, built on an island in a lake, and which is today Mexico City. Tenochtitlan boasted a population of 300,000 at the time of the arrival of the Spanish conquistadors. It was known for its canals and its pyramids, none of which survive today.

The Aztec had many enemies, some of whom helped Spanish conquistador Hernan Cortés conquer the Aztec empire in 1519.

Central America

The most advanced Native American civilization was likely the **Mayan** from Central America. Mayan worship resembled the practices of the Aztec and Inca, although human sacrifices were rare. The Mayans also traded heavily with their neighbors. They developed the most sophisticated writing system of **glyphs** or **pictographs** in the Americas. In recent years, archaeologists have had success deciphering it.

The Mayans also built huge pyramids and other stone figures and sculptures, mostly of the gods they worshiped. The Mayans are known for their **calendars** and for their mathematics. The Mayan calendars were the most accurate on the planet until the sixteenth century. They may have been the first civilization to use zero.

South America

The **Inca** Empire stretched across a vast period of territory down the western coast of South America. The empire was connected by a series of roads. Messengers used these roads to carry news and orders from the capital, Cusco. The Incas are known for inventing the *quipu*, a string-based device that provided them with a method of keeping records. The Inca Empire, like the Aztec Empire, was a centralized state with all income going to the state coffers and all trade going through the emperor. The Incas worshiped the dead, ancestors, and nature and often took part in intricate rituals.

Skill 1.2h Analyze the geographic, political, economic, religious, and social structures of Asia and Africa between 500 and the end of the 18th century.

India

Between the fourth and ninth centuries, Asia was an area of empires ruled by religion, kings and emperors, wars, and contact with other cultures.

During this period, **India** was recovering from the invasion of Alexander the Great. **Chandragupta Maurya** conquered most of what we call India and began one of his country's most successful dynasties. His grandson, **Asoka**, was a more peaceful ruler but still powerful. He was also a great believer in the practices and power of Buddhism, sending missionaries throughout Asia to preach the ways of the Buddha. Succeeding the Mauryas were the Guptas, who ruled India for a longer period of time and brought prosperity and international recognition to its people.

The **Guptas** were great believers in science and mathematics, especially their uses in production of goods. They invented the decimal system and had a concept of zero, two things that put them ahead of the rest of the world on the mathematics timeline. They were the first to make cotton and calico, and their medical practices were much more advanced than those in Europe and elsewhere in Asia. These inventions and innovations created a high demand for Indian goods throughout Asia and Europe.

The idea of a united India continued after the Gupta Dynasty ended. The invading Muslims took over in the eleventh century, ruling the country for hundreds of years through a series of sultanates. The most famous Muslim leader of India was **Tamerlane**, who founded the Mogul Dynasty and began a series of conquests that expanded the borders of India. Tamerlane's grandson **Akbar** is considered the greatest Mogul. He believed in freedom of religion and is perhaps best known for the series of buildings that he had built, including mosques, palaces, forts and tombs. During the years Muslims ruled India, Hinduism continued to be respected, but became a minority religion. Buddhism, however, died out almost entirely from its country of origin.

The imposing mountains in north India served as a deterrent to Chinese expansion. India was more vulnerable to invaders who came from the west or by sea from the south. The Indian people were also vulnerable to the powerful monsoons, which came driving up from the south a few times every year, bringing howling winds and devastation in their wake.

China

China was a country ruled by dynasties controlling various parts of what is now China and Tibet. The **Tang Dynasty** (618-907) was an age or reform and invented the idea of civil service and block printing. Next was the **Song Dynasty**

(960-1279), which produced some of the world's greatest paintings and porcelain pottery. Buddhism declined, but Confucianism rose. Large cities developed and inventions included gunpowder. However, the Song Dynasty failed to unify China. This would prove instrumental in the takeover of China by the **Mongols**, led by Genghis Khan and his most famous grandson, Kublai.

Genghis Khan is known as a conqueror, and **Kublai** is known as a uniter. Both extended the borders of their empire and at its height, the Mongol Empire was the largest the world has ever seen, encompassing all of China, Russia, Persia, and central Asia.

Following Kublai Khan's death in 1294, the Mongols began to lose control of China. The **Ming Dynasty** (1368-1644) ruled successfully, focusing on isolation as did the **Qing Dynasty** (also called the Manchu Dynasty) that followed. As a result, China at the end of the eighteenth century knew very little of the outside world, and vice versa. The Ming Dynasty focused on undoing the damage from the Mongol invasion, although they kept the trade. They also concentrated on growing agriculture and the arts. Artists created beautiful porcelain pottery, but not much of it saw its way into the outside world until much later. The Qing Dynasty (formed 1636; ruled 1644-1912) was the last imperial dynasty of China. Achievements focused on learning, farming, and road-building in order to keep up with an expanding population. Confucianism, Taoism, and ancestor worship— the staples of Chinese society for hundreds of years — continued to flourish during this time.

Japan
Japan developed independently and tried to keep itself that way for hundreds of years. Early Japanese society focused on the emperor and the farm, in that order. Japan was influenced early by China, from which it borrowed many things, including religion (Buddhism), a system of writing, calendar, and even fashion. The Sea of Japan protected Japan from more Chinese and Mongol invasions; including the famous Mongol invasion that was blown back by a typhoon known as the "divine wind."

The power of the emperor declined as it was usurped by the era of the daimyo and soldiers, known as **samurai**. Japan flourished economically and culturally during these years, although the policy of isolation kept the world from knowing such things. Buddhism and local religions were joined by Christianity in the sixteenth century. It wasn't until the mid-nineteenth century that Japan became a world power.

Africa
The Sahara desert and other inhospitable lands restricted African settlements to a few select areas outside of Egypt and northern coastal Africa. Islam had already spread into these areas, and Islamic traders spread the religion through their travels, primarily along the coast of West Africa.

The Kingdom of Zimbabwe (1220-1450) was a kingdom in southern Africa. Its capital, Great Zimbabwe, was a successful trading center. The city is the site of the largest stone dwellings in pre-colonial southern Africa.

More successful was **Ghana**, a Muslim-influenced kingdom that arose in West Africa during the ninth century and lasted for nearly 300 years. Ghanaians had large farms and raised cattle and elephants. They traded with people from Europe and the Middle East. Ghana, along with its neighbor, Mali (1200-1450) had much gold, drawing Islamic traders. The Mali trade center **Timbuktu** grew as a trading post on the trans-Saharan caravan route. The succeeding civilization of the **Songhai** in Mali had relative success in maintaining that trade.

Skill 1.2i   Analyze the art, literature, music, science, and technology of the Renaissance and their diffusion and impact throughout Europe.

The word **Renaissance** literally means "rebirth" and followed the Middle Ages, which some began referring to as the Dark Ages. The Renaissance signaled the rekindling of interest in classical Greek and Roman civilizations. The feudal system declined and was replaced by a focus on artistic and intellectual development. Philosophically, it was a time that put humans at the center instead of religion. It was a cultural revolution, and in the areas of art, literature, music, and science, the world changed for the better.

The Renaissance is believed to have started in Florence. The **Medici** family is sometimes referred to as the Godfathers of the Renaissance because they encouraged great artists and thinkers. Education, especially for some of the merchants, required reading, writing, math, the study of law, and the writings of classical Greek and Roman writers.

Renaissance artists had a lasting impact in Western culture, including Giotto and his development of perspective in paintings; **Leonardo da Vinci** who was a scientist and inventor; **Michelangelo** who was a sculptor, painter, and architect. Other artists include Raphael, Donatello, Titian, and Tintoretto. All of these men pioneered a new method of painting and sculpture—portraying real events and real people as they really looked, not as the artists imagined them to be. One need look no further than Michelangelo's *David* to illustrate this.

Attention was also on literature during the Renaissance. **Humanists**, a group that included **Petrarch, Boccaccio, Erasmus**, and **Sir Thomas More**, advanced the idea of human life on earth and the opportunities it can bring, rather than a constant focus on heaven and its rewards. The monumental works of **Shakespeare, Dante,** and **Cervantes** found their origins in these ideas as well as the ones that drove the painters and sculptors. These works became even more available and popular with the invention of the printing press, which occurred during the Renaissance.

In Germany, Gutenberg's invention of the **printing press** with movable type facilitated the rapid spread of Renaissance ideas, writings and innovations, thus ensuring the enlightenment of most of Western Europe. Contributions were also made by Durer and Holbein in art and by Paracelsus in science and medicine.

The Renaissance also altered music. Music was still composed for the church, but the style expanded, and secular music began to be composed as well. Composers often had patrons who supported them.

Science advanced considerably during the Renaissance, especially in the area of physics and astronomy. **Copernicus, Kepler,** and **Galileo** led a Scientific Revolution in proving that the earth was round, a revelation to medieval and church view of a geocentric universe. Galileo was charged with heresy and sentenced to house arrest for the remainder of his life.

Other contributions of the Italian Renaissance period were in:

Political philosophy - the writings of **Machiavelli**

Medicine - the work of Brussels-born **Andrea Vesalius** earned him the title of "father of anatomy" and had a profound influence on the Spaniard **Michael Servetus** and the Englishman **William Harvey**

The Renaissance ushered in a time of curiosity and learning that expanded people's world view and encouraged exploration. The work of geographers, astronomers and mapmakers studied and applied the work of such men as Hipparchus of Greece, Ptolemy of Egypt, Tycho Brahe of Denmark, and Fra Mauro of Italy.

Skill 1.2j   Analyze the political and religious transformations caused by the Reformation and their impact on Europe.

Following the Renaissance was the Reformation, which began in Germany but quickly spread throughout Europe. The Reformation came about due to dissatisfaction with the Catholic Church. The Reformation period consisted of two phases: the **Protestant Reformation** or **Revolution** and the **Catholic Reformation**.

Protestant Reformation
The Protestant Reformation started because of religious, political, and economic reasons. The religious reasons stemmed from abuses in the Catholic Church: fraudulent clergy with scandalous lifestyles, the sale of religious offices, indulgences (the idea that you could purchase a remission of sin), and general corruption.

The political reasons for the **Protestant Reformation** came from the increase in the power of rulers who were considered absolute monarchs, who desired power and control over the Church. The growth of **nationalism** or patriotic pride in one's own country was another contributing factor.

Economic reasons included the greed of ruling monarchs to possess and control all lands and wealth of the Church, the deep animosity against the burdensome papal taxation, the rise of the affluent middle class and its clashing with medieval Church ideals, and the increase of an active system of intense capitalism.

The Protestant Revolution began in Germany with the revolt of **Martin Luther** against Church abuses. It spread to Switzerland where it was led by **John Calvin**. They called for a reform of religion, which led to the development of **Protestantism**. It gathered momentum in England when the Church refused King Henry VIII's request for an annulment of his marriage to Catherine of Aragon. In 1534, the Anglican Church was born with the king as its leader.

Catholic Reformation

The **Catholic Reformation** was undertaken by the Church to slow or stop the Protestant Revolution. The major efforts to this end were the Council of Trent where Catholics tried unsuccessfully to bring Protestants back to the church and founded the Jesuit order.

Six major results of the Reformation included
1. More opportunities for education
2. Limited power and control of rulers
3. Increase in religious wars
4. Increase in fanaticism and persecution

Skill 1.2k   **Analyze the historical developments of the Scientific Revolution and the ideas of the Enlightenment and their effects on social, religious, political, economic, and cultural institutions.**

Scientific Revolution

The Scientific Revolution and the Enlightenment were two of the most important movements in the history of civilization, resulting in a new sense of self-examination and a wider view of the world than ever before.

The **Scientific Revolution** was a shift in focus from belief to evidence. Scientists and philosophers wanted proof, not just to have faith in what people had always said. Theories and beliefs had to be proven with evidence, and the **Scientific Method** was born.

A Polish astronomer, **Nicolaus Copernicus**, launched the Scientific Revolution when he argued that the Sun, not the Earth, was the center of a solar system and that other planets revolved around the Sun, not the Earth. This flew in the face of established doctrine. Copernicus crystallized a lifetime of observations into a book that was published around the time of his death.

Danish astronomer **Tycho Brahe** was the first to catalog his observations of the night sky. Building on Brahe's data, German scientist **Johannes Kepler** instituted his theory of planetary movement and his famous Laws of Planetary Movement. Using Brahe's data, Kepler confirmed Copernicus's observations that the Earth revolved around the Sun.

The most famous defender of this idea was **Galileo Galilei**, an Italian scientist who conducted many famous experiments in the pursuit of science. He is best known, however, for his defense of the **heliocentric** (sun-centered) idea. He wrote a book comparing the two theories based on his own observations with the relatively new invention — the telescope. He observed four of Jupiter's moons revolving around Jupiter. They certainly did not revolve around the Earth, so why should everything else? The Church was still powerful enough to place Galileo under house arrest.

Galileo died under house arrest, but his ideas didn't die with him. Picking up the baton was an English scientist named **Isaac Newton**, who became perhaps the most famous scientist of all. He is known as the discoverer of gravity and a pioneering voice in the study of optics (light), calculus, and physics. Newton proved the idea of a mechanistic view of the world.

Enlightenment
The Scientific Revolution and Reformation naturally led to the **Enlightenment**, a period of intense self-study that focused on ethics and logic over religion. Scientists and philosophers questioned cherished truths and widely held beliefs in an attempt to discover why the world worked. "I think, therefore I am" ("Cogito ergo sum" in Latin) was a famous sayings from the Enlightenment. It was uttered by **Rene Descartes**, a French scientist-philosopher whose dedication to logic and the rigid rules of observation were a blueprint for the thinkers who came after him.

Another of the giants of the era was Scotland's **David Hume**. A pioneer of the doctrine of empiricism and was a proponent of skepticism. He was naturally suspicious of things that other people told him to be true and constantly set out to discover the truth for himself. These two related ideas influenced a great many thinkers after Hume, and his many writings continue to inspire philosophers to this day.

Immanuel Kant of Germany was a philosopher who took a definitely scientific view of the world. He wrote the movement's most famous essay, "Answering the Question: What Is Enlightenment?" For Kant, the human being was a rational being capable of hugely creative thought and intense self-evaluation. He encouraged all to examine themselves and the world around them. He believed that the source of morality lay not in the nature of the grace of God but in the human soul itself. He believed that man believed in God for practical, not religious or mystical, reasons.

Talk expanded to the rights of the individual as being more important than the aristocracy, which set the stage for the French and American revolutions. A popular idea from the Enlightenment was the **social contract**, the belief that government existed because of the people. The people had an agreement with the government that they would submit to it as long as it protected them and didn't encroach upon their basic human rights. This idea was first introduced by the French philosopher Jean-Jacques Rousseau, but was adopted and explored by England's John Locke and Thomas Hobbes.

John Locke was one of the most influential political writers of the seventeenth century. He put great emphasis on human rights and believed that when government violated those rights people should rebel. He wrote "Two Treatises of Government" in 1689. The book influenced political thought in the American colonies and helped shaped the new U.S. government.

COMPENTENCY 1.3   MODERN WORLD HISTORY

Skill 1.3a   Describe and evaluate the significance of the "Age of Exploration," and the main ideas of the Enlightenment and their influences on social, political, religious, and economic thought and practice.

The **Age of Exploration** (also known as the Age of Discovery) began in the mid-1500s, but had its beginnings centuries before exploration actually took place. The rise and spread of Islam in the seventh century and its subsequent control over Jerusalem led to the holy wars known as the Crusades. Although the Crusades were not a success, those who survived and returned to their homes in Western Europe brought new products such as silks, spices, perfumes, new and different foods.

The revival of interest in classical Greek art, architecture, literature, science, astronomy, medicine during the Renaissance increased trade between Europe and Asia. Ideas and new ways of looking at the world from the Enlightenment were aided by the invention of the printing press, which spread those ideas and knowledge. People wanted to see and experience the world.

For centuries, various mapmakers made maps and charts to describe the world. This also stimulated curiosity. At the same time, the Chinese were using the magnetic compass in their ships. Pacific Islanders were going from island to island, covering thousands of miles in open canoes navigating by sun and stars. Arab traders were sailing the Indian Ocean in their **dhows**.

Trade routes between Europe and Asia were slow and difficult. It took months and even years for the exotic luxuries of Asia to reach the markets of Western Europe. Initially, they were controlled by the Italian merchants in **Genoa** and **Venice**. The **Vivaldo brothers** and **Marco Polo** wrote of their travels, fascinating experiences and new information about exotic lands, people, customs, and desired foods and goods, such as spices and silks. Other countries began looking for cheaper travel and shorter travel routes.

Prince Henry the Navigator of Portugal encouraged, supported, and financed Portuguese seamen who led in the search for an all-water route to Asia. A shipyard was built and navigation was taught. New sailing ships were built that could carry the seamen safely on the ocean waters. The Portuguese experimented with new maps, navigational methods, and instruments. New instruments like the **astrolabe** and the **compass** enabled sailors to determine direction, latitude, and longitude for exact locations.

Prince Henry died in 1460, but the Portuguese continued exploring Africa's west coastline. In 1488, **Bartholomeu Dias** and his men were the first to sail around Africa's Cape of Good Hope.

The Portuguese were successful in reaching India ten years later when **Vasco da Gama** and his men continued the route of Diaz. They rounded Africa's Cape of Good Hope, sailed across the Indian Ocean, and reached India's port of Calicut (Calcutta), proving Asia could be reached from Europe by sea. Another Portuguese explorer, **Ferdinand Magellan,** is credited with the first circumnavigation of the earth.

Christopher Columbus, sailing for Spain, has been credited with the discovery of America although he never set foot on its soil and America was already inhabited by Native Americans. Other Spanish and Portuguese explorers made their marks in parts of the Americas. The British and French followed. European countries claimed the lands by establishing colonies.

France's claims to North America were the result of the efforts of such men as **Champlain, Cartier, LaSalle, Father Marquette** and **Joliet.** Dutch claims were based on the work of **Henry Hudson. John Cabot** gave England its stake in North America. Other English explorers included **John Hawkins, Sir Francis Drake,** and the half-brothers **Sir Walter Raleigh and Sir Humphrey Gilbert.**

The Norsemen led by **Eric the Red** and later, his son Leif the Lucky, were the first Europeans in the New World.

The Age of Exploration and the colonization of the New World allowed people suffering from poverty and persecution places to start new and better lives.

The Age of Exploration led to the development of better maps and charts and improved navigational instruments. It led to increased knowledge, great wealth, and new and different foods and items not previously known in Europe. It was also proof that Asia could be reached by sea and that the earth was round.

With the increase in trade and travel, cities began to grow. Craft workers developed their skills to a high degree, eventually organizing guilds to protect the quality of the work and regulate the buying and selling of their products. City governments developed and flourished.

Skill 1.3b   Compare and contrast the American Revolution and the French Revolution and their enduring worldwide effects on political expectations for self-government and individual liberty.

The American Revolution and the French Revolution were similar yet different. In addition to both occurring in the last half of the 18th century, both promoted the liberty of the common people and a republican government. They were both influenced by new political ideology from the Enlightenment. And both are considered turning important turning points in history.

Several important differences need to be emphasized

1. The American colonists were striking back against unwanted taxation and other government interference. The French people, many who didn't have enough to eat, were striking back against an autocratic regime.
2. The American Revolution involved years of battles, skirmishes, and stalemates. The French Revolution was bloody to a degree but mainly an overthrow of society and its outdated traditions.
3. The American Revolution resulted in a representative government. The French Revolution resulted briefly in five republics plus a consulship, emperor, and monarchy again.

After more than one hundred years of mostly self-government, many colonists resented the increased British control and and policies like taxation without representation. The **American Revolution** resulted in the American colonists achieving independence from Great Britain.

The **French Revolution** was a revolution of social classes within a single country. The middle and lower classes revolted against the political and economic excesses of the rulers and nobility. Conditions that led to revolt included extreme taxation, inflation, lack of food, and the disregard of the rulers, nobility, and Church toward the people. It ended with the establishment of the first in a series of French Republics.

Skill 1.3c   Describe and analyze the emergence of nationalism in the 18th and 19th centuries and its impact on Western, African, and Asian societies.

Nationalism is loyalty to a nation, but it's also a political ideology that has political, economic, and social effects. During the eighteenth and especially the nineteenth centuries, **nationalism** emerged as a powerful force in Europe and the United States. Taken to the extreme, countries can use nationalism as a right to impose its rules and values on other countries.

Nationalism led to countries like Germany and Russia to expand into nearby countries. Other European countries began to expand into Africa, and Asia and benefit from sources of goods, trade, and cheap labor. Africa, especially, suffered at the hands of European imperialists. Asia, too, suffered colonial expansion, most notably in India and Southeast Asia.

And in the United States, nationalism led to Westward Expansion and a war with Mexico to claim land America believed it was entitled to.
Colonial expansion would come back to haunt the European imperialists as colonial skirmishes spilled over into alliances that dragged the European powers into World War I.

Skill 1.3d   Analyze the causes and effects of the Industrial Revolution, including its impact on science, technology, and society.

The **Industrial Revolution** began in Great Britain in the 18th century and eventually spread through Western Europe. Steam and coal-powered machinery led to the accelerated growth of the manufacturing industry. Peoples' lives changed drastically as a largely agricultural society changed to an industrial one. Industrialization fueled colonization as industrialized nations seized raw materials from Africa and Asia to feed industry.

The Industrial Revolution was a transition from an agrarian, handicraft economy to one dominated by industry and machine manufacturing. Industrial changes led to new building materials, energy sources, inventions, and advances in transportation and communication.

The Industrial Revolution was largely confined to Britain from 1760 to 1830 and then spread to Belgium and France. Once Germany, the United States, and Japan achieved industrial power, they advanced beyond Great Britain's initial successes. Eastern European countries lagged into the 20th century, and finally to China and India.

Symbolic of the industrial revolution was the use of **coal** as a source of energy. The conversion of coal to a high carbon fuel called coke made cheaper iron ore smelting possible and simultaneously produced gas lighting. Coal-fueled boilers provided steam-power for factory machinery and locomotives. This allowed goods like cotton textiles to be made cheaply in large quantities, thus increasing availability.

Social changes occurred with industrialization. Many new jobs were created between the later 18th and the mid-19th century, but they were mainly in cities where the factories were located. Large numbers of people migrated to cities. 14 million immigrants arrived in the United States between 1860 and 1900. Urban areas grew rapidly leading to overcrowding and unsanitary conditions.

Industrialization led to economic, political, and social changes. Wealthy industrialists grew richer while the workers labored in factories with dangerous conditions and for low pay. Labor movements formed to argue for better working conditions and an end to child labor.

Industrialization also allowed the countries to be more accessible through transportation options like railroads and steamboats, and communication from telegraphs.

Skill 1.3e   Describe the emergence and origins of new theories regarding politics, economics, literature, and the arts in the 18th, 19th, and 20th centuries.

The overriding theme of life during the eighteenth through the twentieth centuries was progress. Technological advancements brought changes in all aspects of life. Businesses presented opportunities. New ways of thinking impacted politics and the arts. Mark Twain coined the term, the Gilded Age, to describe the social problems beneath a layer of gold.

The driving forces in politics in the eighteenth century were **nationalism** and **liberalism**. Liberalism is the belief that government should support rapid social changes in order to correct social and economic inequalities. Nationalism is an ideology that promotes the welfare of the nation-state over all other considerations, even to the detriment of other peoples. The eighteenth century ended with the American and French Revolutions, which overthrew monarchies in favor of representative governments. These two driving forces dominated the political landscape of the nineteenth and twentieth centuries, with nearly the entire map of Europe being rewritten in a wake of nationalist fervor.

Communism was a major political and economic ideology adopted by the Soviet Union plus China, North Korea, and Vietnam. In communism, society was to be classless with private ownership replaced with public ownership. Communist states controlled most aspect of society, including religion and economics. The government owned factories, ports, machines and ships. This kind of economic theory was in stark contrast to the famous **laissez faire** policy that occupied much of the Western nations during the 1700s, 1800s, and 1900s.

Another impetus that drove many political actions during this time was **colonization**. European powers carved up Africa in the search of greater resources. Asia fell under the yoke of European occupation, as did Central and South America. The United States and Russia became involved in an ongoing struggle that culminated in the Cold War. Differences in political ideology along with the effects of colonialism led to nearly every major war during these 200 years.

Progress also touched the worlds of literature and art. The main development in the nineteenth century was **Romanticism**, an emphasis on emotion and the imagination that was a direct reaction to the logic and reason stressed in the Age of Enlightenment. Famous Romantic authors included **John Keats, William Wordsworth, Victor Hugo,** and Johann Wolfgang von **Goethe**. The horrors of the Industrial Revolution gave rise to the famous realists **Charles Dickens, Fyodor Dosteovsky, Leo Tolstoy,** and **Mark Twain**, who described life as they saw it, for better or for worse.

Twentieth century authors stressed individual action and responsibility. The giants of the 1900s include: **James Joyce, T.S. Eliot, John Steinbeck, Ernest Hemingway, William Faulkner,** and **George Orwell**, all of whom expressed distrust at the power of machines and weapons and most of modern society.

The most famous artistic movement of the 1800s was **Impressionism**. The idea was to present an impression of a moment in time on canvas. Famous impressionists include: **Monet, Degas, van Gogh, Manet, Cezanne,** and **Renoir**.

Pablo Picasso, the young Spanish painter revolutionized art in the early twentieth century with the **Cubism**, which exaggerated perspective and people and things in a way never before seen. A Russian painter, Vasili Kandinski, created what is believed to be the first completely abstract painting.

Following Cubism, a variety of art movements emphasizing different things. Surrealism aimed to depict the subconscious mind on canvas. Dadaism, explored formlessness and mocked the materialistic. Pop art, made famous by **Andy Warhol,** celebrated popular culture.

Skill 1.3f   Analyze the economic, political, social, and geographic factors contributing to the emergence of 19th-century imperialism, and evaluate its impact on Africa, Southeast Asia, China, India, Latin America, and the Philippines.

Land signified power during the 19th century, and European nations wanted more. By the 19th century **European imperialism** was also fueled by the urgent demand for the raw materials needed for the Industrial Revolution. One of the main places for European imperialist expansion was Africa. **Britain, France, Germany,** and **Belgium** claimed countries in Africa. The resources, including people, were then shipped back to the mainland and claimed as colonial gains. The Europeans reasoned that they were educating "savages."

Southeast Asia, particularly Vietnam, was another area of French expansion. India and China were colonized by Great Britain. Yet clashes with the Chinese dynasties led to the British taking over the Hong Kong territory instead. Great Britain, France, and Spain occupied countries in Latin America, including the Caribbean Islands. Spain seized the rich lands of the Philippines.

The time from 1830 to 1914 was characterized by the extraordinary growth and spread of patriotic pride in a nation along with intense, widespread imperialism.

Skill 1.3g   Compare and contrast the social, political, and economic factors that influenced the Russian Revolutions of 1905 and 1917.

Until the early years of the twentieth century Russia was ruled by a succession of **Czars** (also spelled Tsars). Czars were autocratic rulers of Russia in the years before 1917.

Russian society was essentially feudalistic and was structured in three levels. The top level was the czar. The second level was composed of the rich nobles who held government positions and owned vast tracts of land. The third and largest level of the society were the peasants or serfs who lived in poverty. Several unsuccessful attempts to rebel occurred during the 19th century but they were quickly suppressed. The two revolutions of the early twentieth century, in 1905 and 1917, however, had different results.

Discontent with the social structure, living conditions of the peasants, and working conditions despite industrialization were among the causes of the **1905 Revolution**. This general discontent was aggravated by the **Russo-Japanese War** (1904–1905) that led to inflation. Peasants began to starve. Many Russian troops were killed in battles due to poor leadership, lack of training, and inferior weaponry. Czar Nicholas II refused to end the war despite setbacks. An important port, Port Arthur, fell to the Japanese in January, 1905. Japan's victory was complete a couple of months later.

In the same month that Port Arthur fell, trade union leader Father Gapon, organized a protest to demand better working conditions and pay for workers. More than 150,000 peasants joined a demonstration outside the Czar's **Winter Palace**. Before the demonstrators spoke, the palace guard opened fire on the crowd in what would be called the Bloody Sunday Massacre. The people's trust in the Czar was lost, and massive protests and strikes followed.

The strikes eventually brought the Russian economy to a halt. Czar Nicholas II agreed to sign the **October Manifesto** which created a constitutional monarchy, extended some civil rights, and gave the parliament limited legislative power. In time, the Czar disbanded the parliament and violated the promised civil liberties.

The violation of the October Manifesto led to the **1917 Revolution**. There were other factors as well. Defeats during World War I (WWI) caused discontent, loss of life, and a popular desire to withdraw from the war. WWI had also caused a surge in prices and scarcity of many items. Most of the peasants could not afford to buy bread.

In addition, the people believed that the government leaders were incompetent. Czar Nicholas II listened to his wife Alexandra for advice. She was strongly influenced by a self-proclaimed holy man, **Rasputin**, also known as the Mad Monk.

Workers in Petrograd went on strike in 1917 over the need for food. The Czar ordered troops to suppress the strike but the troops sided with the workers. The revolution then took a unique direction. The parliament created a provisional government to rule the country. The military and the workers also created their own governments called **soviets** (popularly elected local councils). The parliament, composed of nobles, soon lost control of the country when they failed to comply with the wishes of the populace.

The most significant differences between the 1905 and 1917 revolutions were the formation of political parties, the use of propaganda, and the support of the military in 1917. The political leaders who had previously been driven into exile returned. **Lenin, Stalin,** and **Trotsky** won the support of the peasants with the promise of "Peace, Land, and Bread." The parliament, on the other hand, continued the country's involvement in the war. Lenin and the **Bolshevik Party** gained the support of the **Red Guard** and together overthrew the provisional government, gained complete control of Russia and established a communist state.

Skill 1.3h. **Analyze the origins and course of World War I and its effects on Europe and the rest of the world, including its impact on science, technology, the arts, politics, society, economics, and geography.**

Imperialistic colonization for industrial raw materials, military build-up (especially by Germany), and diplomatic and military alliances were among the factors that led to World War I. The spark that set off the explosion took place in June, 1914, when a Serbian national assassinated **Archduke Ferdinand**, the heir to the Austro-Hungarian Empire, and his wife as they visited the Balkan city of Sarajevo. The assassin belonged to a Serbian independence movement. War began a few weeks later. Eventually nearly 30 nations were involved, and the war didn't end until 1918.

World War I introduced the use of tanks, airplanes, machine guns, submarines, poison gas, and flame throwers. Fighting on the Western front was characterized by a series of **trenches** that were used throughout the war. After WWI, poison gas would be outlawed in the Geneva Protocol of 1925.

At the Paris Peace Conference, Germany was subjected to harsh reparations, and required to pay the other countries for damages from the war. Germany's arms and territories were taken away. In America, President Wilson lost in his efforts to get the U.S. Senate to approve the peace treaty, which would have made the U.S. a member of the League of Nations.

There were 32 nations involved in the war, not including colonies and territories. It began July 28, 1914 and ended November 11, 1918 with the signing of the Treaty of Versailles. Economically, the war cost a total of $337 billion. Inflation was high, and a huge war debt led to a loss of markets, goods, jobs, and factories.

Politically, old empires collapsed, and new boundaries were drawn. New, independent nations were formed and some predominately ethnic areas came under control of nations of different cultural backgrounds. Some national boundary changes overlapped and created tensions and hard feelings as well as political and economic confusion. Nationalism increased, and Communists seized power in Russia.

Socially, total populations decreased resulting in millions of displaced persons. Villages and farms were destroyed. There was less rigid social distinction and old beliefs and values were questioned. The peace settlement, the Versailles Treaty, established the **League of Nations** to ensure peace. With the United States refusal to join, the League of Nations did not have enough power to be successful.

Skill 1.3i **Analyze the conflict between fascist and Marxist/communist ideologies, and the rise, goals, and policies of dictatorships and totalitarian governments between the two World Wars.**

Socialism and communism have sometimes been used interchangeably. It's true that they are economic and political philosophies. Socialism began as a working class movement that suggested the state should be actively distributing wealth to all citizens. Communism is a branch of socialism in which the community as a whole owns all property. In practice this has translated to ownership by a totalitarian state.

The roots of socialism can be traced to the 19th century when Karl Marx and Fredrich Engels published *The Communist Manifesto*, which said that true freedom and equality came from social control of a country's resources. As time passed, socialism would split into different branches. The believers who gathered around Marx believed in what he called **Scientific Socialism**.

Communism has a more rigid ideology. Its bible, **Das Kapital,** sees Communism emerging as a result of almost cosmic laws. Modern socialism sees change in human society and hopes for improvement, but there is no unchanging millennium at the end of the road. Communism is sure that it will achieve the perfect state and in this certainty it is willing to use any and all means to bring it about. In Russia, it focused on the industrial worker and on state domination over the means of production.

Communists believe that revolution is inevitable and work toward it by emphasizing class antagonisms. Socialism seeks change but insists on the use of democratic procedures within the existing social order of a given society.

Socialism is confident only that the human condition is always changing and makes no easy approximation between ends and means. It does not justify brutalities. This tendency was found in the **Utopian-Socialists** of the early nineteenth century, whose basic aim was the repudiation of the private-property system with its economic inefficiency and social injustice. Like Marx, they envisioned industrial capitalism as becoming more and more inhumane and oppressive. They could not imagine the mass of workers prospering in such a system.

Yet the workers soon developed their own powerful organizations and institutions. They began to bend the economic system to their own benefit. A split did occur — first, between those rejected the earlier utopian ideas as being impractical and second, between those who believed the newfound political awareness of the working class was the key to organizing a realistic revolution.

The next split would occur between those who believed in the absolute inevitability of the coming revolution (the Revolutionary Socialists or as they came to be known, the **Communists**), and those **Democratic-Socialists** who while accepting the basic idea that the current capitalist system could not last, saw in the growing political awareness of the working class the beginnings of an ability to effect peaceful and gradual change in the social order.

The decade following World War I saw tremendous growth in socialism. Economic planning and the nationalization of industry was undertaken in many countries.

This political balance left most industrialized countries with a mixed socialist-capitalist economy. The consequences of World War II, particularly the independence of former European colonies, has opened vast new areas for the attempted development of socialist forms. Most have tried to aspire to the democratic type but very few have succeeded except where democratic traditions were strong.

Socialism, although concentrating on economic relationships, always considered itself a complete approach to human society. In effect, a new belief system and thus a world rather than a national movement. In this respect as well, it owes much to Great Britain for it was in London in 1864 that the first **Socialist International** was organized by Karl Marx. This radical leftist organization died off after limping along for twelve years, by which time its headquarters had moved to New York.

After the passage of about another twelve years, the **Second Socialist International** met in Paris to celebrate the anniversary of the fall of the Bastille in the French Revolution. By this time, serious factions were developing. There were the Anarchists, who wanted to tear down everything, Communists who wanted to tear down the established order and build another in its place, and the Democratic-Socialist majority who favored peaceful political action.

Struggling for internal peace and cohesion right up to the First World War, socialism would remain largely ineffectual at this critical international time. Peace brought them all together again in Bern, Switzerland, but by this time the Soviet Union had been created and the Russian Communists refused to attend the meeting on the grounds that the Second Socialist International opposed the type of dictatorship it saw as necessary in order to achieve revolution. Thus the **Communist International** was created in direct opposition to the Socialist International. The socialists went on to advocate the "triumph of democracy, firmly rooted in the principles of liberty" with the objective of maintaining the peace.

Fascism was a system of government that used authoritarian rule. Oppressing dissent was believed to benefit the nation, and fascism can be compared to an extreme form of nationalism. Fascism has several characteristics

- An origin at a time of serious economic disruption and of rapid social change
- A philosophy that rejects democratic and humanitarian ideals and glorifies the **absolute sovereignty of the state**
- An **aggressive nationalism** that calls for the mobilization and regimentation of every aspect of national life
- The **simulation of mass popular support** accomplished by outlawing all but a single political party and by using suppression, censorship, and propaganda
- A program of vigorous action including economic reconstruction, industrialization, pursuit of economic self-sufficiency

Fascism has always declared itself the uncompromising enemy of communism. However, fascist actions have much in common with communism. Many of the methods of organization and propaganda used by fascists were taken from the experience of the early Russian communists, along with the belief in a single strong political party, secret police, etc. Two of the main people to head fascist governments between the world wars were Benito Mussolini and Adolf Hitler. The governments in Italy and Germany turned into totalitarian governments and dictatorships.

In theory, at least, the chief distinction between fascism and communism is that fascism is **nationalist**, exalting the interests of the state and glorifying war between nations, whereas, communism is **internationalist**, exalting the interests of a specific economic class (the proletariat) and glorifying worldwide class warfare. In practice, however, this fundamental distinction loses some of its validity because in its heyday, fascism was also an internationalist movement.

Skill 1.3j   **Analyze the origins, course, and consequences of World War II, including the human cost of the war (e.g., the Holocaust), the resulting redrawing of boundaries, and the movement of peoples in Europe, Asia, Africa, and the Middle East.**

World War I seriously damaged the economies of European countries, both the victors and the defeated, leaving them deeply in debt. Both sides experienced difficulty paying off war debts. People had trouble finding jobs. Japan and Italy found themselves with few resources for their growing populations.

Atlantic/Europe
Germany suffered from runaway inflation, which ruined the value of its money and wiped out the savings of millions. The U.S. made loans to Germany, which helped the government to restore some order and provided a short existence of some economic stability in Europe, but the Great Depression undid the good that had been done. Mass unemployment, poverty, and despair greatly weakened the democratic governments that had been formed and greatly strengthened the

increasing power and influence of extreme political movements, such as communism, fascism, and national-socialism.

The extreme form of patriotism called nationalism that had been a chief cause of World War I grew stronger after the war ended in 1918. Political, social, and economic unrest fueled nationalism and it became an effective tool that enabled dictators to gain power in the 1930s. In the Soviet Union, **Joseph Stalin** succeeded in gaining political control. **Benito Mussolini** and the Fascist party, promised prosperity and order in Italy and set up a fascist government. In Japan, Emperor **Hirohito** did not have actual control. The military officers did. In Germany, harsh treaty terms, loss of territory, great economic chaos and collapse after World War I enabled **Adolf Hitler** and his National Socialist, or **Nazi,** party to gain power and control.

Fascism relies on a policy of aggressive territorial expansion. Italy invaded **Ethiopia** in 1935, having complete control by 1936. The Soviet Union did not invade or take over any territory but along with Italy and Germany, actively participated in the **Spanish Civil War**, using it as a means to test tactics and weapons, setting the stage for World War II.

In Germany, in direct violation of the World War I peace treaty, Hitler began the buildup of the armed forces. He sent troops into the Rhineland in 1936, then invaded Austria in 1938 and united it with Germany. In 1938, he seized control of the Sudetenland, part of western Czechoslovakia where mostly Germans lived, followed by the rest of Czechoslovakia in March 1939.

Preferring not to embark on another costly war, the European powers opted for a policy of **Appeasement** or making concessions, believing that once Hitler had satisfied his desire for land war could be averted. On September 1, 1939, Hitler began World War II in Europe by invading **Poland**.

By 1940, Germany invaded and assumed controlled of Norway, Denmark, Belgium, Luxembourg, the Netherlands, and France. German military forces struck in what came to be known as the **blitzkrieg**, or lightning war. A shock attack, it relied on the use of surprise, speed, and superiority in firepower. The German blitzkrieg coordinated land and air attacks to paralyze the enemy by disabling its communications and coordination capacities.

France fell in June 1940, and the Franco-German armistice divided France into two zones: one under German military occupation and one under nominal French control (the southeastern two-fifths of the country). The National Assembly, summoned at Vichy, France, ratified the armistice and granted **Philippe Pétain** control of the French State. The **Vichy** government then collaborated with the Germans, eventually becoming little more than a rubber stamp for German policies. Germany occupied the whole of France in 1942, and by early 1944, a

Resistance movement created a period of civil war in France. The Vichy regime was abolished after the liberation of Paris.

With Europe safely conquered, Hitler turned his sights to England. The **Battle of Britain** (June 1940–April 1941) was a series of intense raids directed against Britain by the **Luftwaffe**, Germany's air force. Intended to prepare the way for invasion, the air raids were directed against British ports and Royal Air Force (**RAF**) bases. In September 1940, London and other cities were attacked in the "**blitz**," a series of bombings that lasted for 57 consecutive nights. Sporadic raids continued until April 1941. The RAF was outnumbered but succeeded in blocking the German air force. Eventually Hitler was forced to abandon his plans for invasion, Germany's first major setback in the war.

After success in North Africa and Italy, and following the D-Day Invasion, the Allied forces faced a protracted campaign across Europe. The **Battle of the Bulge**, also known as Battle of the Ardennes (December 16, 1944–January 28, 1945) was the largest World War II land battle on the Western Front and the last major German counteroffensive of the war. The German army's goal was to cut Allied forces in half and to retake the crucial port of Antwerp, Belgium. The attack resulted in a bulge seventy miles deep into Allied lines, but all forward momentum for the Germans was essentially stopped by Christmas.

During the war, Allied forces flew extensive bombing raids deep into German territory. Launched from bases in England, both American and RAF bomber squadrons proceeded to bomb German factories and cities. German cities were reduced to rubble by war's end, and the impact on Germany's production capacity and transportation lines helped swing the tide of war.

Before war in Europe had ended, the Allies had agreed on a military occupation of Germany. It was divided into four zones each one occupied by Great Britain, France, the Soviet Union, or the United States with the four powers jointly administering Berlin. After the war, the Allies agreed that Germany's armed forces would be abolished, the Nazi Party outlawed, and the territory east of the Oder and Neisse Rivers taken away. Nazi leaders were accused of war crimes and brought to trial at **Nuremburg**.

Pacific/Asia

World War II was also being played out in the Pacific as Japan became the aggressor. Japanese forces seized control of Manchuria, a part of China containing rich natural resources. In 1937, Japan began attacking on the rest of China, occupying most of its eastern part by 1938. Japan also brutally occupied Korea.

On December 7, 1941, Japanese forces bombed Pearl Harbor in Hawaii, leading the United States to join the Allies, which included Great Britain, France, and the Soviet Union. The Axis Powers were Japan, Germany, and Italy.

Major consequences of the war included horrendous death and destruction. The Nazi regime launched the Holocaust, a campaign that murdered six million Jews. Other victims of the Nazi death machine included Roma, homosexuals and Soviet citizens. Millions more died of famine, particularly in China and the Soviet Union. Millions were displaced as the boundary lines of countries changed. World War II ended more lives and caused more devastation than any other war.

While the Axis powers were defeated, Great Britain and France were seriously weakened. The Soviet Union and the United States became the world's leading powers. America's **Marshall Plan** helped the nations of Western Europe get back on their feet.

Although allied during the war, the U.S.-Soviet alliance fell apart as Communism spread in Europe and Asia. During the war, it had spread to Lithuania, Estonia, Latvia, and parts of Poland, Czechoslovakia, Finland, and Romania. The war helped Communist governments gain power in Bulgaria, Romania, Hungary, Czechoslovakia, Poland, and North Korea. China fell to **Mao Zedong**'s Communist forces in 1949.

Until the fall of the Berlin Wall in 1989 and the dissolution of Communist governments in Eastern Europe and the Soviet Union, the United States and the Soviet Union were locked into what was called a Cold War. The possibility of the terrifying destruction by nuclear weapons loomed over both nations.

Nineteenth-century nationalism spilled over into the mid-twentieth century, with former colonies of European powers declaring themselves independent, especially in Africa. The Jewish people, who had experienced such horrors during World War II, established an independent Jewish state out of British territory, called Israel.

The **United Nations**, a more successful successor to the League of Nations began in the waning days of the war. It brought the nations of the world together to discuss their problems, rather than fight about them.

Skill 1.3k   Analyze the international developments of the post- World War II era, including decolonization, nationalism, nation building, the development of international organizations, and global migration.

Decolonization refers to the period after World War II when many African and Asian colonies and protectorates gained independence from their colonizers. The independence of India and Pakistan from Britain in 1945 marked the beginning of an especially important period of decolonization that lasted through 1960. Several British colonies in eastern Africa and French colonies in western Africa and Asia also formed independent countries during this period.

Colonial powers had found it efficient to draw political boundaries across traditional ethnic and national lines, thereby dividing local populations and making them easier to control. With the yoke of colonialism removed, many new nations found themselves trying to reorganize into politically stable and economically viable units. The role of nationalism was important in this reorganization, as formerly divided peoples had opportunity to reunite.

In nationalism, a nation is a well-defined group of people sharing a common identity. The process of organizing new nations from the remains of former colonies was called **nation building**.

Nation building did not always result in the desired stability. Pakistan eventually split into Bangladesh and Pakistan along geographic and religious lines. Ethnic conflicts in newly formed African nations arose. As the United States and the Soviet Union emerged as dominant world powers, these countries encouraged dissent in post-colonial nations such as Cuba, Vietnam, and Korea, which became arenas for Cold War conflict.

With the emergence of new independent nations, the role of **international organizations,** such as the newly formed United Nations, grew in importance. The United Nations deployed peacekeeping troops and imposed sanctions and restrictions on member states. The British Commonwealth and the French Union maintained connections between Britain and France and their former colonies. UNICEF formed to help vulnerable children.

Global migration saw an increase in the years during and following World War II as many Jewish people left the hostile climate under Nazi Germany for the United States and the new country of Israel. World War Two left millions of people displaced and caused immense refugee populations.

Skill 1.3l   **Analyze the Cold War from its origins in the post-World War II 1940s to the dissolution of the Soviet Union in 1991, including its impact on social, cultural, political, economic, technological, and geographic developments in the world.**

The Cold War was an ideological struggle between proponents of democracy and communism. The major players were the United States and the Soviet Union, but other countries were involved. It was a "cold" war because no large-scale fighting took place directly between the two big protagonists. Government, resources, and economics were concerns.

The major thrust of U.S. foreign policy from the end of World War II to 1990 was the post-war struggle between non-Communist nations, led by the United States, and Communist nations, led by the Soviet Union. Both the Soviet Union and the United States embarked on an arsenal buildup of atomic and hydrogen bombs as well as other nuclear weapons. Both nations had the capability of destroying each other but because of the continuous threat of nuclear war and accidents, extreme caution was practiced on both sides. The Cold War lasted for 45 years.

In 1946, Josef Stalin stated publicly that the presence of capitalism and its development of the world's economy made international peace impossible. An American diplomat in Moscow, **George F. Kennan,** proposed the idea of **containment**, as a response to Stalin. The goal of the U.S. would be to limit the extension or expansion of Soviet Communist policies and activities. After Soviet efforts to make trouble in Iran, Greece, and Turkey, U.S. President Harry Truman adopted what is known as the **Truman Doctrine** which committed the U.S. to a policy of intervention to contain the spread of communism throughout the world.

The Soviets were opposed to German unification and in April 1948 took serious action to either stop it or to force the Allies to give up control of West Berlin to the Soviets. The Soviets blocked all road traffic access from West Germany to West Berlin, which lay wholly within Soviet-controlled East Germany. To avoid any armed conflict, it was decided to airlift needed food and supplies into West Berlin. The **Berlin Airlift**, lasted from June 1948 to mid-May 1949, and forced the Soviets to lift the blockade and permit vehicular traffic access to the city.

The Soviet Union kept a tight leash on its client countries, including all of Eastern Europe, which made up a military organization called the **Warsaw Pact**. The Western nations responded with a military organization of their own, **NATO** or **North American Treaty Organization**. Another prime battleground was Asia, where the Soviet Union had allies in China, North Korea, and North Vietnam and the U.S. had allies in Japan, South Korea, Taiwan, and South Vietnam. The Korean War and Vietnam War were major conflicts in which both protagonists played big roles, but didn't directly fight each other.

The Cold War continued to varying degrees until 1991 when the Soviet Union collapsed. Eastern European countries were beginning to see their communist governments overthrown by this time, marking the shredding of the **Iron Curtain**, which was the ideological, symbolic and physical division of Europe between East and West. Another symbol of the Cold War was the **Berlin Wall**, dividing Germany. Built in 1961, the Wall literally was torn down in 1989.

Skill 1.3m   **Analyze the emergence of a global economy and its impact on the environment, epidemiology, and demographics, and the development and impact of the information, technology, and communications revolutions.**

Globalism is defined as the principle of the interdependence of all the world's nations and their peoples. Many international organizations have been set up to promote and encourage cooperation and economic progress among nations. When trade tariffs are eliminated trade is stimulated, resulting in increased productivity and economic progress. International systems of banking and finance have been devised to assist governments and businesses in setting currency exchange policies and guidelines.

The global economy had its origins in the early twentieth century when transportation expanded. Trucks, trains, and ships carry cargo all over the world. The introduction of the airplane made a significant impact on globalism. As technology improved, trade routes got longer and demand for things from overseas grew.

Globalization also brought financial and cultural exchange on a worldwide scale. Not only goods but also belief systems, customs, and practices are being exchanged. Immigration between countries continued to climb, which can be problematic when there aren't enough resources.

The problems of **nonrenewable resources**, like coal and oil, became apparent. For example, coal and oil are in worldwide demand these days, and the supplies won't last forever. Transportation and trade requires a fuel source.

Globalization has brought about welcome and unwelcome developments in the field of epidemiology. Vaccines and other cures for diseases can be shipped relatively quickly all around the world. Unfortunately, the preponderance of global travel has also meant that the threat of spreading a disease to the world by an infected person traveling on an international flight has increased.

Skill 1.3n   **Describe the causes and effects of genocide in the 20th century, including, but not limited to, the Armenian genocide, the Holocaust, and post-World War II "ethnic cleansing."**

Genocide is the intended extinction of one people by another. In the twentieth century, it has reached great heights.

The first organized genocide in the 1900s was the **Armenian genocide**, an attempted extermination of a huge number of Armenians at the hands of the young Turks who inherited Turkey from the Ottoman Empire. More than one million Armenian people (nearly half of their population) died between 1915 and 1917.

The Armenians were blamed for early defeats at the hands of Russia and its allies. Armenians were forcibly moved and kept in harsh conditions. A total of twenty-five concentration camps were believed to have existed to hold the Armenians.

The most well-known genocide of the twentieth century is the **Holocaust** of Jews before and during World War II. Germans carried out the Holocaust throughout German-occupied countries during the war. German authorities capitalized on twenty centuries of European hatred, distrust, racism, murder and rape of Jewish people and invented a plan they called the **Final Solution of the Jewish Question.** This solution was the extermination of the Jewish people with a vast system of transportation systems and concentration camps, where Jews were imprisoned and killed in increasingly large numbers.

German doctors carried out experiments on Jewish prisoners, pursuing radical cures for diseases and, more often than not, new methods of torture and mistreatment of prisoners of war. Germans subjected prisoners to the forced **death march** from one location to another, miles away, without providing prisoners food or sustenance.

The number of Jews killed during the Holocaust is six million. This figure includes people from all over Europe. The Holocaust didn't kill just Jews, however. Gypsies, communists, homosexuals, Jehovah's Witnesses, Catholics, psychiatric patients, and even common criminals were systematically incarcerated and, in many cases, killed for being enemies of the state.

The Holocaust ended with Germany's defeat in World War II. The liberating troops of the West and East uncovered the concentration camps and the mass killings. Much of the meticulous record keeping was intact, preserving for all the world the horrors that the Nazis had inflicted.

Ethnic cleansing in Yugoslavia occurred in Kosovo in the 1990s. The country had a majority population of Albanian Muslims. The people with power, including control of the government and the army, were the Serbs. In 1989, Serbian president **Slobodan Milosevic** abrogated the constitutional autonomy of Kosovo. He and the Serb minority in Kosovo didn't like that Muslim Albanians were in control of an area considered sacred to Serbs. The Serbian government expelled ethnic Albanians from the province. The Serbian officials also confiscated all identity documentation from those who were expelled so that any attempt to return could be refused by claiming that without documents to prove Serbian citizenship the people must be native Albanians. The effort even went so far as to destroy archival documents that proved citizenship.

Growing tensions led to armed clashes in 1998 between Serbs and the Kosovo Liberation Army (**KLA**), which had begun killing Serbian police and politicians. The Serbs responded with a ruthless counteroffensive, inducing the UN Security Council to condemn the Serbs' excessive use of force. After diplomatic efforts broke down, **NATO** responded with an 11-week bombing campaign that extended to Belgrade, Yugoslavia, and significantly damaged Serbia's infrastructure. NATO and Yugoslavia signed an accord in June 1999 outlining Serbian troop withdrawal and the return of nearly 1,000,000 ethnic Albanian refugees as well as 500,000 displaced within the province. Kosovo is now its own country. The leaders of this genocide have been convicted of their crimes, as were the Nazi perpetrators before them.

The **Rwandan Genocide** was the 1994 mass extermination of hundreds of thousands of ethnic **Tutsis** and moderate **Hutu** sympathizers in Rwanda and was the largest atrocity during the Rwandan Civil War. About 800,000 Tutsis and moderate Hutus were slaughtered over 100 days.

In the wake of the Rwandan Genocide, the United Nations and the international community drew severe criticism for its inaction. Despite international news media coverage of the violence as it unfolded, most countries, including France, Belgium, and the United States, declined to intervene or speak out against the massacres. Canada continued to lead the UN peacekeeping force in Rwanda. However, the UN Security Council did not authorize direct intervention or the use force to prevent or halt the killing.

The genocide ended when a Tutsi-dominated expatriate rebel overthrew the Hutu government and seized power. Fearing reprisals, hundreds of thousands of Hutu and other refugees fled into eastern Zaire (now the Democratic Republic of the Congo). People who had actively participated in the genocide hid among the refugees, fueling the First and Second Congo Wars. From 1995 to 2014, the International Criminal Tribunal for Rwanda tried perpetrators.

Skill 1.3o   Explain and evaluate the strategic importance of the Middle East and the volatile political relations within the region.

The Middle East is defined by its name and geographic position. Its position enables it to exert tremendous influence on not only the trade that passes through its realm of influence, but also the political relations between its countries and those of different parts of the world.

From the beginnings of civilization, the Middle East has been a destination for attackers, adventure-seekers, and those starving for food and a technologically advanced series of other resources, from iron to oil. Today, the countries of the Middle East play an important role in the economics of the world.

First and foremost is the importance of **oil**. Saudi Arabia, Iran, Iraq, Kuwait, Qatar, Dubai, and the United Arab Emirates are huge exporters of oil. The vast majority of the world's developed nations would be helpless without oil, so these nations want to keep oil flowing from the Middle East into their countries.

The countries of the Middle East, despite their economic similarities, have important differences in their government, belief systems, and global outlooks. Iran and Iraq fought a devastating war in the 1980s. **Iraq** invaded **Kuwait** in the late 1990s.

The **Iranian Revolution** in 1979 transformed a constitutional monarchy, led by the Shah, into an Islamic populist theocratic republic. The new ruler was Ayatollah Ruhollah Khomeini. This revolution occurred in two essential stages. In the first, religious, liberals, and leftist groups and those who sought a limitation of the Shah's power and a constitutional democracy cooperated to oust the **Shah** (king). In the second stage, the Ayatollah rose to power and created an Islamic state.

The Shah was said to be a puppet of the U.S. government. A series of protests in 1978 escalated until more than two million people gathered in Tehran in protest against the Shah. In a very short period of time, the Ayatollah Khomeini had gathered his revolutionaries and completed the overthrow of the monarchy.

The revolution accomplished certain goals: reduction of foreign influence and a more even distribution of the nation's wealth. It did not change repressive policies or levels of government brutality. It reversed policies toward women, restoring ancient policies of repression. Religious repression became rife, particularly against members of the Bahai Faith. The revolution has also isolated Iran from the rest of the world, being rejected by both capitalist and communist nations. This isolation, however, allowed the country to develop its own internal political system, rather than having a system imposed by foreign powers.

A large factor in the instability in the Middle East is ethnic strife. Each country has its own ethnic mix. A good example of this is Iraq, which has a huge minority of **Kurdish** people. Saddam Hussein, the former dictator of Iraq, persecuted the Kurds. Saddam Hussein went so far as to use chemical weapons on the Kurds. Iraq is also an example of a religious conflict, with the minority Shiites now in power and Hussein's Sunnis out of power. These two people agree very little outside the basics of Islamic faith.

Religious conflict between **Israelis** and **Palestinians** continues a centuries-old fight over religion and geography. This conflict goes back to the beginnings of Islam, in the seventh century. Muslims claimed Jerusalem, capital of the ancient civilization of Israel, as a holy city, in the same way that Jews and Christians did. Muslims seized control of Jerusalem and held it for a great many years, prompting Christian armies from Europe to fight for control of the area during the Crusades.

In 1917 present day Israel and Jordan was made a British colony. After the Holocaust the United Nations proposed the **Partition Plan**, this would create two states — one for Arabs and one for Jews — out of Britain's territory. Israel accepted this deal but the Arab countries did not and immediately invaded Israel. Israel won its War for Independence in 1949 after defeating the armies of Egypt, Jordan, Syria, Iraq, Lebanon, and Saudi Arabia.

Since Israel's War for Independence Israel has won three major wars with its neighbors. Nearly daily conflict continues, much as it has for thousands of years.

In 1988, the Arab population of the West Bank and Gaza Strip formed the State of Palestine. This could be the basis for the **Two-State Solution** that has proved so elusive.

In response to the 9/11 terror attacks America invaded Afghanistan in 2001. Afghanistan was ruled by the Taliban, who protected Osama bin Laden and the Al-Qaeda network. America forced the Taliban to retreat and since that time American troops, diplomats and economic agents have attempted to build Afghanistan into a functioning and stable democracy.

In 2003 America invaded Iraq and deposed Iraq's dictator, Saddam Hussein. Saddam was captured and tried for his crimes against humanity. These crimes included genocide against the Kurdish people in northern Iraq. Since 2003 America has been engaged in similar nation building efforts as in Afghanistan.

DOMAIN 2   U.S. HISTORY

COMPETENCY 2.1   PRE-REVOLUTIONARY ERA AND THE WAR FOR
                  INDEPENDENCE

**Skill 2.1a   Describe the major American Indian cultural groups and their
contributions to early American society.**

Native American tribes lived in varying degrees of togetherness throughout what
we now call the United States. They adopted different customs, pursued different
avenues of agriculture and food gathering, and made slightly different weapons.
They fought among themselves and with other peoples. To varying degrees, they
had established cultures long before Columbus or any other European explorer
arrived on the scene.

Perhaps the most famous of the Native American tribes is the **Algonquians**.
They were one of the first to interact with the newly arrived English settlers in
Plymouth and beyond. The Algonquians lived in wigwams and wore clothing
made from animal skins. They were proficient hunter-gatherers, and trappers
who also knew quite a bit about farming. Beginning with a brave man named
Squanto, they shared this agricultural knowledge with the English settlers,
including how to plant and cultivate corn, pumpkins, and squash. Other famous
Algonquians included **Pocahontas,** her father, Powhatan. **Tecumseh** and Black
Hawk were known for their fierce fighting ability.

The **Iroquois**, who were fierce fighters lived in the Northeast. They lived in long
houses and wore clothes made of buckskin. The Iroquois were expert farmers
who grew the "**Three Sisters**" (corn, squash, and beans). Five of the Iroquois
tribes formed a Confederacy, a shared form of government. The Iroquois formed
the **False Face Society**, a group of medicine men who shared their medical
knowledge with others but kept their identities secret while doing so.

The **Seminoles** and **Creeks**, a huge collection of people who lived in **chickees**
(open, bark-covered houses) and wore clothes made from plant fibers lived in the
Southeast. They were expert planters and hunters and were proficient at
paddling the dugout canoes they made. They created beautiful bead necklaces
and are known for their struggle against Spanish and English settlers, led by the
great **Osceola**.

The **Cherokee** also lived in the Southeast. They were one of the most advanced
tribes, living in domed houses and wearing deerskin and rabbit fur. Accomplished
hunters, farmers, and fishermen, the Cherokee were known the continent over
for their intricate and beautiful basketry and clay pottery. They also played a
game called lacrosse, which survives to this day in countries around the world.

The **Plains Tribes** lived in what we now call the Midwest. Tribes such as the **Sioux, Cheyenne, Blackfeet, Comanche,** and **Pawnee** compose the Plains Tribes. They lived in teepees and wore buffalo skins with feather headdresses. They hunted wild animals on the Plains, especially the buffalo. They were well known for their many ceremonies, including the Sun Dance, and for the peace pipes that they smoked. Famous Plains people include: **Crazy Horse** and **Sitting Bull**, authors of Custer's defeat at Little Big Horn, **Sacagawea**, leader of the Lewis & Clark expedition, and **Chief Joseph**, the famous Nez Perce leader.

Dotting the deserts of the Southwest were a handful of tribes, including the famous **Pueblo**. The Pueblo lived in houses that bear their tribe's name, wore clothes made of wool and woven cotton, farmed crops in the middle of desert land, created exquisite pottery and Kachina dolls, and had one of the most complex religions of all the tribes. They are perhaps best known for the challenging vista-based villages that they constructed from the sheer faces of cliffs and rocks and for their **adobes**, mud-brick buildings that housed their living and meeting quarters.

The **Apaches** lived in the Southwest. Their famous leader was **Geronimo** and they lived in homes called wickiups, which were made of bark, grass, and branches. They wore cotton clothing, were excellent hunter-gatherers, and were adept at basketry. The Apache believe everything in nature holds special powers.

The **Navajo**, also residents of the Southwest, lived in **hogans** (round homes built with forked sticks) and wore clothes of rabbit skin. Their major contribution to the overall culture of the continent was in sand painting, weapon making, accomplished silversmiths, and weavers.

The **Inuit** lived in tents made from animal skins or, in some cases, **igloos** in the Northwest. They wore clothes made of animal skins, usually seals or caribou. They were excellent fishermen and hunters who crafted efficient kayaks and umiaks to take them through waterways and harpoons with which to hunt animals. They left behind tall totem poles and great carvings made of ivory.

Skill 2.1b Explain and analyze the struggle for the control of North America among European powers and the emergence of the 13 Colonies under English rule.

Throughout the 1700s the British searched for the **Northwest Passage**, an open-water route across North America to the wealth of Asia. It was not until 1806 that the **Lewis and Clark Expedition** proved conclusively that there was no Northwest Passage.

However, the lack of an open-water passage did not deter exploration or settlement. **Spain, France, England,** and the **Dutch** led the way in expanding Western European civilization in the New World. The first three nations had strong monarchial governments and were struggling for dominance and power in Europe. With the defeat of Spain's mighty Armada in 1588, England became undisputed ruler of the seas. Spain lost its power and influence in Europe and it was left to France and England to carry on the rivalry, leading to eventual British control of the American continent.

Spain's influence extended across Florida, along the Gulf Coast of Texas all the way west to California and south to the tip of South America. **French** control centered from New Orleans north to what is now northern Canada **England** settled the eastern seaboard of North America, including parts of Canada and the U.S. from Maine to Georgia. Each of the three nations controlled various islands of the West Indies. **The Dutch** had New Amsterdam for a period but later ceded it to Britain.

Spanish settlement had its beginnings in the Caribbean with the establishment of colonies in Puerto Rico, Cuba, and on Hispaniola at Santo Domingo (which became the capital of the West Indies). The first permanent settlement in what is now the United States was in 1565 at **St. Augustine**, Florida. A later permanent settlement in the southwestern United States was in 1609 at Santa Fe, New Mexico. At the peak of Spanish power, the area in the United States claimed, settled, and controlled by Spain included Florida and all land west of the Mississippi River.

There were a number of reasons for Spanish involvement in the Americas, among them:

- the spirit of adventure
- the desire for land
- expansion of Spanish power, influence, and empire
- the desire for great wealth
- expansion of Roman Catholic influence and conversion of native peoples

France and England laid claim to some of the same areas. Nonetheless, ranches and missions were built and the Indians who came in contact with the Spaniards were introduced to animals, plants, and seeds from the Old World that they had never seen before. Animals brought in included horses, cattle, donkeys, pigs, sheep, goats, and poultry.

The Spanish cut barrels were in half, filled them with earth and transported and trees bearing apples, oranges, limes, cherries, pears walnuts, olives, lemons, figs, apricots and almonds to transplant. Sugar cane and flowers made it to America along with bags bringing seeds of wheat, barley, rye, flax, lentils, rice, and peas.

All Spanish colonies belonged to the King of Spain, who was considered **an absolute monarch** who claimed to rule by divine right. The belief held that God had given him the right to rule and as king he answered only to God for his actions. He appointed personal representatives, or **viceroys**, to rule for him in his colonies. They ruled in his name with complete authority and were richly rewarded with land grants, privileges of trading, and the right to operate the gold and silver mines.

Indians were enslaved to work in the mines and on the plantations. They either rapidly died due to a lack of immunity from European diseases or escaped into nearby jungles or mountains. As a result, African slaves were brought in, particularly to the West Indies.

Spain's control over its New World colonies lasted more than 300 years, longer than England or France. Spanish influence remains in the names of places, art, architecture, music, literature, law, and cuisine. Spanish settlements in North America were not private enterprises. B They were established to expand and defend the wealth of the Spanish Empire. The treasure and wealth found in Spanish New World colonies went back to Spain to be used to buy whatever goods and products were needed. Spain did not set up its own industries to manufacture what was needed. As the amount of gold and silver was depleted, Spain could not pay for the goods needed and was unable to produce goods for themselves.

At the same time, Spanish treasure ships at sea were seized by English and Dutch "pirates" who took the wealth to fill the coffers of their own countries. On land: Russian seal hunters came down the Pacific coast, the English moved into Florida and beyond the Appalachians, French traders and trappers made their way from Louisiana and other parts of New France into Spanish territory. Facing encroachment on all sides, and without self-sustaining economic development and colonial trade, the Spanish settlements in the U.S. never really prospered.

By the 1750s in Europe, Spain was no longer the most powerful nation. The remaining rivalry was between Britain and France. For nearly 25 years, between 1689 and 1748, a series of "armed conflicts" involving these two powers took place. These conflicts spilled over to North America. The War of the League of Augsburg in Europe, 1689–1697, was called King William's War. The War of the Spanish Succession, 1702–1713, was called Queen Anne's War. The War of the Austrian Succession, 1740– 1748, was called King George's War in the colonies. They fought for possession of colonies in North America, and for control of the seas, but none of these conflicts were decisive.

The part of North America claimed by **France** was called New France and consisted of the land west of the Appalachian Mountains. This area of French claims and settlement included the St. Lawrence Valley, the Great Lakes, the Mississippi Valley, and the entire region of land westward to the Rockies. They established the permanent settlements of Montreal and New Orleans. This gave France control of the two major gateways into the vast, rich interior of North

America. The St. Lawrence River, the Great Lakes, and the Mississippi River (along with its tributaries) made it possible for the French explorers and traders to roam at will, trapping, trading, and furthering the interests of France.

Most of France's settlements were in Canada along the **St. Lawrence River**. Only scattered forts and trading posts were found in the upper Mississippi Valley and Great Lakes region. The French rulers originally intended New France to have vast estates owned by nobles and worked by peasants with the peasants living on the estates in compact farming villages — the New World's version of the of feudalism. However, New France's settled areas wound up mostly as a string of farmhouses stretching from Quebec to Montreal along the St. Lawrence and Richelieu Rivers.

French fur traders settled in the uninhabited regions of New France. The traders made friends with the local Indians, spent winters with them and got the furs needed for trade. In the spring, the fur traders would return to Montreal to trade their furs for the products brought by the cargo ships from France. Most of the wealth for New France and its "Mother Country" was from the fur trade. Manufacturers and workmen in France, ship-owners and merchants, as well as the fur traders and their Indian allies, all benefited. However, the freedom of roaming and trapping in the interior was a powerful enticement for younger, stronger men. This resulted in the French not fortifying the areas settled along the St. Lawrence.

French rivalry with the **British** grew stronger in the eighteenth century. New France was united under a single government and enjoyed the support of many Indian allies. The French traders were diligent in preserving the forests and game that the Indians depended on for life. By the early 1750s, in Western Europe, France was the most powerful nation. Its armies were superior to all others and its navy gave the British stiff competition for control of the seas. The stage was set for confrontations in both Europe and America.

The final conflict began in North America in 1754 in the Ohio River Valley. It was known in America as the **French and Indian War** and in Europe as the Seven Years' War, since it began there in 1756. In America the British colonies were well established and consolidated in a smaller area. British colonists outnumbered French colonists 23 to 1. Except for a small area in Canada, French settlements were scattered over a much larger area (roughly half of the continent) and were smaller. However, the French settlements were united under one government and were quick to act and cooperate when necessary. In addition, the French had many more Indian allies than the British. The British colonies had separate, individual governments and very seldom cooperated. In Europe, at that time, France was the more powerful of the two nations.

Both sides had stunning victories and humiliating defeats. If one person could be given the credit for British victory, it would have to be **William Pitt**. He was a strong leader, enormously energetic, supremely self-confident, and set on a complete British victory. Despite the advantages and military victories of the French, Pitt succeeded. He formed a strong army and sent more troops to America, strengthened the British navy, gave officers of the colonial militias equal rank to the British officers, and took the offensive. Of all the British victories, perhaps the most crucial and important was winning Canada.

The French depended on the St. Lawrence River for transporting supplies, soldiers, and messages. The St. Lawrence River was the link between New France and the Mother Country. Tied to this waterway system were the connecting links of the Great Lakes, Mississippi River and its tributaries, along which were scattered French forts, trading posts, and small settlements. In 1758, the British captured Louisburg on Cape Breton Island. New France was doomed. Louisburg gave the British navy a base of operations, preventing French reinforcements and supplies getting to their troops. Other forts fell to the British: Frontenac, Duquesne, Crown Point, Ticonderoga, Niagara, those in the upper Ohio Valley, and, most importantly, Quebec and finally Montreal. Spain entered the war in 1762 to aid France, but it was too late. British victories occurred all around the world: in India, in the Mediterranean, and in Europe.

Spain, France, and Britain met in Paris in 1763 to draw up the **Treaty of Paris** to end the Seven Years' War. Great Britain got most of India and all of North America east of the Mississippi River, except for New Orleans. From Spain Britain received control of Florida and returned to Spain the captured territories of Cuba and the Philippines. France lost nearly all of its possessions in America and India but was allowed to keep four islands: Guadeloupe, Martinique, Haiti on Hispaniola, and Miquelon and St. Pierre off the coast of Canada. France gave Spain New Orleans and the vast territory of Louisiana, west of the Mississippi River. Britain was now the most powerful nation.

Skill 2.1c **Analyze the effects of English, French, Dutch, and Spanish colonial rule on social, economic, and governmental structures in North America, and the relationships of these colonies with American Indian societies.**

Colonists from England, France, Holland, Sweden, and Spain all settled in North America, on lands once frequented by Native Americans. Spanish colonies were mainly in the south, French colonies were mainly in the extreme north and in the middle of the continent, and the rest of the European colonies were in the northeast and along the Atlantic coast. These colonists got along with their new neighbors with varying degrees of success.

The French colonists seemed the most willing to work with the Native Americans. Even though their pursuit of animals to fill the growing demand for the fur trade was overpowering, they managed to find a way to keep their new neighbors happy. The French and Native Americans even fought together against England.

The Dutch and Swedish colonists were interested mainly in surviving in their new homes. The **Dutch West India Company** founded a colony in what is now New York, establishing it as New Holland. It was eventually captured by English settlers and named New York, but many of the Dutch families that had been granted large segments of land by the Dutch government were allowed to keep their estates.

The English and Spanish colonists had the worst relations with Native Americans, mainly because the Europeans made a habit of taking land, signing and then breaking treaties, massacring, and otherwise abusing their new neighbors. The Native Americans shared their agriculture and jewel-making secrets with the Europeans and got grief and deceit in return.

The English colonies were divided generally into the three regions: **New England**, **Middle Atlantic**, and the **South**. The culture of each was distinct and affected attitudes, politics, religion, and economic activities. The geography of each region also contributed to unique characteristics.

The **New England** colonies consisted of **Massachusetts, Rhode Island, Connecticut,** and **New Hampshire**. Life in these colonies was centered on the towns. Every family farmed its own plot. Because they had a short summer growing season and a limited amount of good soil, other economic activities such as manufacturing, fishing, shipbuilding, and trade became important. The vast majority of the settlers shared similar origins, coming from England and Scotland. Towns were carefully planned and laid out the same way. The form of government was the **town meeting** where all adult males met to make laws. The legislative body, the **General Court,** consisted of an upper and lower house.

The **Middle or Middle Atlantic** colonies included **New York, New Jersey, Pennsylvania, Delaware,** and **Maryland**. New York and New Jersey were at one time the Dutch colony of New Netherland, and Delaware at one time was New Sweden. These five colonies were considered "melting pots," with settlers from many different nations and backgrounds. The main economic activity was farming with the settlers scattered over the countryside cultivating rather large farms. The Indians were not as much of a threat as in New England. Soil was very fertile, land gently rolled, and there was a mild climate that provided a longer growing season. The farms produced a large surplus of food and this colonial region became known as the "breadbasket" of the New World. New York and Philadelphia seaports were constantly filled with ships being loaded with meat, flour, and other foodstuffs for the West Indies and England.

There were other economic activities such as shipbuilding, iron mines, and factories which produced paper, glass, and textiles. The legislative body in Pennsylvania was **unicameral** (one house). In the other four colonies, the legislative body had two houses (**bicameral**). Local government units were in counties and towns.

The **Southern** colonies were **Virginia, North and South Carolina,** and **Georgia.** Virginia was the first permanent successful English colony and Georgia was the last. Three significant events took place in 1619. First, sixty women were sent to Virginia to marry and establish families. Second, twenty Africans, the first of hundreds of thousands, arrived. Third, the Virginia colonists were granted the right to self-government and they elected their own representatives to the **House of Burgesses**, their own legislative body.

The major economic activity in this region was farming. The soil was fertile and the climate was mild with a long growing season. Large plantations in the coastal or tidewater areas used large numbers of slaves. The wealthy slave-owning planters set the pattern of life in this region, but most of the people lived inland away from coastal areas and were small farmers.

The settlers in these four colonies came from diverse backgrounds and cultures. Virginia was colonized mostly by people from England while Georgia was started as a haven for debtors from English prisons. Pioneers from Virginia settled in North Carolina while South Carolina welcomed people from England and Scotland, French Protestants, Germans, and emigrants from islands in the West Indies. Products from farms and plantations included rice, tobacco, indigo, cotton, some corn and wheat. Other economic activities included lumber and naval stores (tar, pitch, rosin, and turpentine) from the pine forests and fur trade on the frontier. Cities such as Savannah and Charleston were important seaports and trading centers.

Daily life of the colonists differed greatly between the coastal settlements and the inland or interior. Southern planters and the people living in the coastal cities and towns had a way of life similar to that of English towns. The influence was seen and heard in the way people dressed and talked, the architectural styles of houses and public buildings, and the social divisions or levels of society. Planters and city dwellers enjoyed an active social life and had strong emotional ties to England.

Life on the frontier had marked differences. All facets of daily life—clothing, food, home, economic and social activities—were connected to what was needed to sustain life and survive in the wilderness. The people produced practically everything themselves. They were self-sufficient and extremely individualistic and independent. There were few, if any, levels of society or class distinctions as they considered themselves to be equal to all others, regardless of station in life. The roots of equality, independence, individual rights and freedoms were extremely strong and well developed.

Skill 2.1d   Describe the institutionalization of African slavery in the Western Hemisphere and analyze its consequences in sub-Saharan Africa.

Slavery in the English colonies began in 1619 when twenty Africans arrived in Jamestown, Virginia. From then on, slavery had a foothold, especially in the agricultural South, where a large amount of labor was needed for the extensive plantations. Free men refused to work for wages on the plantations when land was available for settlement on the frontier. Slavery became profitable in the South but not in the other two colonial regions.

Slavery began in America in 1619 and ended in 1865, after the South's defeat in the Civil War and the passage of the Thirteenth Amendment, which outlawed slavery.

Skill 2.1e   Analyze the causes for the War for Independence, the conduct of the war, and its impact on Americans.

The war for independence occurred due to a number of changes, the two most important ones being economic and political. By the end of the French and Indian War in 1763, Britain's American colonies were thirteen out of a total of thirty-three scattered around the earth. Like all other countries, Britain strove for having a strong economy and a favorable balance of trade. That required wealth, self-sufficiency, and a powerful army and navy. The English colonies, with only a few exceptions, were considered commercial ventures founded to make a profit for the crown, or the company, or whoever financed its beginnings. The colonies provided raw materials for the industries in the Mother Country and were a market for finished products. This **mercantilism** assisted the Mother Country in becoming economically and militarily powerful. Great Britain's strong merchant fleet provided training for the Royal Navy and bases of operation.

Trade was the major reason for British encouragement and support of colonization, especially in North America. Between 1607 and 1763, the British Parliament enacted different laws to assist the government in maintaining a positive trade balance. One series of laws required that most of the manufacturing be done exclusively in England. Another prohibited exporting any wool or woolen cloth from the colonies, and prohibited the manufacture of beaver hats or iron products. This forced money to flow from the colonies back to the mother country.

The **Navigation Acts of 1651** put restrictions on shipping and trade within the British Empire by requiring that trade was allowed only on British ships. This increased the strength of the British merchant fleet and greatly benefited the American colonists. Since they were British citizens, they could have their own vessels, and build and operate them as well. By the end of the war in 1763, the shipyards in the colonies were building one-third of the merchant ships under the British flag.

The **Navigation Act of 1660** restricted the shipment and sale of colonial products to England only. In 1663, another Navigation Act stipulated that the colonies had to buy manufactured products only from England and that any European goods going to the colonies had to go to England first. These acts were a protection from enemy ships and pirates and from competition from European rivals.

The New England and Middle Atlantic colonies at first felt threatened by these laws but soon found new markets for their goods and began their own **triangular trade**. Colonial vessels started the first part of the triangle by sailing to Africa, loaded with kegs of rum from colonial distilleries. On Africa's West Coast, the rum was traded for either gold or slaves. The second part of the triangle was from Africa to the West Indies where slaves were traded for molasses, sugar, or money. The third part of the triangle was home, bringing sugar or molasses (to make more rum), gold, and silver.

The major concern of the British government was that the trade violated the 1733 **Molasses Act**. Planters had wanted the colonists to buy all of their molasses in the British West Indies but these islands could give the traders only about one eighth of the amount of molasses needed for distilling the rum. The colonists were forced to buy the rest from the French, Dutch, and Spanish islands. By buying from outside colonies Americans avoided the high taxes placed on British molasses. If Britain had enforced the Molasses Act, economic chaos and ruin would have occurred. For this act and all the other mercantile laws, the government followed the policy of "salutary neglect," deliberately failing to enforce the laws.

In 1763, after the war, Britain needed money to pay their war debt, the defense of the empire, and the governing of thirty-three colonies scattered around the globe. It was decided to adopt a new colonial policy and pass laws to raise revenue. The earlier laws passed had been for the purposes of regulating production and trade, which generally put money into colonial pockets. These new laws would take money out of their pockets—unjustly and illegally so, in colonial eyes.

Colonial governments differed, depending on the type of colony. Each colony had a lower legislative assembly that was elected and a higher council and governor that were elected or appointed in different ways, depending on the how the colony was organized initially. In most colonies, the councils and governors were appointed by the King of England or by British property owners or agencies. In corporate colonies, the council and governors were elected by colonial property owners who maintained close connections with England.

Colonies were allowed to regulate much of their daily lives through representation in the colonial assemblies but Britain maintained control of international affairs and international trade by controlling the upper levels of colonial government.

The first glimmers of dissent from the colonies came during the French and Indian War when **colonial militias** were raised to fight the French in America. Conflict arose with Britain over who should control these militias. The colonies wanted the assemblies to have control. Shortly after the start of the war in 1754, the French and their Indian allies defeated Major **George Washington** and his militia at Fort Necessity. This left the entire northern frontier of the British colonies vulnerable and open to attack. In the wake of this, **Benjamin Franklin** proposed to the thirteen colonies that they unite permanently to better defend themselves.

Delegates from seven of the thirteen colonies met at Albany, New York, along with the representatives from the Iroquois Confederation and British officials. Franklin's proposal, known as the **Albany Plan of Union**, was rejected by the colonists, along with a similar proposal from the British. Delegates simply did not want each of the colonies to lose its right to act independently.

Before 1763, except for trade and the supply of raw materials, the colonies had mostly been left to themselves. England looked on them merely as part of an economic or commercial empire. Little consideration was given to how they were to conduct their daily affairs, so the colonists became very independent, self-reliant, and skillful at handling those daily affairs. This, in turn, gave rise to leadership, initiative, achievement, and vast experience. In fact, there was a far greater degree of independence and self-government in America than could be found in Britain or the major countries on the Continent or any other colony anywhere.

In America, representatives to the colonial legislatures were elected from the districts in which they lived. Only qualified property-owning males were allowed to vote. Each colony had a royal governor appointed by the king, representing his interests in the colonies. Nevertheless, the colonial legislative assemblies controlled the purse strings by having the power to vote on all issues involving money to be spent by the colonial governments.

The colonists' protest of, "**No taxation without representation**" was meaningless to the English. The colonists were incensed at this English attitude and considered their colonial legislative assemblies equal to Parliament, a position which was totally unacceptable to the English.

In 1763, Parliament decided to garrison a standing army in North America to reinforce British control. In 1765, the **Quartering Act** was passed requiring the colonists to provide supplies and living quarters for British troops. In addition, efforts by the British were made to keep the peace by establishing good relations with the Indians. Consequently, a proclamation was issued which prohibited any American colonists from making any settlements west of the Appalachians until provided for through treaties with the Indians.

The **Sugar Act of 1764** required efficient collection of taxes on any molasses that were brought into the colonies. The Act gave British officials free license to conduct searches of the premises of anyone suspected of violating the law. The colonists were taxed on newspapers, legal documents, and other printed matter under the **Stamp Act of 1765**. Nine colonies assembled in New York to call for the repeal of the Act. At the same time, a group of New York merchants organized a protest to stop the importation of British goods. Similar protests arose in Philadelphia and Boston and other merchant cities, often erupting in violence. As Britain's representatives in the colonies, the governors and members of the cabinet and council were sometimes the targets of these protests. The ensuing uproar of rioting and mob violence caused Parliament to repeal the tax.

The **Declaratory Act**, attached to the repeal, plainly stated that Parliament still had the right to make all laws for the colonies. Other acts leading up to armed conflict included the **Townshend Acts** passed in 1767 taxing lead, paint, paper, and tea brought into the colonies. This, too, increased anger and tension. In response Britain sent troops to New York City and Boston. In Boston, mob violence brought about the deaths of five people and the wounding of eight others in the so-called **Boston Massacre**.

A growing patriot movement gained foothold and the issue of independence arose in common thought. When Britain proposed that the East India Company be allowed to import tea to the colonies without customs duty, the colonists were faced with a dilemma. They could purchase the tea at a much lower price than the smuggled Dutch tea they had been drinking, however tea was still subject to the Townshend Act, and to purchase it would be an acceptance of this act. The **Boston Tea Party** was the result, where a group of colonists seized a shipment of British tea in Boston Harbor and dumped it into the sea.

Britain responded with a series of even more restrictive acts, driving the colonies to come together in the **First Continental Congress** to make a unified demand that Britain remove these **Intolerable Acts**, as they were called by the colonists.

In 1774, the passage of the **Quebec Act** extended the limits of that Canadian colony's boundary southward to include territory located north of the Ohio River. Boston's port was closed; the royal governor of the colony of Massachusetts was given increased power, and the colonists were compelled to house and feed British soldiers. The propaganda activities of the patriot organizations **Sons of Liberty** and **Committees of Correspondence** kept the opposition and resistance before everyone's eyes.

Delegates from twelve colonies met in Philadelphia September 5, 1774, in the **First Continental Congress**. They opposed acts of lawlessness and wanted some form of peaceful settlement with Britain. The Continental Congress affirmed America's loyalty to the Mother Country and Parliament's power over colonial foreign affairs. They insisted on repeal of the **Intolerable Acts** and demanded an end to all trade with Britain until the repeal took effect. The reply from George III, the last king of America, was an insistence of colonial submission to British rule.

Britain stood firm and sought to dissolve the colonial assemblies that came forth in opposition to British policies. When British soldiers in America were ordered to break up the illegal meeting of the Massachusetts' assembly outside Boston, they were met with armed resistance at **Lexington and Concord** in April 1775, and the Revolutionary War was underway. **The Second Continental Congress** met a month later in Philadelphia to conduct the business of war and government. Many of the delegates recommended a declaration of independence from Britain. The group established an army and commissioned George Washington as its commander.

British forces attacked patriot strongholds at Breed's Hill and **Bunker Hill** near Boston. Although the colonists withdrew, the loss of life for the British was nearly fifty percent of their army. The next month King George III declared the American colonies to be in a state of rebellion. The war quickly began in earnest.

The colonial army was quite small in comparison to the British army, and although it lacked formal military training, the colonists had learned a new method of warfare from the Indians. Many battles were fought in the traditional style of two lines of soldiers facing off and firing weapons, but the advantage the patriots had was the understanding of guerilla warfare: fighting from behind trees and other defenses, and more importantly, fighting on the run.

In 1776, colonial representatives met for the Second Continental Congress. On July 3, 1776, British General Howe arrived in New York harbor with 10,000 troops to prepare for an attack on the city. The next day, the **Declaration of Independence** was drafted and independence was declared July 4, 1776.

The first American victory of the Revolutionary War followed a surprise attack on British and Hessian troops under the command of George Washington at **Trenton**, New Jersey. Washington and his men crossed the icy **Delaware River** on Christmas Day, 1776, and attacked the next day, completely surprising the British. The victory helped to restore American morale.

Washington labored against tremendous odds to wage a victorious war. American troops spent the winter of 1777–1778 at **Valley Forge.** The encampment became a symbol of endurance in adversity. The turning point in the Americans' favor occurred in 1777 with the American victory at **Saratoga**.

This victory led the French to align with the American cause. With the aid of Admiral deGrasse and French warships blocking the entrance to Chesapeake Bay, British General Cornwallis was trapped at **Yorktown**, Virginia. Cornwallis surrendered in 1781 and the war was over. The Treaty of Paris of 1783 officially ended the war.

COMPETENCY 2.2	THE DEVELOPMENT OF THE CONSTITUTION AND THE EARLY REPUBLIC

Skill 2.2a　　**Describe and evaluate the impact of the Enlightenment and the unique colonial experiences on the writing of the Declaration of Independence, Articles of Confederation, the Federalist Papers, the Constitution, and the Bill of Rights.**

Democracy is loosely defined as "rule by the people," either directly or through representatives. The basic concept of democracy existed in the thirteen English colonies with the practice of independent self-government.

The **Declaration of Independence** is an outgrowth of ancient Greek ideas of democracy, individual rights Renaissance ideas and the European Enlightenment. Particularly the Enlightenment ideology of the political thinker **John Locke**. **Thomas Jefferson** (1743–1826), the principle author of the Declaration, borrowed much from Locke's theories and writings. Jefferson was attracted to Locke's great emphasis on human rights and the belief that when governments violate those rights people should rebel. Locke wrote *Two Treatises of Government* in 1690, which had tremendous influence on political thought in the American colonies and helped shaped the U.S. Constitution and Declaration of Independence.

Jefferson argued that King George III had repeatedly violated the rights of the colonists as subjects of the British Crown and that American colonists were left with no choice but to abolish such government and institute a new government.

Locke and Jefferson both stressed that the individual citizen's rights are prior to and more important than any obligation to the state. Government is the servant of the people. The officials of government hold their positions at the sufferance of the people. The rights of the people must be preserved and protected by that government.

The Declaration of Independence (July 1776) was intended to demonstrate the reasons why the colonies sought independence from Great Britain. The Colonists had tried all means to resolve their dispute peacefully. It was the right of a people, when all other methods had been tried and failed, to separate themselves from that power that was keeping them from full expression of their rights to "**life, liberty, and the pursuit of happiness**".

The **Articles of Confederation** was the first political system under which the newly independent colonies were organized. It was passed by the Continental Congress on November 15, 1777, ratified by the thirteen states, and took effect on March 1, 1781.

The newly independent states were unwilling to give too much power to a national government. They did not want to replace one harsh ruler with another. Under the Articles of Confederation, each state had one vote in the Congress. Congress had the power to declare war, appoint military officers, and coin money. It was also responsible for foreign affairs. The Articles of Confederation limited the powers of Congress by giving the states final authority. Although Congress could pass laws, at least nine of the thirteen states had to approve a law before it went into effect. Congress could not pass any laws regarding taxes. To get money, Congress had to ask each state for it, and no state could be forced to pay.

The Articles created a loose alliance among the thirteen states. The national government was weak, in part, because it didn't have a strong chief executive to carry out laws passed by the legislature. Many different disputes arose and there was no way of settling them. Delegates met to try to fix the Articles; instead they ended up scrapping them and created a new form of government. They drafted the Constitution that established the foundation of the new government.

The first order of business at the **Constitutional Convention** was the agreement among all the delegates that the convention would be kept secret. The delegates wanted to be able to discuss, argue, and agree among themselves before presenting the completed document to the American people.

Between the official notes kept and the complete notes of future President **James Madison**, an accurate picture of the events of the Convention is part of the historical record.

The delegates went to Philadelphia representing different areas and different interests. They all agreed on a strong central government but with limited powers. They also agreed that no one part of government could control the rest. It would be a **republican** form of government (sometimes referred to as representative democracy) in which the supreme power was in the hands of the voters who would elect the men who would govern for them.

One of the first serious controversies involved the small states versus the large states over representation in Congress. Virginia's Governor Edmund Randolph proposed that state population determine the number of representatives sent to Congress, a plan known as the **Virginia Plan**. New Jersey delegate William Paterson countered with what is known as the **New Jersey Plan**, where every state would have equal representation.

After much debate, the **Great Compromise** was reached. It is also known also as the **Connecticut Compromise**, and was proposed by Roger Sherman. It was agreed that Congress would have two houses. The Senate would have two senators from each state. The House of Representatives would have its members elected based on population. Both houses could draft bills to debate and vote on with the exception of bills pertaining to money, which must originate in the House of Representatives.

Another controversy involved economic differences between North and South. One concerned the counting of the African slaves for determining representation in the House of Representatives. The southern delegates wanted slaves counted to determine representation in the House of Representatives but didn't want them counted to determine taxes to be paid. The northern delegates argued the opposite: count the slaves for taxes but not for representation. The resulting agreement was known as the **"three-fifths" compromise**. Three-fifths of the slaves would be counted for both taxes and determining representation in the House.

The last major compromise was the **Commerce Compromise**. The economic interests of the northern part of the country were industry and business whereas the South's economic interests were primarily agriculture. The northern merchants wanted the government to regulate and control commerce with foreign nations and with the states. Southern planters opposed this idea as they felt that any tariff laws passed would be unfavorable to them.

The acceptable compromise to this dispute was that Congress was given the power to regulate commerce with other nations and between the states, including levying tariffs on imports. However, Congress did not have the power to levy tariffs on any exports. This increased the South's concern about the effect it would have on the slave trade. The delegates finally agreed that the importation of slaves would continue for 20 more years with no interference from Congress. Any import tax could not exceed 10 dollars per person. After 1808, Congress would be able to decide whether to prohibit or regulate any further importation of slaves.

Nine states needed to **ratify** (approve) for the Constitution to go into effect. Those favoring the Constitution and a strong central government were **Federalists**. The opposition (**Anti-Federalists**) had three major objections:

- The states felt they were being asked to surrender too much power to the national government.
- The voters did not have enough control and influence over the men who would be elected by them to run the government.
- There was no "bill of rights" guaranteeing hard-won individual freedoms and liberties.

Promoters of the Constitution wrote articles called the *Federalist Papers* to convince the public of the need to ratify the Constitution. The Constitution also incorporated the separation of powers of the three branches of government and the built-in system of checks and balances to keep power balanced.

Skill 2.2b   Examine the issues regarding ratification of the Constitution, and compare and contrast the positions of the Federalists and Anti-Federalists.

Among the leaders of the Federalists were Alexander Hamilton and John Jay. These two, along with James Madison, wrote a series of letters to New York newspapers, urging that that state ratify the Constitution. These became known as the *Federalist Papers*.

In the Anti-Federalist camp were Thomas Jefferson and Patrick Henry. These men and many others like them worried that a strong national government would descend into the kind of tyranny that they had just worked so hard to abolish. In the same way that they took their name from their foes, they wrote a series of arguments against the Constitution called the **Anti-Federalist Papers.**

In the end, both sides got most of what they wanted. The Federalists got their strong national government, which was held in place by the famous "checks and balances." The Anti-Federalists got the **Bill of Rights**, the first ten Amendments to the Constitution and a series of laws that protect some of the most basic of human rights.

COMPETENCY 2.3   THE EMERGENCE OF A NEW NATION

Skill 2.3a   Describe the differing visions of the early political parties and explain the reasons for the respective successes and failures of those parties.

It is important to realize that political parties are unmentioned in the United States Constitution. George Washington himself warned against the creation of "factions" in American politics that cause "jealousies and false alarms" and result in damage to the body politic. Thomas Jefferson echoed this warning, yet he would lead a political party.

In 1789, the Electoral College unanimously elected George Washington as the first President. The early presidential administrations established much of the forms procedures still present today, including the development of the party system. George Washington established a Cabinet: individual advisers overseeing the various functions of the executive branch and who advise the President, who makes a final decision. Divisions within Washington's Cabinet and within Congress during his administration eventually led to the development of political parties.

By the time Washington retired from office in 1796, the new political parties would come to play an important role in choosing his successor. The election of 1796 was the first one in which political parties played a role.

Washington's Vice President, **John Adams**, was elected to succeed him. Adams' administration was marked by the new nation's first entanglement in international affairs. Britain and France were at war, with Adams' Federalist Party supporting the British and Vice President Thomas Jefferson's Republican Party supporting the French. The U.S. was nearly brought to the brink of war with France, but Adams managed to negotiate a treaty that avoided conflict. In the process, however, he lost the support of his party and was defeated after one term by Thomas Jefferson.

Americans had good reason to fear the emergence of political parties. They had witnessed how parties worked in Great Britain. Parties, called "factions" in Britain were made up of a few people who schemed to win favors from the government. They were more interested in their own personal profit and advantage than in the public good. Thus, the new American leaders wanted to prevent the rise of any factions. It was, ironically, disagreements between two of Washington's chief advisers, **Thomas Jefferson** and **Alexander Hamilton** that spurred the formation of the first political parties in the United States.

The two parties that developed through the early 1790s were led by Washington's Secretary of State, Thomas Jefferson and Washington's Secretary of the Treasury Alexander Hamilton.

Hamilton wanted the federal government to be stronger than the state governments. Jefferson believed that the state governments should be supreme. Hamilton supported the creation of the first Bank of the United States. Jefferson opposed it because he felt that it gave too much power to wealthy investors who would help run it.

Jefferson interpreted the Constitution strictly; he argued that nowhere did the Constitution give the federal government the power to create a national bank. He believed that the common people, especially the farmers, were the backbone of the nation. He thought that the rise of big cities and manufacturing would corrupt American life.

Hamilton interpreted the Constitution more loosely. He pointed out that the Constitution gave Congress the power to make all laws "necessary and proper" to carry out its duties. He reasoned that since Congress had the right to collect taxes, then Congress had the right to create the bank. Hamilton wanted the government to encourage economic growth. He favored the growth of trade, manufacturing, and the rise of cities as necessary parts of economic growth. Hamilton believed that government should focus more on business leaders than farmers.

When Congress began to pass many of Hamilton's ideas and programs, Jefferson and James Madison decided to organize support for their own views. Jefferson was interested in meeting with several important New York politicians such as New York Governor George Clinton and Aaron Burr, a strong critic of Hamilton. Jefferson asked Clinton and Burr to help defeat Hamilton's program by getting New Yorkers to vote for Jefferson's supporters in the next election. Soon, leaders in other states began to organize support for either Jefferson or Hamilton. Jefferson's supporters called themselves **Democratic-Republicans** (often this was shortened just to Republicans, though in actuality it was the forerunner of today's Democratic Party). Hamilton and his supporters were known as **Federalists** because they favored a strong federal government. The Federalists had the support of the merchants and ship owners in the Northeast and some planters in the South. Small farmers, craft workers, and some of the wealthier landowners supported Jefferson and the Democratic-Republicans.

By the beginning of the 1800s, the Federalist Party, torn by internal divisions, began to decline. After the 1800 election when Thomas Jefferson became President, the Federalist Party began to collapse. By 1816, after losing a string of important elections, (Jefferson was reelected in 1804, and James Madison, a Democratic-Republican was elected in 1808), the Federalist Party ceased to be an effective political force, and soon passed off the national stage.

By the late 1820s, new political parties had grown up. The **Democratic-Republican** Party was the major party for two decades, but differences within the party caused a split after 1824. Those who favored strong national growth took the name **Whigs** and united around President John Quincy Adams. Many business people in the Northeast as well as some wealthy planters in the South, supported the Whigs.

Those who favored slower growth and were more worker and small farmer oriented, formed the new Democratic Party. Andrew Jackson was its first leader as well as the party's first President. This party was the forerunner of today's Democratic Party.

In the mid-1850s, the slavery issue began to come to head and in 1854, those opposed to slavery, the Whigs, and some northern Democrats opposed to slavery, united to form the Republican Party. Before the Civil War, the Democratic Party was more heavily represented in the South and was thus pro-slavery.

By the Civil War, the present form of the major political parties had been formed. Though there would be drastic changes in ideology and platforms over the years, no other political party would manage to gain enough strength to seriously challenge the "Big Two" parties.

Skill 2.3b **Compare the significant political and socioeconomic ideas and issues during the Jeffersonian and Jacksonian periods and contrast how they were implemented in policy and practice.**

European events have helped shaped U.S. policies, especially how America's foreign policy. After 1815, the U.S. became much more independent from European influence and was treated with growing respect by European nations. These nations were impressed that the young United States showed no hesitancy in going to war with the world's greatest naval power.

The election of Andrew Jackson as President signaled a swing of the political pendulum from government influence of the wealthy, aristocratic Easterners to the interests of the Western farmers and pioneers and the era of the "common man." Jacksonian democracy expanded the **franchise** (right to vote) to poorer white men.

After the War of 1812, Henry Clay and his supporters favored economic measures that came to be known as the **American System**. These economic measures involved tariffs that protected American farmers and manufacturers from having to compete with foreign products and stimulated industrial growth and employment. With more people employed, more farm products would be consumed, prosperous farmers would be able to buy more manufactured goods, and the additional monies from tariffs would make it possible for the government to make needed internal improvements. In 1816 Congress passed a high tariff and chartered a second **Bank of the United States**. When Andrew Jackson became President, he fought to close the bank.

One of the many duties of the bank was to regulate the supply of money for the nation. President Jackson believed that the bank was a monopoly that favored the wealthy. Congress voted in 1832 to renew the bank's charter but Jackson vetoed the bill, withdrew the government's money, and the bank collapsed.

Jackson also faced the "null and void," or **nullification** issue from South Carolina. In 1828 Congress passed a law that placed high tariffs on goods imported to the United States. Southerners, led by then Vice-President John C. Calhoun (himself a South Carolinian), felt that the tariff favored the manufacturing interests of New England. In response he denounced the tariff as an abomination, and claimed that any state could nullify any federal law it considered unconstitutional. The tariff was lowered in 1832, but not low enough to satisfy South Carolina, which promptly threatened to secede from the Union. Although Jackson agreed with the rights of states, he also believed in the preservation of the Union. A year later, the tariffs were lowered and the crisis was averted.

Skill 2.3c   Describe American foreign policy prior to the Civil War.

In the early years of the American nation, three primary ideas determined American foreign policy. The first of these, **isolationism,** was perhaps also the most long-lasting. The founding fathers and the earliest Americans (after the Revolution) tended to believe that the U.S. had been created and destined for a unique role, what Thomas Jefferson called the "City on the Hill." They understood personal and religious freedom to be a unique experiment. Although many hoped the nation would grow, this expectation did not extend to efforts to plant colonies in other parts of the world.

The second idea was that of **"No Entangling Alliances."** George Washington's farewell address had initially espoused the intention of avoiding permanent alliances in any part of the world. This was echoed in Jefferson's inaugural address. In fact, when James Madison led the nation into the War of 1812, he refrained from entering an alliance with France, which was also at war with England at the time.

The United States' unintentional and accidental involvement in what was known as the **War of 1812** came about due to the political and economic struggles between France and Great Britain. Napoleon's goal was complete conquest and control of Europe, including and especially Great Britain. Napoleon drove British troops from Continental Europe. However, the British fleet still controlled the seas, the seas across which France conduct commerce and transport French military power. America traded with both nations, especially with France and its colonies. The British decided to destroy the American trade with France, mainly for two reasons. First, products and goods from the U.S. gave Napoleon what he needed to keep up his struggle with Britain. France was the enemy and it was felt that the Americans were aiding Britain's enemy. Second, Britain felt threatened by the increased strength and success of the U.S. merchant fleet. They became major competitors with the ship owners and merchants in Britain.

The British issued the **Orders in Council** which was a series of measures that barred American ships entrance to any French ports in Europe, India and the West Indies. At the same time, Napoleon began efforts to blockade the British Isles. He issued a series of Orders that prohibited all trade with the British. He threatened seizure of every ship entering French ports after they stopped at any British port or colony, even threatened to seize every ship inspected by British cruisers or that paid duties to the British government. The British stopped American ships and **impressed** (capture and forced labor of the crew) American seamen to service on British ships. Americans were outraged.

In 1807, Congress passed the **Embargo Act** that prohibited American ships from sailing to foreign ports. The act couldn't be completely enforced and it also hurt business and trade in America, so it was repealed in 1809. Two additional acts were signed by James Madison attempted to get Britain and France to remove restrictions they had put on American shipping. The catch was that whichever nation removed restrictions, the U.S. agreed not to trade with the other one. Napoleon was the first to do this so Madison issued orders that prohibited trade with Britain. Although Britain eventually rescinded the Orders in Council, war came in June of 1812.

During the war, Americans were divided over not only whether it was necessary to fight, but also over what territories should be fought for and taken. The nation was still young and unprepared for war. The primary American objective to conquer Canada ended in failure. Two naval victories and one military victory stand out for the United States. Oliver Perry gained control of Lake Erie and Thomas MacDonough fought on Lake Champlain. Both of these naval battles successfully prevented the British invasion of the United States from Canada. Nevertheless, British troops did land below Washington on the Potomac, marched into the city and burned government buildings, including the White House. Andrew Jackson's victory at New Orleans was a great morale booster to Americans. It gave the impression that the U.S. had won the war. The battle actually took place after Britain and the United States had reached an agreement and it had no impact on the war's outcome.

The war ended Christmas Eve, 1814, with the signing of the Treaty of Ghent. The peace treaty did little for the United States other than bring peace, release prisoners of war, restore all occupied territory, and set up a commission to settle boundary disputes with Canada. Interestingly, the war proved to be a turning point in American history.

In President Monroe's message to Congress on December 2, 1823, he delivered what is called the **Monroe Doctrine**. The United States informed the powers of the Old World that the American continents were no longer open to European colonization. The Monroe Doctrine holds that any effort to extend European political influence into the New World would be considered by the United States "dangerous to our peace and safety." The United States would not interfere in European wars or internal affairs, and expected Europe to stay out of American affairs.

The American experience had created a profound wariness of any encroachment onto the continent by European countries. The Monroe Doctrine was a clear warning: no new colonies in the Americas.

The nineteenth century was the age of "**Manifest Destiny**" – the belief in the divinely given right of the nation to expand westward and incorporate more of the continent into the nation. This belief had been expressed, at the end of the Revolutionary War, in the demand that Britain cede all lands east of the Mississippi River to America. The goal of westward expansion was further confirmed with the **Northwest Ordinance** (1787) and the **Louisiana Purchase** (1803). Manifest Destiny was the justification of the **Mexican-American War**

(1846–48) which resulted in the annexation of Texas and California, as well as much of the southwest. The feelings of **nationalism** became stronger during this period.

Skill 2.3d **Identify and describe the political, social, religious, economic, and geographic factors that led to the formation of distinct regional and sectional identities and cultures.**

Regionalism can be defined as the political division of an area into partially autonomous regions or to loyalty to the interests of a particular region. **Sectionalism** is generally defined as excessive devotion to local interests and customs.

Religious interests, economic life, and geography began to be understood as definitive of particular regions. The northeast tended toward industrial development. The south tended to rely upon agriculture. The west was an area of untamed open spaces where people settled and practiced agriculture and animal husbandry.

Each of these regions came to be defined, at least to some extent, on the basis of the way people made their living and the economic and social institutions that supported them. In the industrialized north, the factory system tended to create a division between the tycoons of business and industry and the poor industrial workers.

The south was characterized by cities that were centers of social and commercial life. The agriculture that supported the region was practiced on "plantations" that were owned by the wealthy and worked by slaves or indentured servants.

The west was a vast expanse to be explored and tamed. Life on a western ranch was distinctly different from either life in the industrial north or the agricultural south. The challenges of each region were also distinctly different. The role of children in the economy was different; the role of women was different; the importance of trade was different. And religion was called upon to support each unique regional lifestyle.

The regional differences between North and South came to a head over the issue of slavery. The rise of the abolitionist movement in the North, the publication of **Uncle Tom's Cabin**, and issues of trade and efforts by the national government to control trade for the regions coalesced around the issue of slavery in a nation that was founded on the principle of the inalienable right of every person to be free. As the South defended its lifestyle and its economy and the right of the states to self-determine, the North became stronger in its criticism of slavery. The result was a growing sectionalism.

As the nation extended its borders into the lands west of the Mississippi, thousands of settlers streamed into this part of the country. They brought with them ideas and concepts and adapted them to the development of the unique characteristics of the region. Equality for everyone, as stated in the Declaration of Independence, did not apply to minority groups, black Americans, women or American Indians. Voting rights and the right to hold public office were restricted in varying degrees in each state. All of these factors decidedly affected the political, economic, and social life of the country and all three were focused in the attitudes of the three sections of the country on slavery.

Skill 2.3e   Describe the purpose, challenges, and economic incentives associated with settlements of the West, including the concept of Manifest Destiny.

In the United States, territorial expansion occurred in the expansion westward under the banner of "**Manifest Destiny**." In addition, the U.S. was involved in the **War with Mexico**, the **Spanish-American War**, and support of the Latin American colonies of Spain in their revolt for independence. In Latin America, the Spanish colonies were successful in their fight for independence and self-government

After the U.S. purchased the Louisiana Territory, Jefferson appointed Captains **Meriwether Lewis and William Clark** to explore it, to find out exactly what had been bought. With the help of local guides, including a Native American woman named **Sacagawea**, the expedition called the **Corps of Discovery** went all the way to the Pacific Ocean. They returned two years later with maps, journals, and artifacts. This led the way for future explorers to make available more knowledge about the territory and resulted in the Westward Movement and the later belief in the doctrine of Manifest Destiny.

It was the belief of many that the United States was destined to control all of the land between the two oceans. This mass migration westward put the U.S. government on a collision course with the Indians, Great Britain, Spain, and Mexico. The fur traders and missionaries ran up against the Indians in the northwest and the claims of Great Britain for the Oregon country.

The Red River cession was the next acquisition of land and came about as part of a treaty with Great Britain in 1818. The area included parts of North and South Dakota and Minnesota. In 1819, Florida, both east and West, was ceded to the U.S. by Spain along with parts of Alabama, Mississippi, and Louisiana. Texas was annexed in 1845 and after the war with Mexico in 1848, the government paid $15 million for what would become the states of California, Utah, Nevada and parts of four other states.

The U.S. and Britain had shared the Oregon territory. By the 1840s, with the increase in the free and slave populations and the demand of the settlers for entry into the U.S., the conflict had to be resolved. In a treaty, signed in 1846, the **Oregon Territory** was ceded to the U.S. The acquisition extended the western border to the Pacific Ocean. The northern U.S. boundary was established at the 49th parallel. The states of Idaho, Oregon, and Washington were formed from this territory. In 1853, the **Gadsden Purchase** rounded out the present boundary of the 48 conterminous states with payment to Mexico of $10 million for land that makes up the present states of New Mexico and Arizona.

Spain had claimed the American Southwest since the 1540s. Spain had spread northward from Mexico City, and, in the 1700s, had established missions, forts, villages, towns, and very large ranches. After the purchase of the Louisiana Territory in 1803, Americans began to move into Spanish territory. A few hundred American families in what is now Texas were allowed to live there but had to agree to become loyal subjects to Spain. In 1821, Mexico successfully revolted against Spanish rule, won independence, and chose to be more tolerant toward the American settlers and traders. The Mexican government encouraged and allowed extensive trade and settlement, especially in Texas. Many of the new settlers were Southerners who brought their slaves with them. Slavery was outlawed in Mexico and was illegal in Texas, although the Mexican government looked the other way.

Friction increased between land-hungry Americans who swarmed into western lands and the Mexican government, which controlled these lands. The clash was not only political but also cultural and economic. The Spanish influence permeated all parts of the southwestern life: law, language, architecture, and customs. By this time Manifest Destiny was in the hearts and on the lips of those seeking new areas of settlement and a new life. Americans were demanded U.S. control of not only the Mexican Territory but also Oregon. Peaceful negotiations with Great Britain secured Oregon but it took two years of war to gain control of the southwestern U.S.

In addition, the Mexican government owed debts to U.S. citizens whose property was damaged or destroyed during its struggle for independence from Spain. By the time war broke out in 1845, Mexico had not paid its war debts. The government was weak, corrupt, irresponsible, torn by revolution, and not in decent financial shape. Mexico was also bitter over American expansion into Texas and the **1836 revolution**, which resulted in Texas independence. In the 1844 Presidential Election, the Democrats pushed for annexation of Texas and Oregon and after winning, they started the procedure to admit Texas to the Union.

When Texas statehood occurred, diplomatic relations between the U.S. and Mexico ended. President Polk wanted U.S. control of the entire southwest, from Texas to the Pacific Ocean. He sent a diplomatic mission with an offer to purchase New Mexico and Upper California but the Mexican government refused to receive the diplomat. Consequently, in 1846, each nation claimed aggression on the part of the other and war was declared. The treaty signed in 1848 and a subsequent one in 1853 completed the southwestern boundary of the United States, extending to the Pacific Ocean, as President Polk wished.

Skill 2.3f   Map and analyze the expansion of U.S. borders and the settlement of the West, and describe how geographic features influenced this expansion.

Westward expansion occurred for a number of reasons, the most important was economic. Cotton had become most important to most of the people who lived in the South. The effects of the Industrial Revolution, which began in England, were being felt in the United States. With the invention of power-driven machines, the demand for cotton fiber greatly increased because yarn was needed in spinning and weaving. Eli Whitney's **cotton gin** made the separation of the seeds from the cotton much more efficient. This, in turn, increased the demand and more farmers became involved in the raising and selling of cotton.

The innovations and developments of better methods of long-distance transportation moved the cotton in greater quantities to textile mills in England as well as the areas of New England and Middle Atlantic States. As prices increased along with increased demand, southern farmers cleared more land to grow cotton. People moved west. They settled the areas and began to farm the fertile soil. This, in turn, demanded increased need for a large supply of cheap labor. The system of slavery expanded, both in numbers and in the movement to lands "west" of the South.

Cotton farmers and slave owners were not the only ones headed west. Many others joined in the migration—trappers, miners, merchants, ranchers, and others who sought their fortune. The Lewis and Clark expedition stimulated the westward push. Fur companies hired men, known as "Mountain Men", to search for pelts to supply the market and meet the demands of the East and Europe. These men, in their own ways, explored and discovered the many passes and trails that would eventually be used by settlers in their treks west. The California Gold Rush also had a large influence on the movement west.

The availability of cheap land and the expectation of great opportunity prompted thousands, including immigrants, to travel across the Mississippi River and settle the Great Plains and California. The primary focuses of the new western economy were farming, mining, and ranching. Both migration and the economy were facilitated by the expansion of the railroad and the completion of the **transcontinental railroad** in 1869.

There were also religious reasons for westward expansion. Missionaries who traveled west with the fur traders encouraged settlement. By the 1840s, the population increases in the Oregon territory were about a thousand people a year. People of many different religions and cultures as well as Southerners with slaves made their way west for political reasons.

Skill 2.3g   Analyze the evolution of American Indian policy up to the Civil War.

During the American Revolution the British competed for the allegiance of Native Americans east of the Mississippi River. Many Native Americans sided with the British in the hope of stopping the expansion of the American colonies into the lands they occupied.

By the terms of the **Treaty of Paris** which ended the Revolutionary War, a large amount of land occupied and claimed by American Indians was ceded to the United States.

During the nineteenth century the nation expanded westward. This expansion and settlement of new territory forced the Native Americans to continue to move farther west. The Native Americans were gradually giving up their homelands, their sacred sites, and the burial grounds of their ancestors. Some of the American Indians chose to move west. Many, however, were relocated by force.

The Indian Removal Act of 1830 authorized the government to negotiate treaties with Native Americans to provide land west of the Mississippi River in exchange for lands east of the river. This policy resulted in the relocation of more than 100,000 Native Americans. Theoretically, the treaties were expected to result in voluntary relocation of the native people. In fact, many of the native chiefs were forced to sign the treaties.

One of the worst examples of "Removal" was the **Treaty of New Echota**. This treaty was signed by a faction of the Cherokees rather than the actual leaders of the tribe. When the leaders attempted to remain on their ancestral lands, the treaty was enforced by President Martin Van Buren. The removal of the Cherokees came to be known as "**The Trail of Tears**" and resulted in the deaths of more than 4,000 Cherokees, mostly due to disease.

The next phase of the government's policy toward the American Indians was to purchase their land in treaties in order to continue national expansion. This created tension with the states and with settlers. Migration and settlement were not easy. As the settlers moved west they encountered Native American tribes who insisted on their natural rights to lands their ancestors had lived on for generations. Resentment of the encroachment of new settlers was particularly strong among the tribes that had been ordered to relocate to "Indian Country" prior to 1860.

Skill 2.3h   Describe and analyze the impact of slavery on American society, government, and economy, and the contributions of enslaved Africans to America, and trace the attempts to abolish slavery in the first half of the 19th century.

Slavery in the English colonies began in 1619 when twenty Africans arrived in the colony of Virginia at Jamestown. From then on, slavery had a foothold, especially in the agricultural South, where a large amount of cheap labor was needed to keep the extensive plantations profitable. Free men refused to work for wages on the plantations when land was available for settling on the frontier. Therefore the plantation class turned to slave labor.

At the Constitutional Convention, one of the slavery compromises concerned how to count slaves to decide the number of representatives for the House and the amount of taxes to be paid. Southerners pushed for counting the slaves for representation but not for taxation. The Northerners pushed for the opposite. The resulting compromise, sometimes referred to as the **three-fifths compromise**, was that both groups agreed that three-fifths of the slaves would be counted for both taxation and representation.

The other compromise over slavery was part of the disputes over how much regulation the central government would control over commercial activities such as trade with other nations and the slave trade. It was agreed that Congress would regulate commerce with other nations including taxing imports. Southerners were worried about taxing slaves coming into the country and the possibility that Congress would prohibit the slave trade altogether. The agreement allowed the states to continue to import slaves for the next twenty years until 1808, at which time Congress would make the decision as to the future of the slave trade. During the 20-year period, no more than $10 per person could be levied on slaves coming into the country.

These two slavery compromises were a necessary concession to have Southern support and approval for the Constitution and new government. Many Americans felt that the system of slavery would eventually die out in the U.S., but by 1808, cotton was increasingly important in the primarily agricultural South and slavery was firmly entrenched in Southern culture. It is also evident that as early as the Constitutional Convention, active anti-slavery feelings and opinions were very strong, leading to extremely active groups and societies.

The first serious clash between North and South occurred during 1819–1820 when James Monroe was president. It concerned the admission of Missouri as a state. In 1819, the U.S. consisted of 21 states: 11 free states and 10 slave states. The Missouri Territory allowed slavery and if admitted would cause an imbalance in the number of U.S. Senators. Alabama had already been admitted as a slave state and that had balanced the Senate with the North and South each having 22 senators. The first **Missouri Compromise** resolved the conflict by approving admission of Maine as a free state along with Missouri as a slave state, thus continuing to keep a balance of power in the Senate with the same number of free and slave states.

An additional provision of this compromise was that with the admission of Missouri, slavery would not be allowed in the rest of the Louisiana Purchase territory north of latitude 36 degrees 30'. This was acceptable to the Southern Congressmen since it was not profitable to grow cotton on land north of this latitude line. It was thought that the crisis had been resolved until it was discovered that Missouri's state constitution discriminated against free blacks. Anti-slavery supporters in Congress went into an uproar and were determined to exclude Missouri from the Union. Henry Clay, known as the **Great Compromiser**, then proposed a second Missouri Compromise which was accepted and opened the way for Missouri's statehood—a temporary reprieve on the slavery issue.

Restless pioneers moved into new frontiers of the West, seeking land, wealth, and opportunity. Many were from the South and were slave owners who brought their slaves with them. A faction arose supporting the doctrine of "**popular sovereignty**" which stated that people living in territories and states should be allowed to decide for themselves whether slavery should be permitted.

By 1836, Texas was an independent republic with its own constitution. During its fight for independence, Americans were sympathetic to and supportive of the Texans and some volunteers crossed into Texas to help the struggle. Problems arose when the state petitioned Congress for statehood. Texas wanted to allow slavery but Northerners in Congress opposed admission to the Union because it would disrupt the balance between free and slave states and give Southerners in Congress increased influence.

In 1849, California applied for admittance to the Union and the furor began. The result was the **Compromise of 1850**, a series of laws designed as a final solution to the slavery issue. Concessions made to the North included the admission of California as a free state and the abolition of the slave trade in Washington, D.C. The laws also provided for the creation of the New Mexico and Utah territories. As a concession to Southerners, the residents there would decide whether to permit slavery when these two territories became states. In addition, Congress authorized implementation of stricter measures to capture runaway slaves.

A few years later, Congress took up consideration of new territories between Missouri and present-day Idaho. Those opposed to slavery used the Missouri Compromise to argue that the land considered for territories was part of the area the Compromise had designated as banned to slavery. But on May 25, 1854, Congress passed the infamous **Kansas-Nebraska Act** which nullified this provision, created the territories of Kansas and Nebraska, and provided for the people of these two territories to decide for themselves whether to permit slavery. Feelings were so deep and divided that any further attempts to compromise would meet with little, if any, success. Political and social turmoil swirled everywhere. Kansas was called "**Bleeding Kansas**" because of the extreme violence and bloodshed throughout the territory caused by the two governments there, one pro-slavery and the other anti-slavery.

The Supreme Court in 1857 handed down the Dred Scott decision. **Dred Scott** was a slave whose owner had taken him from slave state Missouri, then to the free state of Illinois, into the Minnesota Territory, which was free under the provisions of the Missouri Compromise, and then finally back to slave state Missouri. Abolitionists argued that since Scott had lived in a Free State and free territory, he was a free man. Two lower courts had ruled before the Supreme Court, one ruled in favor and one against. The Supreme Court decided that residing in a Free State and free territory did not make Scott a free man because Scott (or any slave) was not a U.S. citizen or a state citizen of Missouri. Therefore, he did not have the right to sue in state or federal courts. The Court went a step further and ruled that the old Missouri Compromise was now unconstitutional because Congress did not have the power to prohibit slavery in the territories.

Anti-slavery supporters were stunned. They had just recently formed the new Republican Party and one of its platforms was to keep slavery out of the territories. According to the decision in the Dred Scott case, this basic party principle was unconstitutional. The only way to ban slavery in new areas was by a Constitutional amendment, requiring ratification by three-fourths of all states.

In 1858, **Abraham Lincoln** and Stephen A. Douglas ran for an Illinois senate seat and participated in a series of debates, which directly affected the outcome of the 1860 Presidential election. Douglas, a Democrat, was up for re-election and knew that if he won this race, he had a good chance to be president in 1860. Lincoln, a Republican, was not an abolitionist, but he believed that slavery was morally wrong and he firmly believed in and supported the Republican Party principle that slavery must not be allowed to extend any further.

Douglas, on the other hand, originated the doctrine of "**popular sovereignty**" and was responsible for the inflammatory Kansas-Nebraska Act. In the course of the debates, Lincoln challenged Douglas to show that popular sovereignty reconciled with the Dred Scott decision. Either way he answered Lincoln, Douglas would lose crucial support. If he supported the Dred Scott decision, Southerners would support him but he would lose Northern support. If he stayed with popular sovereignty, Northern support would be his but Southern support would be lost. His reply to Lincoln, that Territorial legislatures could exclude slavery through refusal to pass laws to support slavery, gave him enough support to be re-elected to the Senate. But it cost him the Democratic nomination for president in 1860.

Southerners came to realize that Douglas supported and was devoted to popular sovereignty but not necessarily to the expansion of slavery. Two years later, Lincoln received the nomination of the Republican Party for president.

In 1859, abolitionist **John Brown** and his followers seized the federal arsenal at Harper's Ferry in what is now West Virginia. His purpose was to take the guns stored in the arsenal, give them to slaves, and lead them in a widespread rebellion. He and his men were captured by Colonel Robert E. Lee of the United States Army and after a trial with a guilty verdict, he was hanged. This merely served to widen the gap between the two sections.

The final straw came with the election of Lincoln to the presidency the next year. Due to a split in the Democratic Party, there were four candidates from four political parties. Lincoln received a minority of the popular vote and a majority of electoral votes. The Southern states, one by one, voted to secede from the Union as they had promised they would do if Lincoln and the Republicans were victorious.

Skill 2.3i   **Describe and compare and contrast early 19th-Century social and reform movements and their impact on antebellum American society (e.g., the Second Great Awakening, the temperance movement, the early women's movement, utopianism).**

The spirit of nineteenth century reform found expression in the effort to protect the rights and opportunities of all. Many other social reform movements began during this period, including education, women's rights, labor, and working conditions, temperance, prisons and insane asylums.

The labor organization movement began during the 1830s–1850s and resulted in the establishment of a ten-hour workday in several states. A new understanding of education led to movements for public education for all children. The public school system became common in the North.

The most intense and controversial movement was the abolitionists' efforts to end slavery. This effort split the country, hardened Southern defense of slavery, and led to four years of bloody war. The abolitionist movement, affected admittance of states into the Union and the government's continued efforts to keep a balance between total numbers of free and slave states. Congressional legislation after 1820 reflected this.

The **Industrial Revolution** had spread from Great Britain to the United States. Before 1800, most manufacturing activities were done in small shops or in homes. However, starting in the early 1800s, factories with modern machines were built. This made it possible to produce goods faster. The eastern part of the country became a major industrial area although some industry developed in the

West. At about the same time, improvements began to be made in roads, railroads, canals, and steamboats. The increased ease of travel facilitated the westward movement as well as boosted the economy with faster and cheaper shipment of goods and products. Some of the innovations included the Erie Canal that connected the interior and Great Lakes with the Hudson River and the coastal port of New York. .

Robert Fulton's **Clermont**, the first commercially successful steamboat, led the way in changing the fastest way to ship goods. Later, steam-powered railroads became the biggest rival of the steamboat as a means of shipping. The railroad became the most important transportation method to open up the West. With expansion into the interior of the country, the United States became the leading agricultural nation in the world. The hardy pioneer farmers produced a vast surplus and emphasis went to producing products with a high-sales value. Implements such as the cotton gin and reaper aided in production efficiencies. Travel and shipping were greatly assisted in areas not yet touched by railroad by improved or new roads, such as the National Road in the East and in the Oregon and Santa Fe Trails in the West.

People were exposed to works of literature, art, newspapers, drama, live entertainment, and political rallies. With better communication and travel, more information was desired about previously unknown areas of the country, especially the West. The discovery of gold and other mineral wealth resulted in a literal surge of settlers.

More industries and factories required more labor. Women, children, and entire families worked the long hours and days. By the 1830s, the factories were even larger and employers began to hire immigrants who came to America in huge numbers. Efforts were made to organize a labor movement to improve working conditions and increase wages.

Utopianism is the dream of or the desire to create the perfect society. By the nineteenth century few believed this was possible. One of the major causes of utopianism is the desire for moral clarity. Against the backdrop of the efforts of a young nation to define itself and to ensure the rights and freedoms of its citizens, within the context of the second Great Awakening, it is easy to see how the reform movements, the religious sentiment, and the gathering national storm would lead to the desire to create the perfect society. **Robert Owen** was one of the utopian movement's major proponents.

The Second Great Awakening was an evangelical Protestant revival that preached personal responsibility for one's actions, both individually and socially. This movement was led by preachers such as Charles Finney who traveled the country preaching the gospel of social responsibility. Social responsibility was a point of view taken up by the "mainline Protestant denominations" (Episcopal, Methodist, Presbyterian, Lutheran, Congregational). Part of the social reform movement that led to an end to child labor, to better working conditions, and to other changes in social attitudes, arose from this new recognition that the Christian faith should be expressed for the good of society.

Closely allied to the Second Great Awakening was **the temperance movement**. This movement had the purpose of ending the sale and consumption of alcohol, and the purpose arose from religious beliefs, the violence that women and children experienced from heavy drinkers, and from the effect of alcohol consumption on the work force. The Society for the Promotion of Temperance was organized in Boston in 1826.

Public schools were established in many states to educate more children. With more literacy and more participation in literature and the arts, the young nation developed a unique culture, one that was less dependent on Europe.

Horace Mann grew up a poor child with little opportunity for education except for his small community library. He took full advantage of the library and was admitted to Brown University, from which he graduated in 1819. Mann practiced law for several years and served in the Massachusetts House of Representatives. He served on the committee of the first school funded by public tax dollars in Dedham, Massachusetts, and in 1837 was appointed secretary to the newly formed State Board of Education. Mann became an outspoken proponent of educational reform, and fought for better resources for schools and teachers. Mann planned the Massachusetts Normal School system for training new teachers. The compulsory public education that is taken for granted today was a new idea in antebellum (pre-Civil War) America, and Mann faced opposition to his ideas. Shortly after Massachusetts adopted this system, New York followed suit. This lay the foundation for the present state-based educational system.

Dorothea Dix was an advocate for public treatment and care for the mentally ill. In the early 1840s, Dix called attention to the deplorable treatment and conditions the mentally ill in Massachusetts were subjected to in a pamphlet entitled *Memorial*. Her efforts resulted in a bill that expanded the state hospital. Dix traveled to several other states, encouraging and overseeing the founding of state mental hospitals. She proposed federal legislation that would have sold public land with the proceeds being distributed to the states to fund care for the mentally ill. The legislation was approved by Congress, however, using public money for social welfare was a contentious issue, and President Franklin Pierce vetoed it.

It was during this period that efforts were made to transform the prison system and its emphasis on punishment into a penitentiary system that attempted rehabilitation.

A group of women emerged in the 1840s who began the first women's rights movement in the nation's history. Among the early leaders of the movement were **Elizabeth Cady Stanton, Lucretia Mott,** and **Ernestine Rose**. At this time few states recognized **women's suffrage** (rights to vote), property rights, sue for divorce, or execute contracts. In 1869, **Susan B. Anthony**, Ernestine Rose and Elizabeth Cady Stanton founded the **National Woman Suffrage Association**.

The **Seneca Falls Convention** was a gathering of women and men in 1848, in the New York mill town of Seneca Falls. The aim was to address the rights of women in the U.S. The growing momentum of the anti-slavery movement and discussion over the rights of black citizens had drawn attention to the rights of female citizens, who could not vote or hold important positions in American government. Some 300 people attended the convention, which culminated in the publication of a "Declaration of Sentiments," which was modeled on the Declaration of Independence and called for equal participation for women. The Seneca Falls Convention is considered an early milestone in the feminist movement.

The following is a partial list of well-known Americans who contributed their leadership and talents in various fields and reforms during this period:

- Emma Hart Willard, Catherine Esther Beecher, and Mary Lyon for **education for women**
- Dr. Elizabeth Blackwell, the **first woman doctor**
- Antoinette Louisa Blackwell, the **first female minister**
- Elihu Burritt and William Ladd for **peace movements**
- Horace Mann, Henry Barnard, Calvin E. Stowe, Caleb Mills, and John Swett for **public education**
- Benjamin Lundy, David Walker, William Lloyd Garrison, Isaac Hooper, Arthur and Lewis Tappan, Theodore Weld, Frederick Douglass, Harriet Tubman, James G. Birney, Henry Highland Garnet, James Forten, Robert Purvis, Harriet Beecher Stowe, Wendell Phillips, and John Brown for **abolition of slavery and the Underground Railroad**
- Louisa Mae Alcott, James Fenimore Cooper, Washington Irving, Walt Whitman, Henry David Thoreau, Ralph Waldo Emerson, Herman Melville, Richard Henry Dana, Nathaniel Hawthorne, Henry Wadsworth Longfellow, John Greenleaf Whittier, Edgar Allan Poe, Oliver Wendell Holmes, **famous writers**
- John C. Fremont, Zebulon Pike, Kit Carson, **explorers**
- Henry Clay, Daniel Webster, Stephen Douglas, John C. Calhoun, American **statesmen**
- Robert Fulton, Cyrus McCormick, Eli Whitney, **inventors**
- Noah Webster, American **dictionary and spellers**

COMPETENCY 2.4   CIVIL WAR AND RECONSTRUCTION

Skill 2.4a   Interpret the debates over the doctrines of nullification and state secession.

The doctrine of **nullification** states that the states have the right to nullify (declare invalid) any act of Congress they believe to be unjust or unconstitutional.

The nullification crisis of the mid-nineteenth century resulted from a new tariff on imported manufactured goods that was enacted by the Congress in 1828. The tariff protected the manufacturing and industrial interests of the North but raised the prices of needed goods in the South.

John C. Calhoun, Andrew Jackson's vice president, led South Carolina to adopt the Ordinance of Nullification which declared the tariff null and void within state borders. The issue came to the brink of military action but was resolved by the enactment of a new tariff in 1832.

The South believed in a state's right to nullify any federal law which was contrary to local interests. The South based this belief on the assumption that the United States was a union of independent commonwealths, and that the general government was merely the agent of the several states — not their superior. The North, however, assumed the Federal government to be supreme and that the Union was inseparable.

When economic issues and the issue of slavery came to a head, the North declared slavery illegal. The South acted on the principles of the doctrine of nullification, declared the new laws null, and acted upon their presumed right as states to secede from the union and form their own government. The North saw secession as a violation of the national unity contract.

Skill 2.4b   Compare and contrast the strengths and weaknesses of the Union and Confederacy.

South Carolina was the first state to **secede** from the Union and the first shots of the war were fired on Fort Sumter in Charleston Harbor. Both sides quickly prepared for war. The North had in its favor: a larger population, superiority in finances, transportation infrastructure, manufacturing, agricultural, and natural resources. The North possessed most of the nation's gold, had about 92% of all industries and almost all known supplies of copper, coal, iron, and various other minerals. Since most of the nation's railroads were in the North and mid-West, men and supplies could be moved wherever needed. Food could be transported from the farms of the mid-West to workers in the East and to soldiers on the battlefields. Trade with nations overseas could go on as usual due to Union control of the navy and the merchant fleet. The Northern states numbered 24 and included western (California and Oregon) and border (Maryland, Delaware, Kentucky, Missouri, and West Virginia) states.

Eleven southern states that included South Carolina, Georgia, Florida, Alabama, Mississippi, Louisiana, Texas, Virginia, North Carolina, Tennessee, and Arkansas made up the **Confederacy**. Although outnumbered in population, the South was completely confident of victory. The Confederacy knew that all they had to do was fight a defensive war. The idea was to force the Union to commit to invade an area almost the size of Western Europe bog down the invaders until the Union would tire of the struggle and give up. Another advantage of the South was that a number of its best officers were graduates of the U.S. Military Academy at West Point and had years of army experience. Some had even exercised varying degrees of command in the Indian wars and the war with Mexico. Southerners were conditioned to living outdoors and were more familiar with horses and firearms than many men from northeastern cities. Since cotton was such an important crop, Southerners felt that Britain and France would help the Confederacy because their textile mills were so dependent on raw cotton.

The South had specific reasons and goals for fighting the war, more so than the North. The major aims of the Confederacy never wavered: to win independence, to govern themselves as they wished, and to preserve slavery. The Union was not as clear in their reasons for war. At the beginning, most believed, along with Lincoln, that preservation of the Union was paramount. Only a few extremely fanatical abolitionists looked on the war as a way to end slavery. However, by war's end, more and more northerners had come to believe that freeing the slaves was just as important as the restoration of the Union.

Skill 2.4c   Describe the major military and political turning points of the war.

The war strategies for both sides were relatively simple. The South planned a defensive war, wearing down the North until it agreed to peace on Southern terms. The exception was to gain control of Washington, D.C., go north through the Shenandoah Valley into Maryland and Pennsylvania in order to drive a wedge between the northeast and mid-west. This would interrupt the lines of communication and end the war quickly. The North had three basic strategies

1. Blockade the Confederate coastline in order to cripple the South
2. Seize control of the Mississippi River and interior railroad lines to split the Confederacy in two
3. Seize the Confederate capital of Richmond, Virginia, then drive southward to join up with Union forces marching eastward from the Mississippi Valley.

The South won decisively until the Battle of Gettysburg, July 1–3, 1863. Prior to Gettysburg, Lincoln's commanders, **McDowell and McClellan**, were less than effective, and **Burnside and Hooker** had not been what was needed. **General Lee**, on the other hand, had many able officers such as **Jackson and Stuart**. Jackson died at Chancellorsville and was replaced by **Longstreet**. Lee decided to invade the North and depended on **J.E.B. Stuart** and his cavalry to keep him informed of the location of Union troops and their strengths. Four things worked against Lee at Gettysburg

1. The Union troops gained the best positions and the best ground first, making it easier to make a stand there.
2. Lee's move into Northern territory put him and his army a long way from food and supply lines. They were more or less on their own.
3. Lee thought that his Army of Northern Virginia was invincible and could fight and win under any conditions.
4. Stuart and his men did not arrive at Gettysburg until the end of the second day of fighting. They detoured around Union soldiers and that delayed the information Lee needed.

Consequently, Lee made the mistake of ignoring Longstreet. A Lee refused to regroup back into Southern territory to the supply lines. Lee felt that regrouping was retreating and almost an admission of defeat.

It was not the intention of either side to fight at Gettysburg but the battle began when a Confederate brigade stumbled onto a unit of Union cavalry while looking for shoes. On the third day Lee launched the final attempt to break Union lines. **General George Pickett** sent his division of three brigades against Union troops on Cemetery Ridge under command of General Winfield Scott Hancock. Union lines held and Lee and the defeated Army of Northern Virginia made their way back to Virginia. Lincoln's commander George Meade successfully turned back a Confederate charge but failed to pursue Lee and the Confederates. This battle was the turning point for the North because after this battle Lee never again had the troop strength to launch a major offensive.

The day after Gettysburg, on July 4, Vicksburg, Mississippi surrendered to Union **General Ulysses Grant.** The Union had severed the western Confederacy from the eastern part. In September 1863, the Confederacy won its last important victory at Chickamauga. In November, the Union victory at Chattanooga made it possible for Union troops to go into Alabama and Georgia that split the eastern Confederacy in two. Lincoln gave Grant command of all Northern armies in March of 1864. Grant led his armies into battles in Virginia while Sheridan and his cavalry did as much damage as possible. In a skirmish at Yellow Tavern, Virginia, Sheridan's and Stuart's forces met Stuart was fatally wounded. The Union won the Battle of Mobile Bay. In May 1864, **William Tecumseh Sherman** began his march to successfully demolish Atlanta, and then on to Savannah. He and his troops turned northward through the Carolinas to meet Grant in Virginia. On April 9, 1865, Lee formally surrendered to Grant at **Appomattox Courthouse**, Virginia.

Skill 2.4d   Describe and analyze the physical, social, political, and economic impact of the war on combatants, civilians, communities, states, and the nation.

The Civil War took more American lives than any other war in history, the South lost one-third of its soldiers in battle compared to about one-sixth for the North. More than half of the total deaths were caused by disease and the horrendous conditions of field hospitals. Both sections paid a tremendous economic price but the South suffered more severely from direct damages.

The effects of the Civil War were tremendous. It changed the methods of waging war and has been called the first modern war. It introduced weapons and tactics that were used extensively in wars of the late 1800s and early 1900s. Civil War soldiers were the first to fight in trenches, first to fight under a unified command, first to wage a defense called "major cordon defense", a strategy of advance on all fronts. They were also the first to use repeating and breech loading weapons. Observation balloons were first used during the war along with submarines, ironclad ships, and mines. Telegraphy and railroads were put to use first in the Civil War. It was considered a modern war because of the vast destruction and was "total war", involving the use of all resources of the opposing sides.

By executive proclamation and constitutional amendment, slavery was officially ended. **Sectionalism**, especially in the area of politics, remained strong for another 100 years but not to the degree nor with the violence as existed before 1861.

The North's victory established that no state has the right to end or leave the Union. Lincoln never proposed to punish the South. He was most concerned with restoring the South to the Union in a program that was flexible and practical rather than rigid and unbending. His plans consisted of two major steps

1. All Southerners who took an **oath of allegiance** to the Union promising to accept all federal laws and proclamations dealing with slavery would receive a full pardon. The only ones excluded from this were men who had resigned from civil and military positions in the federal government to serve in the Confederacy. Those who were part of the Confederate government, those in the Confederate army above the rank of lieutenant, and Confederates who were guilty of mistreating prisoners of war and blacks.

2. A state would be able to write a new constitution, elect new officials, and return to the Union equal to all other states on certain conditions: a minimum number of persons (at least 10% of those who were qualified voters in their states before secession from the Union who had voted in the 1860 election) must take an oath of allegiance.

Congressional Radicals, such as Charles Sumner in the Senate, considered the Southern states as complete political organizations and were now in the same position as any unorganized territory and should be treated as such. Radical House leader Thaddeus Stevens considered the Confederate States, not as territories, but as conquered provinces and felt they should be treated that way. President Johnson refused to work with Congressional moderates, insisting on having his own way. As a result, the Radicals gained control of both houses of Congress and when President Johnson opposed their harsh measures, the House of Representatives impeached him and the Senate came within one vote of the two-thirds majority needed to convict him.

Skill 2.4e   Compare and contrast plans for Reconstruction with its actual implementation.

After the Civil War, the nation was faced with repairing the torn Union and readmitting the Confederate states. **Reconstruction** was the period between 1865 and 1877 when the federal government implemented plans to provide civil rights to freed slaves and set the terms under which the former Confederate states would rejoin the Union.

Plans for Reconstruction began in 1861. The Republican Party favored the extension of voting rights to black men, but was divided as to how far to extend the right. Moderates, such as Lincoln, wanted only literate blacks and those who had fought for the Union to be allowed to vote. Radical Republicans wanted to extend the vote to all black men. Conservative Democrats did not want to give black men the vote at all. Moderates wanted to allow all Confederate soldiers except former leaders to vote, while the radicals wanted to require from all eligible voters an oath that they had never borne arms against the US, which would have excluded all former rebels. On the issue of readmission into the Union, moderates favored a much lower standard, with the radicals demanding nearly impossible conditions for return.

Lincoln's moderate plan for Reconstruction was actually part of his effort to win the war. Lincoln and the moderates felt that if it remained easy for states to return to the Union, and if moderate proposals on black suffrage were made, that Confederate states might be swayed to re-join the Union rather than continue to fight. The radical plan was to ensure that Reconstruction did not actually start until after the war.

In 1865 Abraham Lincoln was assassinated, leaving his Vice-President Andrew Johnson to oversee the beginning of the actual implementation of Reconstruction. Johnson struck a moderate pose and was willing to allow former Confederates to keep control of their state governments. Unfortunately, after Johnson became president the radical Republicans gained control of Congress in 1866 and the harsh measures of radical Reconstruction were implemented.

There was economic and social chaos in the South after the war. The U.S. Army provided some relief of food and clothing for both white and blacks but the major responsibility fell to the **Freedmen's Bureau**. Though the bureau agents to a certain extent helped southern whites, their main responsibility was to the freed slaves. They were to assist the freedmen to become self-sufficient and protect them from being taken advantage of by others. Northerners looked on it as a real, honest effort to help the South out of the chaos it was in. Most white Southerners charged the bureau with causing racial friction and deliberately encouraging the freedmen to consider former owners as enemies.

As a result southern leaders adopted a set of laws known as "black codes", containing many of the provisions of the prewar "slave codes." The codes denied the freedmen their basic civil rights. The black codes were one piece of an expansive effort to keep the freedmen subordinate to whites.

Three amendments were added to the Constitution. The **13th Amendment** (1865) outlawed slavery throughout the entire United States. The **14th Amendment** (1868) made blacks American citizens. The **15th Amendment** (1870) gave black American men the right to vote and made it illegal to deny anyone the right to vote based on race.

In 1866, the Radical Republicans in control of Congress passed the Reconstruction Acts, which placed the governments of the Southern states under the control of the federal military. Republicans began to implement their policies such as granting all black men the vote, and denying the vote to former confederate soldiers. Congress made ratification of the 13th, 14th and 15th Amendments a condition of readmission into the Union by the rebel states. The Republicans found support in the South among Freedmen (as former slaves were called) white southerners who had not supported the Confederacy (called **Scalawags**) and northerners who had moved to the south, known as **Carpetbaggers**.

Military control continued throughout President Grant's administration (1869–1877), despite increased conflict inside and outside the Republican Party. Conservatives in Congress and in the states opposed the liberal policies of the Republicans. Some Republicans became concerned over corruption issues among Grant's appointees and dropped support for him.

The presidential election of 1876 between Republican **Rutherford B. Hayes** and Democrat Samuel J. Tilden. The election produced no clear winner. Through legal and political battles Hayes was declared the winner. Three southern states: Florida, Louisiana, and South Carolina awarded their electoral votes to Hayes. Those votes were enough to swing the election to Republican candidate Hayes. In exchange for these electoral votes Hayes promised to withdraw federal troops from the South — thus ending Reconstruction. The withdrawal led to the legal codification of segregation and white supremacy.

Under President Rutherford B. Hayes, federal troops were removed from the South. Without this support, the Republican governments were replaced by so-called **Redeemer** governments. The rise of the Redeemer governments marked the beginning of the **Jim Crow** laws and official segregation. Blacks were still allowed to vote, but ways were found to make it difficult for them to do so, such as literacy tests and poll taxes. For example, during Reconstruction South Carolina had 92,801 African-Americans registered voters. By 1898 that number fell to 2,823. This pattern was repeated throughout the old Confederacy once federal troops were withdrawn. Reconstruction, which had set as its goal the reunification of the South with the North and the granting of civil rights to freed slaves was a limited success, at best, and in the eyes of blacks was considered a failure.

Federal troops were stationed throughout the South and protected African-American and the new Southern governments. Bitterly resentful, white Southerners fought the new political system by joining a secret society called the **Ku Klux Klan**, using violence to keep black Americans from the vote, employment and education.

Before being allowed to rejoin the Union, the Confederate states were required to agree to all federal laws. Between 1866 and 1870, all of the states had returned to the Union. Northern interest in Reconstruction faded. Reconstruction officially ended when President Hayes ordered the last federal troops to leave the South in 1877.

Skill 2.4f **Explain and assess the development and adoption of segregation laws, the influence of social mores on the passage and implementation of these laws, and the rise of white supremacist organizations.**

The **Emancipation Proclamation** in 1863 and the 13th Amendment in 1865 ended slavery in the United States, but these measures did not erase the centuries of racial prejudices among whites that held blacks to be inferior in intelligence and morality. These prejudices, along with fear of economic competition from newly freed slaves, led to a series of state laws that permitted or required physical segregation of blacks and whites.

The **Black Codes** aimed to keep blacks subservient to whites. Freedmen, as newly freed slaves were called, were afforded some civil rights protection during the Reconstruction period; however, beginning around 1876, Redeemer governments began to take office in Southern states after the removal of federal troops that had supported Reconstruction goals. The Redeemer state legislatures began passing segregation laws which came to be known as **Jim Crow** laws.

The Jim Crow laws varied from state to state, but the most significant of them required separate school systems and libraries for blacks and whites and separate ticket windows, waiting rooms and seating areas on trains and, later, other public transportation. Restaurant owners were permitted or sometimes required to provide separate entrances and tables and counters for blacks and whites, so that the two races did not see one another while dining. Public parks and playgrounds were constructed for each race. Landlords were not allowed to mix black and white tenants in apartment houses in some states.

The Jim Crow laws were given credibility in 1896 when the Supreme Court handed down its decision in the case *Plessy vs. Ferguson*. In 1890, Louisiana had passed a law requiring separate train cars for blacks and whites. To challenge this law, in 1892 Homer Plessy, a man who had a black great grandparent and so was considered legally "black" in that state, purchased a ticket in the white section and took his seat. Upon informing the conductor that he was black, he was told to move to the black car. He refused and was arrested. His case was eventually heard by the Supreme Court.

The Court ruled against Plessy, thereby ensuring that the Jim Crow laws would continue to proliferate and be enforced. The Court held that segregating races was constitutional as long as the facilities for each were identical. This became known as the **"separate but equal"** principle. In practice, facilities were seldom equal. Black schools were funded at far lower levels. Streets and parks in black neighborhoods were not maintained. This trend continued throughout the following decades. Even the federal government adopted segregation as official policy when President Woodrow Wilson segregated the civil service in the 1910s.

Legal segregation was a part of life for generations of Americans until the "separate but equal" doctrine was challenged. In 1954, in the Supreme Court case of *Brown vs. Board of Education*, the "separate but equal" doctrine was overturned in the field of education. This case arose when a Topeka, Kansas man attempted to enroll his third-grade daughter in a segregated white neighborhood elementary school and was refused. Even with the new legal interpretation, some states refused to integrate their schools. In Virginia, the state closed some schools rather than integrate them. In Arkansas, Governor Orville Faubus mobilized the National Guard to prevent the integration of Little Rock High School. President Eisenhower sent federal troops to enforce integration.

The civil rights movement, led by **Martin Luther King, Jr**. and others, culminated in the **Civil Rights Act of 1964**. This act ended legal segregation in the United States; however, some forms of de facto segregation continue to exist, particularly in the area of housing.

Some organized groups opposed integration of blacks into white society. The most notable of these was the **Ku Klux Klan**. First organized in Reconstruction South, the KKK was a loose group made up mainly of former Confederate soldiers who opposed the Reconstruction government and espoused a doctrine of white supremacy. KKK members intimidated, and sometimes killed, their proclaimed enemies. In 1871, President Grant took action to use federal troops to halt the activities of the KKK and actively prosecuted them in federal court. Klan activity waned, and the organization disappeared.

In 1915, the Klan was resurrected following the film *The Birth of a Nation*. The new clan added an anti-immigrant and anti-Catholic slant to its platform and was organized on a national level. Reaching its peak in the 1920s, this new Klan obtained widespread political and social influence, especially throughout the South and Midwest. The Klan saw membership decline through the Great Depression and the Second World War, when they emerged as sympathizers with Nazi sentiment and lost public support. The Klan still exists.

Skill 2.4g **Analyze the relationship of the 13th, 14th, and 15th Amendments to Reconstruction, and compare and contrast their initial and later interpretations.**

The **13th Amendment** abolished slavery and involuntary servitude, except as punishment for crime. The Amendment was ratified by the necessary number of states on December 18, 1865. It followed the Emancipation Proclamation that had freed slaves held in states that were considered to be in rebellion. This amendment freed slaves in states and territories controlled by the Union.

The **14th Amendment** provides for **Due Process and Equal Protection** under the law. It was ratified on July 28, 1868. The Amendment requires that states provide equal protection under the law to all persons. The Amendment overturned the Dred Scott case. The full potential of this amendment was realized in the 1950s and 1960s, when it became the basis of ending segregation in the Supreme Court case *Brown v. Board of Education*. This amendment includes the stipulation that all children born on American soil are U.S. citizens.

After the Civil War, many Southern states passed laws that attempted to restrict the movements of blacks and prevent them from bringing lawsuits or testifying in court. In the *Slaughterhouse Cases* (1871) the Supreme Court first interpreted the 14th Amendment and ruled that the Amendment applies only to rights granted by the federal government. It was not until the 1960s that the Supreme Court held that the 14th Amendment applies to all people everywhere. In the *Civil Rights Cases*, the Court held that the guarantee of rights did not outlaw racial discrimination by individuals and organizations. In the next few decades the Court overturned several laws barring blacks from serving on juries or discriminating against the Chinese immigrants in regulating the laundry businesses.

The separate but equal doctrine was reversed in the area of education in the case of *Brown v. Board of Education*. Since this ruling, the Court has extended the equal protection clause to a number of other historically disadvantaged groups.

The second section of the 14th Amendment establishes the "**one man, one vote**" apportionment of congressional representation. This ended the counting of blacks as three fifths of a person. Section III of the Amendment prevents anyone who took "an oath to support the Constitution of the United States" then served the Confederacy from holding any local, state (such as the Electoral College), federal or military office. Section IV stipulated that the government would not pay "damages" for the loss of slaves or for debts incurred by the Confederate government (e.g., with English or French banks).

The **15th Amendment** (ratified February 1870) gave voting rights to black men. It states the right of citizens of the United States to vote shall not be denied or abridged by the United States or by any **state** on account of **race**, **color**, or previous condition of **servitude**.

All three of these Constitutional Amendments were part of the Reconstruction effort to create stability and rule of law to provide, protect, and enforce the rights of former slaves throughout the nation.

COMPETENCY 2.5 THE "GILDED AGE"

Skill 2.5a Describe and analyze the role of entrepreneurs and industrialists and their impact on the United States economy.

There was a marked degree of industrialization before and during the Civil War, but at war's end, industry in America was small. After the war, dramatic changes took place. Machines replaced hand labor and an extensive nationwide railroad service made possible the wider distribution of goods. New products were made available in large quantities and large amounts of money from bankers and investors were available for expansion of business operations. American life was definitely affected by this phenomenal industrial growth. Cities became the centers of this new business activity. Cities attracted mass population movements and tremendous growth. This new boom in business resulted in huge fortunes for few Americans and extreme poverty for many others. The discontent this caused resulted in a number of new reform movements from which came measures controlling the power and size of big business and help for the poor.

Industry before, during, and after the Civil War was centered mainly in the North, The use of machines in industry enabled workers to produce a large quantity of goods much faster than ever before. With the increase in business, hundreds of workers were hired, assigned to perform a certain job in the production process. This was a method of production called **division of labor.** Due to increased rates of production businesses lowered prices for their products and made products affordable for more people.

The typewriter, the telephone, barbed wire, the electric light, the phonograph, and the gasoline automobile were examples of new products/inventions that became available. The **automobile** had the greatest effect on America's economy. The late 1800s and early 1900s also saw the increased buildup of military strength and the U.S. became a world power.

As business grew, methods of sales and promotion were developed. Salespersons went to all parts of the country to promote various products. Large department stores opened in the growing cities and offered many products at affordable prices. People who lived too far from the cities could use a mail order service. The developments in communication, such as the telephone and telegraph, increased the efficiency and prosperity of big business.

Individuals invested heavily in stocks and bonds in an eager desire to share in the profits. Their investments made available the needed capital for companies to expand their operations. From this, banks made loans to businesses, resulting in significant contributions to economic growth. At the same time, during the 1880s, government made little effort to regulate businesses. This gave rise to **monopolies** where larger businesses eliminated their smaller competitors and assumed control of their industries.

Some owners in the same business would join or merge to form one company. Others formed what were called **trusts**, a type of monopoly in which rival businesses were controlled but not formally owned. Monopolies had some good effects on the economy. Out of them grew the large, efficient corporations, which made important contributions to the growth of the nation's economy. Monopolies enabled businesses to keep their sales steady and avoid sharp fluctuations in price and production. Leaders of monopolies participated in unfair business practices that took advantage of others. They could require suppliers to supply goods at a low cost and then sell the finished products at high prices, making huge profits and reducing quality of the product to save money.

The industrial boom produced several extremely wealthy and powerful **captains of industry** such as **Andrew Carnegie, John D. Rockefeller**, Jay Gould, J.P Morgan and Philip Armour. Most workers put in long hours in dangerous conditions doing monotonous work for low wages. Most were unable to afford to participate in the new comforts and forms of entertainment that were available. Farmers believed they were also being exploited by the bankers, suppliers and the railroads. This produced enough instability to fuel several recessions and two severe depressions.

Skill 2.5b   Describe and analyze the effects of industrialization on the American economy and society, including increased immigration, changing working conditions, and the growth of early labor organizations.

The nation witnessed significant industrial growth during and after the Civil War. Steam power generation, sophisticated manufacturing equipment, the ability to move about the country quickly by railroad, and the invention of the steam powered tractor, resulted in a phenomenal growth in industrial output. The new steel and oil industries provided a significant impetus to industrial growth and added thousands of new jobs.

Between 1870 and 1916, more than 25 million immigrants came into the United States, adding to the phenomenal population growth that took place. This tremendous growth aided business and industry in two ways. First, demand for products rose with the increase in consumers. Second, with increased production and expanding business, more workers were available for newly created jobs. The completion of the nation's **transcontinental railroad** in 1869 contributed greatly to the nation's economic and industrial growth. Railroads could ship raw materials quickly and finished products were sent to all parts of the country. During the last 40 years of the nineteenth century inventors registered almost 700,000 new patents. Innovations in new industrial processes and technology grew at a pace unmatched at any other time in American history. **Thomas Edison** was the most prolific inventor of that time. He used a systematic and efficient method to invent and improve on technology in a profitable manner.

One result of industrialization was the growth of the **labor movement**. There were boycotts and strikes. Some became violent when the police or the militia were called in to stop the strikes. Labor and farmer organizations were created and became a political force. Industrialization brought an influx of immigrants from Asia (particularly Chinese and Japanese) and from Europe (particularly Jews, the Irish, and Russians). High rates of immigration led to the creation of communities in various cities like "little Russia" or "little Italy." Industrialization led to overwhelming growth of cities as workers moved closer to their places of work.

Skilled laborers were organized into a labor union called the **American Federation of Labor** in an effort to gain better working conditions and wages for its members. Farmers joined organizations such as the **National Grange** and farmers alliances. Because both new farmlands rapidly sprouted on the plains and prairies and the development and availability of new farm machinery and newer and better methods of farming farmers produced more food than people could buy. They tried to sell their surpluses abroad but faced stiff competition from other nations. Items farmers needed for daily life were expensive. They had to borrow money to carry on farming and were constantly in debt. Higher interest rates, shortage of money, falling farm prices, dealing with the "middlemen", and the increasingly high charges by the railroads to haul farm products to large markets all contributed to the desperate need for reform to relieve the plight of American farmers.

Skill 2.5c   Explain and analyze the causes for, and the impact of, Populism and Progressivism.

Populism is the philosophy that is concerned with the common-sense needs of average people. Populism often finds expression as a reaction against perceived oppression of the average people by the wealthy elite in society. The prevalent claim of populist movements is that the people should be put first. Populism flourished in the late nineteenth and early twentieth centuries. Several political parties were formed out of this philosophy, including: the Greenback Party, the Populist Party, the Farmer-Labor Party, the Single Tax movement, the Share Our Wealth movement of **Huey Long**, the Progressive Party, and the Union Party. In the 1890s, the People's Party won the support of millions of farmers and other working people. This party challenged the social ills of the monopolists of the Gilded Age.

The late 1800s and early 1900s was a period of significant reforms and changes in the areas of politics, society, and the economy. In the 1890s, the reformers gained increased public support and were able to achieve some influence in government. Since some of these individuals referred to themselves as **progressives**, the period from 1890 to 1917 is referred to by historians as the **Progressive Era**.

In the late 1890s a new type of journalism appeared. It emphasized sensationalism rather than facts and helped push the U.S. in one direction or another. It was called **yellow journalism** and was used to incite Americans and encourage the declaration of war against Spain when the battleship Maine was blown up in Havana, Cuba. During the Spanish-American War yellow journalism promoted the acquisition of territories, such as Puerto Rico and the Philippines.

The **muckrakers** were investigative journalists who published scathing exposes of political and business wrongdoing and corruption. The efforts of these reformers were far-reaching. In an attempt to be more responsive to voters many states enacted the initiative, referendum, and recall. On the national level, **17th Amendment** was ratified and provided U.S. Senators would be chosen by popular election. The **19th Amendment**, which granted women the right to vote, was also ratified.

Major economic reforms of the period included aggressive enforcement of the **Sherman Antitrust Act**, passage of the Elkins and the Hepburn acts, that gave the Interstate Commerce Commission greater power to regulate the railroads, the **Pure Food and Drug Act** that prohibited the use of harmful chemicals in food, and The Meat Inspection Act that regulated the meat industry to protect the public against tainted meat. More than two-thirds of the states passed laws to ban child labor. Workmen's compensation was mandated, and the **Department of Commerce and Labor** was created.

President **Theodore Roosevelt** set aside 238 million acres of federal lands to protect them from development. Wildlife preserves were established, the national park system was expanded, and the **National Conservation Commission** was created. The Newlands Reclamation Act provided federal funding for the construction of irrigation projects and dams in semi-arid areas of the country.

The Wilson Administration carried out additional reforms. The **Federal Reserve Act** created a national banking system that could provide a stable money supply. The Sherman and the Clayton Antitrust acts defined unfair competition, made corporate officers liable for the illegal actions of employees, and exempted labor unions from antitrust lawsuits. The Federal Trade Commission was established to enforce these measures. The **16th Amendment** established the income tax.

Skill 2.5d   Explain the development of federal Indian policy – including the environmental consequences of forced migration into marginal regions – and its consequences for American Indians.

This forced migration of the Native Americans to new lands, combined with the near-extermination of the buffalo, caused a downturn in Prairie Culture. Conflict was intense and frequent until 1867 when the government established two large tracts of land called **reservations** in Oklahoma and the Dakotas to which all tribes would be confined. With the Civil War over, troops were sent west to enforce the relocation and reservation containment policies. As white settlers attempted to move onto Indian lands, the tribes resisted confinement.

Numerous conflicts, often called the **Indian Wars** broke out between the U.S. army and many different native tribes. Two notable battles were the **Battle of Little Bighorn** in 1876, in which native people defeated General Custer and his forces, and the massacre of Native Americans in 1890 at **Wounded Knee**. Many treaties were signed with the various tribes, but most were broken by the government. In 1876, the U.S. government ordered all surviving Native Americans to move to reservations.

Continuing conflict led to passage of the **Dawes Act of 1887**. This law was intended to break up the Indian communities and bring about assimilation into white culture by deeding portions of the reservation lands to individual Indians who were expected to farm the land. The policy continued until 1934.

During the late nineteenth century the government began a practice of trying to "civilize" Indian children by educating them in Indian boarding schools. The children were forbidden to speak their native languages, were forced to convert to Christianity, and generally compelled to give up all aspects of their native culture and identity. Conditions at these schools were harsh. Many children were beaten and abused by the staff.

Armed resistance essentially came to an end by 1890. **Geronimo** surrendered and the massacre at Wounded Knee led to a change of strategy by the Indians. Thereafter, they strove to preserve their culture and traditions.

During World War I, many Native Americans were drafted into military service. Most served heroically. This fact, combined with a desire to see the native peoples effectively merge into mainstream society, led to the enactment of the **Indian Citizenship Act of 1924**, which granted Native Americans citizenship.

The policies of extermination and relocation, as well as the introduction of disease among Native Americans significantly decreased their numbers by the end of the nineteenth century.

Skill 2.5e Analyze the impact of industrialism and urbanization on the physical and social environments of the United States.

The increase in business and industry was greatly affected by the rich natural resources that were found throughout the nation. Industrial machines were powered by the abundant water supply. The construction industry depended heavily on lumber from the forests. Coal and iron ore were needed for the steel industry, which used steel in such things as skyscrapers, automobiles, bridges, railroad tracks, and machines. Other minerals such as silver, copper, and petroleum played a large role in industrial growth, especially petroleum, from which gasoline was refined as fuel for the increasingly popular automobile.

The abundance of resources, the growth of industry, and the pace of capital investments led to the growth of cities. Populations shifted from rural agricultural to urban industrial areas. By the early 1900s one-third of the nation's population lived in cities. Industry needed workers in its factories, mills and plants and rural workers were being displaced by advances in farm machinery and automation.

Densely populated urban areas, often without adequate sanitation or clean water, led to public health challenges that required cities to establish sanitation, water and public health departments to cope with and prevent epidemics. Political organizations also saw the advantage of mobilizing the new industrial working class and created vast patronage programs that sometimes became notorious for corruption in big-city machine politics, such as **Tammany Hall** in New York.

(See also Skills 2.5b and 2.5c)

COMPETENCY 2.6   THE U.S. AS A WORLD POWER

Skill 2.6a   Evaluate the debate about American imperialistic policies before, during and following the Spanish-American War.

Once the American West was firmly under government control, the United States started to look beyond its shores. Overseas markets were became important as American industry produced goods more efficiently and in greater quantities. The U.S. modernized and increased its Navy, which by 1900 ranked third in the world and gave the U.S. the means to become an imperial power. The first overseas possession, **Midway Island,** was annexed in 1867.

By the 1880s, the U.S. pushed to expand trade and influence to Central and South America. In the 1890s, President Grover Cleveland invoked the **Monroe Doctrine** to intercede in Latin American affairs when it appeared Great Britain was going to exert its influence and power in the Western Hemisphere. In the Pacific, the United States supported American sugar planters who overthrew the Kingdom of **Hawaii.** Eventually Hawaii was annexed as a U.S. territory.

During the 1890s, Spain controlled such overseas possessions as Puerto Rico, the Philippines, and Cuba. Cubans rebelled against Spanish rule and the U.S. government found itself participating in the **Spanish-American War** in 1898.

When the revolution began in Cuba, Spain attempted to put it down. When reports of gross atrocities reached America, public sentiment clearly favored the Cuban people. President McKinley refused to recognize the rebellion but affirmed the possibility of American intervention. In February 1898, the American battleship *Maine* was blown up in Havana harbor. There was no proof that the Spanish were responsible but popular sentiment accused Spanish agents and war became inevitable.

Two months later, Congress declared war on Spain and the U.S. was quickly victorious. The peace treaty gave the U.S. Puerto Rico, the Philippines, Guam, and Hawaii. Victory over the Spanish proved fruitful for American territorial ambitions. Congress passed legislation renouncing claims to annex Cuba but annexed **Puerto Rico**, kept a permanent deep-water naval harbor at Guantanamo Bay, Cuba, the Philippines and various other Pacific islands formerly possessed by Spain. The decision to occupy the **Philippines**, rather than grant it immediate independence, led to a guerrilla war. The **Philippines Insurrection** lasted until 1902. U.S. rule over the Philippines lasted until 1942.

Skill 2.6b   **Analyze the political, economic, and geographic significance of the Panama Canal, the "Open Door" policy with China, Theodore Roosevelt's "Big Stick" Diplomacy, William Howard Taft's "Dollar" Diplomacy, and Woodrow Wilson's Moral Diplomacy.**

Until the middle of the nineteenth century, American foreign policy and expansionism was essentially restricted to North America. America had shown no interest in establishing colonies in other lands. Specifically, the U.S. had stayed out of the rush to claim African territories. The variety of imperialism that found expression under the administrations of McKinley and Theodore Roosevelt was not precisely comparable to the imperialistic goals of European nations. There was a type of idealism in American foreign policy that sought to use military power in territories and other lands only in the interest of human rights and to spread democratic principles. Much of the concern and involvement in Central and South America, as well as the Caribbean, was to link the two coasts of the nation and to protect the American economy from European encroachment.

The French began construction of **Panama Canal** in 1880. The effort collapsed and the U.S. completed the Panama Canal in 1914. The Canal was an enormous task of complex engineering. The significance of the Canal is that it connects the Gulf of Panama in the Pacific Ocean with the Caribbean Sea and the Atlantic Ocean. It eliminated the need for ships to sail around the tip of South America, effectively reducing the sailing distance from New York to San Francisco by 8,000 miles (over half of the distance) and reducing shipping time and cost.

The U.S. helped Panama win independence from Colombia in exchange for control of the Panama Canal Zone. A large investment was made in eliminating disease from the area, particularly yellow fever and malaria. After WWII, control of the Canal became an issue of contention between the U.S. and Panama. Negotiations toward a settlement began in 1974, resulting in the Torrijos-Carter Treaties of 1977 that began the process of handing the Canal over to Panama. On December 31, 1999, control of the Canal was handed over to the Panama Canal Authority.

The **Open Door Policy** refers to maintaining equal commercial and industrial rights for the people of all countries in a particular territory. The Open Door policy generally refers to China U.S. relations and was first suggested by the U.S. around the time of the **Opium War** (1829–1842). The essential purpose of the policy was to permit equal access to trade for all nations while protecting the integrity of the Chinese empire. This policy was in effect from about 1900 until the end of WWII. After the war, China was recognized as a sovereign state. When the Communist Party came to power in China, the policy was rejected until the late 1970s when China began to re-adopt a policy of encouraging foreign trade.

Big Stick Diplomacy was a term adopted from an African proverb that meant "speak softly and carry a big stick." It described President Theodore Roosevelt's policy of the U.S. assumption of international police power in the Western Hemisphere to safeguard American economic interests in Latin America. The policy led to the expansion of the U.S. Navy and greater involvement in world affairs.

Dollar Diplomacy describes U.S. efforts under President Taft to extend foreign policy goals into Latin America and East Asia via economic power. The designation derives from Taft's claim that U.S. interests in Latin America had changed from "warlike and political" to "peaceful and economic." Taft justified this policy in terms of protecting the Panama Canal. The practice of dollar diplomacy was from time to time anything but peaceful, particularly in Nicaragua. When revolts or revolutions occurred, the U.S. sent troops to resolve the situation. Immediately upon resolution, bankers were sent in to loan money to the new regimes. The policy persisted until the election of Woodrow Wilson in 1913.

Wilson repudiated the dollar diplomacy approach to foreign policy within weeks of his inauguration. His **Moral Diplomacy** became the model for American foreign policy. Wilson envisioned a federation of democratic nations as the foundation stones of world stability. Wilson promoted the power of free trade and international commerce as the key to a strong economy and engagement in world markets as a means of acquiring a voice in world events. This approach to foreign policy was based on three elements: a combat-ready military to meet the needs of the nation, promotion of democracy abroad, and economic growth through international trade.

Skill 2.6c **Evaluate the political, economic, social, and geographic consequences of World War I in terms of American foreign policy and the war's impact on the American home front.**

U.S. involvement in the WW I did not occur until late in the war. When the war began in 1914, President Woodrow Wilson declared a policy of neutrality. Wilson was re-elected to a second term based the slogan "He kept us out of war". The development of the German *unterseeboot* (submarine) or **U-boat** allowed them to efficiently attack merchant ships that supplied Germany's enemies. German submarines began unlimited warfare against American merchant shipping. A German U-boat sunk the British passenger liner RMS **Lusitania**, more than 1,000 civilians and more than 100 Americans were killed. This attack outraged the American public and turned public opinion against Germany. The attack on the Lusitania became a rallying point for those advocating U.S. involvement in the European conflict.

Great Britain intercepted and decoded a secret message from Germany to Mexico that urged Mexico to go to war against the U.S. The publishing of this information, known as the **Zimmerman Note,** along with continued German destruction of American ships resulted in the eventual entry of the U.S. into the conflict (Tripoli, Cuba, Philippines, etc.). The U.S. made a massive defense mobilization, with America's economy directed to the war effort.

In December 1917, the government assumed control of all of the railroads in the nation and consolidated them into a single system with regional directors. The goal of this action was to increase efficiency and enable the rail system to meet the needs of both commerce and military transportation. This was done with the understanding that private ownership would be restored after the war. The restoration occurred in 1920. In 1918, telegraph, telephone and cable services were also taken over by the federal government; they were returned to original management and ownership in 1919.

The government sold **Liberty Bonds** to the people to obtain money to fight the war. More than one-fifth of Americans bought bonds. After the war Victory Bonds were sold, and for the first time millions of people began to save money.

The war effort required massive production of weapons, ammunition, radios, and other equipment. During wartime work hours were shortened, wages were increased, and labor conditions improved. But when the war ended, industrial owners and managers attempted a return to pre-war conditions, the workers revolted. These conditions contributed to the **Red Scare** and the establishment of new labor laws.

The United States war effort included more than four million who served in the military in some capacity, two million who served overseas. 53,402 Americans were killed in battle and an additional 204,002 were wounded. While there were several peace and non-intervention movements most Americans energetically supported the war effort.

President Wilson proposed a program called the **Fourteen Points** as a method of bringing the war to an end with an equitable peace settlement. There were five points setting out general ideals, eight pertained to resolution of territorial and political problems, and the fourteenth point established an organization of nations to keep world peace.

When Germany agreed to an armistice, it assumed that the peace settlement would be drawn up on the basis of these Fourteen Points. However, the peace conference in Paris in 1919 ignored these points and Wilson had to be content with the establishment of the **League of Nations**. Italy, France, and Great Britain, suffered and sacrificed far more in the war than America and wanted retribution. The treaty was harsh toward the **Central Powers.** It took away arms and territories and required reparations payments. Germany was punished more than the others and was forced to assume the responsibility for the war.

President Wilson failed to get the U.S. Senate to approve the **Treaty of Versailles**. The approval of the treaty would have made the U.S. a member of the League of Nations but Americans had just come off a bloody war to ensure that democracy would exist throughout the world. Americans did not want to accept any responsibility that resulted from its new position of power and were afraid that membership in the League of Nations would embroil the U.S. in future disputes in Europe.

COMPETENCY 2.7   THE 1920s

Skill 2.7a   Analyze domestic events that resulted in, or contributed to, the Red Scare, Marcus Garvey's Back to Africa movement, the Ku Klux Klan, the American Civil Liberties Union, the National Association for the Advancement of Colored People, and the Anti-Defamation League.

The 1920s was a period of relative prosperity, under the leadership of Warren G. Harding and Calvin Coolidge. Harding had promised a return to "normalcy" in the aftermath of World War I and the radical reactions of labor. During most of the decade, the output of industry boomed and the automobile industry put almost 27 million cars on the road. Per capita income rose for almost everyone except farmers.

The decade was also characterized by profound change. **Jazz** became the popular musical form. Professional boxing, radio and silent movies provided new entertainment for the public. The Charleston (dance) and the **flapper look** were popular. The **National Origins Act of 1924** restricted European immigration for the first time in history. In Tennessee, the **Monkey Trial** convicted John Scopes for teaching evolution in science classes. The Bolshevik Revolution in Russia was also on the minds of the people.

Part of the return to "normalcy" promised by Harding, was to restore order in the aftermath of a wave of radicalism. During the war, patriotism prevailed. This strong patriotism provided fertile ground for the Red Scare to grow. During the war, about nine million people in the nation were employed in war-related industries. An additional four million served in the military. When the war ended, most of these people were without jobs and the war industries were without work. There was a small depression in 1920–21, which gave rise to worker unrest. Two groups were highly visible at the time: the **International Workers of the World (IWW)** and the Socialist party, led by **Eugene Debs**. Because both groups had opposed the war, the intensely patriotic population viewed them as unpatriotic and dangerous.

A huge wave of labor strikes sought a return to war-time working conditions when the work day was shorter, wages were higher, and conditions were better. Many of these labor strikes turned violent. The majority of the population viewed the early strikes as the work of radicals who were labeled "reds" (communists). As the news spread and other strikes occurred, the **Red Scare** swept the country. Americans feared a Bolshevik-type revolution in America. As a result, people were jailed for expressing views that were considered anarchist, communist or socialist. In an attempt to control the potential for revolution, civil liberties were scrutinized and thousands were deported. The Socialist Party came to be viewed as a group of anarchist radicals. Several state and local governments passed a variety of laws designed to reduce radical speech and activity. Congress considered more than 70 anti-sedition bills, though none were passed.

Within a year, the Red Scare had essentially run its course.

Marcus Garvey, an English-educated Jamaican, established an organization called the *Universal Negro Improvement and Conservation Association and African Communities League* (usually called the Universal Negro Improvement Association). In 1919 this "Black Moses" claimed followers numbering about two million. He spoke of a "new Negro" who was proud to be black. He published a newspaper in which he taught about the "heroes" of the race and the strengths of African culture. He told blacks that they would be respected only when they were economically strong. He created a number of businesses to achieve this goal. He then called blacks to work with him to build an all-black nation in Africa. His belief in black separatism was not shared by a number of black leaders. In 1922 he and other members of the organization were jailed for mail fraud. His sentence was commuted and he was deported to Jamaica as an undesirable alien.

The **Ku Klux Klan** entered a second period in 1915. Using the new film medium, this group tried to spread its message with *The Birth of a Nation*. They published a number of anti-Semitic newspaper articles and became a structured membership organization. Its membership did not begin to decline until the Great Depression. Membership in the 1920s reached approximately four million and the group's political influence was significant, essentially controlling some southern legislatures and state governments.

Several groups were formed to protect the civil rights and liberties guaranteed to all citizens by the U.S. Constitution. The **American Civil Liberties Union** was formed in 1920. It was originally an outgrowth of the American Union Against Militarism, which opposed American involvement in WWI and provided legal assistance to conscientious objectors and those prosecuted under the Espionage Act of 1917 and the Sedition Act of 1918. With the name change there was attention to additional concerns and activities. The agency began to try to protect immigrants threatened with deportation and citizens threatened with prosecution for communist activities. They also opposed efforts to repress the Industrial Workers of the World and other labor unions.

The National Association for the Advancement of Colored People (NAACP) was founded in 1909 to assist African Americans. In the early years, the work of the organization focused on working through the courts to overturn Jim Crow statutes that legalized racial discrimination. The group organized voters to oppose Woodrow Wilson's efforts to weave racial segregation into federal government policy. Between WWI and WWII, much energy was devoted to stop the lynching of blacks throughout the country.

The Anti-Defamation League was created in 1913 to stop discrimination against the Jewish people. The organization has historically opposed all groups considered anti-Semitic and/or racist. This has included the Ku Klux Klan, the Nazis, and a variety of others.

Skill 2.7b   Analyze the significance of the passage of the 18th and 19th Amendments as they related to the changing political and economic roles of women in society.

The end of World War I and the decade of the 1920s saw tremendous changes in the United States. The shift from farm to city life occurred in tremendous numbers. The 18th Amendment to the Constitution, the so-called Prohibition Amendment, prohibited selling alcoholic beverages throughout the U.S. The 19th Amendment gave women the right to vote in all elections. The decade of the 1920s also showed a marked change in roles and opportunities for women with more women seeking and finding careers outside the home.

The influence of the automobile, the entertainment industry, and the rejection of the morals and values of pre-World War I life resulted in the fast-paced **Roaring Twenties.** There were significant effects on events leading to the **Great Depression** of the 1930s and another world war. Many Americans desired the pre-war life and supported political policies and candidates in favor of the return to what was considered normal, ending the government's strong role and adopting a policy of isolation the country from world affairs.

Prohibition of the sale of alcohol increased bootlegging, gangs, illegal speakeasies, and jazz music. The customers of these clubs were considered "modern," reflected by extremes in clothing, hairstyles, and attitudes towards authority and life. Movies and other types of entertainment, along with increased interest in sports figures and the accomplishments of national heroes (such as aviator **Charles Lindbergh**) influenced Americans to admire, emulate, and support individual accomplishments.

Skill 2.7c   Assess changes in American immigration policy in the 1920s.

Immigration has played a crucial role in the growth and settlement of the United States. With a large interior territory to fill and ample opportunity, the U.S. encouraged immigration throughout most of the nineteenth century, maintaining an almost completely open policy. Famine in Ireland and Germany in the 1840s resulted in more than 3.5 million immigrants from these two countries alone between the years of 1830 and 1860.

Following the Civil War, rapid expansion in rail transportation brought the interior states within easy reach of new immigrants who still came primarily from Western Europe and entered the U.S. on the east coast. As immigration increased, several states adopted individual immigration laws, and in 1875 the U.S. Supreme Court declared immigration a federal matter. After a huge surge in European immigration in 1880, the United States began to regulate immigration, first by passing a tax on new immigrants, then by instituting literacy requirements and barring those with mental or physical illness. A large influx of Chinese immigration to the Western states resulted in the complete exclusion of immigrants from that country in 1882. In 1891, the Federal Bureau of Immigration was established. Even with these new limits in place, U.S. immigration remained relatively open to those from European countries, and increased steadily until World War I.

With much of Europe left in ruins after WWI, immigration into the U.S. exploded in the years after the war. In 1920 and 1921, some 800,000 new immigrants arrived. Unlike previous immigrants who came mainly from western European countries, the new wave of immigrants was from southern and eastern Europe. The U.S. responded to this sudden shift in the makeup of new immigrants with a **quota system**, first enacted by Congress in 1921. This system limited immigration in proportion to the ethnic groups that were already settled in the U.S. according to previous census records. This national-origins policy was extended and further defined by Congress in 1924.

This policy remained the official policy of the U.S. for the next forty years. Occasional challenges to the law from non-white immigrants re-affirmed that the intention of the policy was to limit immigration primarily to white, western Europeans, who the government felt were best able to assimilate into American culture. Strict limitations on Chinese immigration were extended throughout the period, and only relaxed in 1940. In 1965, Congress overhauled immigration policy, removing the quotas and replacing them with a preference-based system. Immigrants reuniting with family members and those with special skills or education were given preference. As a result, immigration from Asian and African countries began to increase. The 40-year legacy of the 1920s' immigration restrictions had a direct and dramatic impact on the makeup of modern American society.

Skill 2.7d   Describe new trends in literature, music, and art, including the Harlem Renaissance and the Jazz Age.

Millions of African Americans left the rural South and migrated North during **The Great Migration**. They left in search of opportunity and fled violence and oppression. Many settled in Harlem in New York City. By the 1920s, Harlem had become a center of life and activity for persons of color. The music, art, and literature of this community gave birth to a cultural movement known as **the Harlem Renaissance**. The artistic expressions that emerged from this community in the 1920s and 1930s celebrated the black experience, black traditions, and the voices of black America. Major writers and works of this movement included: Langston Hughes (The Weary Blues), Nella Larsen (Passing), Zora Neale Hurston (Their Eyes Were Watching God), Claude McKay, Countee Cullen, and Jean Toomer.

Many refer to the decade of the 1920s as **The Jazz Age**. Jazz is essentially free-flowing improvisation on a simple theme with a four-beat rhythm. It originated in the poor districts of New Orleans as an outgrowth of the Blues. The decade was a time of optimism and exploration of new boundaries. It was a clear movement in many ways away from conventionalism. Jazz, uniquely American, was the country's popular music at the time and its musical style typified the mood of society. The leading jazz musicians of the time included: Buddy Bolden, Joseph "King" Oliver, Duke Ellington, Louis Armstrong, and Jelly Roll Morton.

As jazz grew in popularity, it gave birth to **Swing** and the era of **Big Band** by the mid-1920s. Some of the most notable musicians of the Big Band era were: Bing Crosby, Frank Sinatra, Don Redman, Fletcher Henderson, Count Basie, Benny Goodman, Billie Holiday, Ella Fitzgerald, and The Dorsey Brothers.

In painting and sculpture, the new direction of the decade was **realism**. Some realist styles were influenced by modernism, and others reacted against it. **The Eight** or **The Ashcan School** developed around the work and style of Robert Henri. Their subjects were everyday urban life presented without adornment or glamor. **The American Scene Painters** produced a tight, detailed style of painting that focused on images of American life that were understandable to all. In the Midwest, a school within this group was called **regionalism**. One of the leading artists of regionalism was Grant Wood, best known for *American Gothic*. Other important realists of the day were Edward Hopper and Georgia O'Keeffe.

Skill 2.7e   Assess the impact of radio, mass production techniques, and the growth of cities on American society.

The British patent for the **radio** was awarded in 1896, but it was not until WWI that the equipment and capability of the radio was recognized. One of the first developments in the twentieth century was the use of commercial AM radio stations for aircraft navigation. Radio was used to communicate orders and information between army and navy units on both sides of the war during WWI. Broadcasting became practical in the 1920s and radio receivers were introduced on a wide scale.

The relative economic boom of the 1920s made it possible for many households to own a radio. The beginning of broadcasting and the proliferation of receivers revolutionized communication. The news was transmitted into every home with a radio and could be transmitted very quickly. By the time of the Stock Market Crash in 1929, approximately 40% of households had a radio.

Another innovation of the 1920s was the introduction of **mass production**, the production of large amounts of standardized products on production lines. **Henry Ford** used mass production to build the Model T Ford and made cars less expensive.

From an economic perspective, mass production decreases labor costs, increases the rate of production, and increases profit. Mass production reduces the chance of human error and variation but it is inflexible. Once a process is established, it is difficult to modify a design or a production process. From the viewpoint of labor, mass production can create job shortages.

During the period before and after 1900, a large number of people migrated to the cities of America. The new immigrants were not farmers. Polish immigrants became steelworkers in Pittsburgh. Serbian immigrants became meatpackers in Chicago. Russian Jewish immigrants became tailors in New York City. Slovaks assembled cars in Detroit. Italians worked in the factories of Baltimore.

Several factors promoted urbanization during the 1920s. The decline of agriculture, the drop in price for grain and produce, and the end of financial support for farming after WWI caused many farmers to go bankrupt. Many sold or lost their farms and migrated to cities to find work. Continuing industrialization drew more workers to the areas near or surrounding industrial or manufacturing centers. Cities were became the locus of political, cultural, financial and economic life. New forms of transportation to places of work and shopping facilitated the growth of cities.

As the population grew in cities, the demographic composition of those areas began to change. Workers flocked to the cities to be closer to the factories that employed them. As the populations of poorer workers increased, the wealthy moved from the city to the suburbs. The availability of automobiles and the extension of public transportation beyond the city limits enabled the middle and upper classes to leave city centers.

Urbanization brings certain needs in its wake, including: adequate water supply, management of sewage and garbage, the need for public services, such as fire and police, road construction and maintenance, bridges to connect parts of cities, and taller buildings were needed. This last led to the invention of steel-framed buildings and of the elevator. In addition, electricity and telephone lines were needed, department stores and supermarkets grew, and the need for additional schools were related to urbanization. With the large migration and low wages came overcrowding, often in old buildings. **Slums** began to appear. Soon public health issues began to arise.

COMPETENCY 2.8   THE GREAT DEPRESSION AND THE NEW DEAL

Skill 2.8a   Analyze the differing explanation for the 1929 stock market crash, Herbert Hoover's and Congress' responses to the crisis, and the implementation of Franklin Delano Roosevelt's New Deal policies.

The 1929 Stock Market crash was the powerful event that is generally interpreted as the beginning of the Great Depression in America. The crash was unexpected but it was not without identifiable causes. The 1920s had been a decade of social and economic growth and hope. But the attitudes and actions of the 1920s regarding wealth, production, and investment created several trends that quietly set the stage for the 1929 disaster.

Uneven distribution of wealth: In the 1920s, the distribution of wealth between the rich and the middle-class was grossly disproportionate. In 1929, the combined income of the top 0.1% of the population was equal to the combined income of the bottom 42%. The top 0.1% of the population controlled 34% of all savings, while 80% of American had no savings. Capitalism enriched the wealthy at the expense of the workers. Between 1920 and 1929, the amount of disposable income per person rose 9%. The top 0.1% of the population, however, enjoyed an increase in disposable income of 75%. One reason for this disparity was the increased manufacturing productivity during the 1920s. Average worker productivity in manufacturing increased 32% during this period. Yet wages in manufacturing increased only 8%. The wages of the workers rose very slowly, failing to keep pace with increasing productivity. As production costs fell and prices remained constant, profits soared. But profits were retained by the companies and the owners.

The legislative and executive branches of the Coolidge administration tended to favor business and the wealthy. The **Revenue Act of 1926** significantly reduced income taxes for the wealthy. Despite the rise of labor unions, even the Supreme Court ruled in ways that further widened the gap between the rich and the middle class. In the case of *Adkins v. Children's Hospital* (1923), the Court ruled that minimum wage legislation was unconstitutional.

Buying on credit caught on very quickly. Buying on credit can create artificial demand for products people cannot ordinarily afford. The 1920s economy also relied on investment and **luxury spending**. If people lose confidence in the economy luxury spending can come to an abrupt halt. In the 1920s, investing was robust but investors began to expect greater returns on their investments and this led many to speculative investments in risky opportunities.

The automotive and radio industries drove the 1920s economy. The government tended to support new industries rather than agriculture. During WWI, the government had subsidized farms and farmers had been encouraged to buy and farm more land and to use new technology to increase production. The nation fed much of Europe during and after the war. When the war ended, these farm policies were cut off. Prices plummeted, farmers fell into debt, and farm prices declined. The agriculture industry was on the brink of ruin before the stock market crash.

The concentration of production and economic stability in the automotive industry and the production and sale of radios was expected to last forever. When these two industries declined due to decreased demand, they caused the collapse of other industries upon which they were dependent (e.g., rubber tires, glass, fuel, construction, etc.).

The other factor contributing to the Great Depression was the economic condition of Europe. The U.S. lent money to European nations to rebuild. Many of these countries used this money to purchase U.S. food and manufactured goods but they were unable to pay their debts. While the U.S. provided money, food, and goods to Europe, America was unwilling to buy European goods. This locked Europe in an economic spiral where they could not break their dependency on American loans. **Trade barriers** were enacted to maintain a favorable trade balance.

Risky speculative investments in the stock market was the second major factor contributing to the stock market crash of 1929 and the Depression. Stock market speculation was spectacular throughout the 1920s. In 1928 and 1929 stock prices doubled and tripled. The opportunities to achieve such profits were irresistible. This created an investment craze that drove the market higher and higher.

Several other factors are cited by some scholars as contributing to the Great Depression. In 1929, the Federal Reserve increased interest rates. Also, as interest rates rose and the stock market began to decline, people began to hoard money.

In September 1929, stock prices began to slip but people remained optimistic. On Monday, October 21, prices began to fall quickly. The volume traded was so high that the tickers were unable to keep up. Investors were frightened, and they started to sell very quickly. This caused further collapse. For the next two days prices stabilized somewhat. On **Black Thursday**, October 24, prices plummeted again. By this time investors had lost confidence. On Friday and Saturday an attempt to stop the crash was made by some leading bankers. But on Monday the 28th, prices began to fall again, declining 13% in one day. The next day, **Black Tuesday, October 29**, saw 16.4 million shares traded. Stock prices fell so far, that at many times no one wanted to buy at any price.

The **Great Depression** of the 1930s resulted in bank failures, loss of jobs due to cut-backs in production and a lack of money. This lack of currency led to a sharp decline in spending, which in turn affected businesses, factories and stores, drove unemployment. Farm products were unaffordable so the farmers suffered even more. Foreign trade sharply decreased and in the early 1930s, the U.S. economy was effectively paralyzed. Europe was affected even more so.

In the immediate aftermath of the stock market crash, many urged President Herbert Hoover to provide government relief. Hoover responded by urging the nation to be patient. By the time he signed relief bills in 1932, it was too late, and Hoover's bid for re-election in 1932 failed.

The new president, **Franklin D. Roosevelt,** won the White House on his promise to the American people of a "new deal." Roosevelt's **New Deal** programs aimed in part to provide relief to hard-hit workers through government-sponsored work programs such as the Civilian Conservation Corps. Many of Roosevelt's policies faced strong opposition, and some programs were struck down by the Supreme Court. Roosevelt was elected to four terms. His New Deal was the start of the social and economic recovery and reform legislative acts designed to gradually ease the country back to prosperity. The legislation was intended to accomplish three goals: **relief, recovery, and reform.**

The first step in the **New Deal** was to relieve suffering. This was accomplished through a number of job creation projects. The second step, the recovery aspect, was to stimulate the economy. The third step was to create social and economic change through innovative legislation.

Congress passed the **Glass-Steagall Act**, which separated banking and investing. The **Securities and Exchange Commission** was created to regulate dangerous speculative practices on Wall Street. **The Wagner Act** guaranteed a number of rights to workers and unions in an effort to improve worker-employer relations. The **Social Security Act of 1935** established pensions for the aged and infirm as well as a system of unemployment insurance.

The National Recovery Administration attempted to accomplish several goals:

- Restore employment
- Increase general purchasing power
- Provide character-building activity for unemployed youth
- Encourage decentralization of industry and thus divert population from crowded cities to rural or semi-rural communities
- To develop river resources in the interest of navigation and cheap power and light
- To complete flood control on a permanent basis
- To enlarge the national program of forest protection and to develop forest resources
- To control farm production and improve farm prices
- To assist home builders and home owners

- To restore public faith in banking and trust operations
- To recapture the value of physical assets, whether in real property, securities, or other investments

These objectives and their accomplishment implied a restoration of public confidence and courage.

"Alphabet organizations" were set up to work out the details of the recovery plan. The most prominent were:

- **Agricultural Adjustment Administration** (AAA) - designed to readjust agricultural production and prices thereby boost farm income
- **Civilian Conservation Corps** (CCC) - designed to give wholesome, useful activity in the forestry service to unemployed young men
- **Civil Works Administration** (CWA) and the **Public Works Administration** (PWA) - designed to give employment in the construction and repair of public buildings, parks, and highways
- **Works Progress Administration** (WPA) - whose task was to move individuals from relief rolls to work projects or private employment

The **Tennessee Valley Authority** (TVA) was of a more permanent nature. Its goal was to improve the navigability of the Tennessee River and increase productivity of the timber and farm lands in its valley. This program built 16 dams that provided water control and hydroelectric generation.

The **Public Works Administration** employed Americans to work on more than 34,000 public works projects. Projects included the construction of a highway that linked the Florida Keys and Miami, the Boulder Dam (now the Hoover Dam) and numerous highway projects. The nation's economy, however, did not fully recover until America entered World War II.

Skill 2.8b   **Describe and assess the human toll of the Great Depression, including the impact of natural disasters and agricultural practices on the migration from rural Southern and Eastern regions to urban and Western areas.**

Unemployment reached 25% nationwide. People lost their homes and created makeshift domiciles of cardboard, scraps of wood and tents. These communities were called **Hoovervilles**. Families stood in bread lines, rural workers left the dust bowl of the plains to search for work in California, and banks failed. More than 100,000 businesses failed between 1929 and 1932. The despair that swept the nation left an indelible scar on all who endured the Depression.

Everyone who lived through the Great Depression was permanently affected in some way. Many never trusted banks again. Many people of later generations hoarded cash so they would not risk losing everything again. Some permanently rejected the use of credit.

In several parts of the country, economic disaster was exacerbated by natural disaster. The Florida Keys were hit by the "**Labor Day Hurricane**" in 1935. The **Great Hurricane of 1938** struck Long Island, caused more than 600 fatalities, and resulting in millions of dollars in damage to the coast from New York City to Boston.

By far the worst natural disaster of the decade came to be known as the **Dust Bowl.** Due to prolonged drought in the Great Plains and a reliance on unsustainable farming techniques, a series of devastating dust storms occurred in the 1930s. These storms resulted in destruction, economic ruin, and dramatic ecological change. Plowing the plains for agriculture had removed the grass and exposed the soil. When the drought occurred, the soil dried out and became dust. Wind blew away the dust. Between 1934 and 1939 winds blew the soil to the east, all the way to the Atlantic Ocean. The dust storms, called "black blizzards," created huge clouds of dust that were visible as far as Chicago. Topsoil was stripped from millions of acres. Crops were ruined, the land was destroyed, and people lost and abandoned homes and farms.

In Texas, Arkansas, Oklahoma, New Mexico, Kansas and Colorado more than half a million people were homeless. Fifteen percent of Oklahoma's population left. Because so many of the migrants were from Oklahoma, the migrants came to be called **Okies** no matter where they came from. Estimates of the number of people displaced by this disaster range from 300,000 to 2.5 million.

Skill 2.8c Analyze the effects of, and controversies arising from, New Deal policies, including the social and physical consequences of regional programs (e.g., the Tennessee Valley Authority, the Central Valley Project).

There were negative reactions to some of the measures taken to pull the country out of the Depression. Farmers lost tillable land and some water supply to the construction of the aqueduct and the Hoover Dam. Tennesseans were initially unhappy with the changes in river flow and navigation when the Tennessee Valley Authority (TVA) began construction of dams, the directing of water to form reservoirs, and hydroelectric plants. Some businesses business leaders were unhappy with the introduction of minimum wage laws and controls on working conditions for laborers. The numerous import/export tariffs of the period were the subject of controversy.

However, much that was accomplished under the New Deal had positive long-term effects on economic, ecological, social and political issues for the next several decades. The Tennessee Valley Authority and the Central Valley Project in California provided reliable sources and supplies of water to major cities. The

New Deal promoted rural electrification. Electricity was brought to communities that had never before had it. For the middle class and the poor, the labor regulations, the establishment of the Social Security Administration, and the separation of investment and banking have served the nation admirably for more than six decades.

Skill 2.8d   Trace and evaluate the gains and losses or organized labor in the 1930s.

The charter of the National Recovery Administration included a statement defending the right of labor unions to exist and to negotiate with employers. This was interpreted by thousands as support for unions. But the Supreme Court declared this unconstitutional. There were, however, several major events or actions that were particularly important to the history of organized labor during the decade.

The **Wagner Act** (The National Labor Relations Act) established a legal basis for unions, set collective bargaining as a matter of national policy required by the law, provided for secret ballot elections for choosing unions, and protected union members from employer intimidation and coercion. This law was later amended by the **Taft-Hartley Act** (1947) and by the **Landrum-Griffin** Act (1959). The Wagner Act was upheld by the Supreme Court in 1937.

The **strike** was a common tactic of the union. Half a million mill workers walked off the job in the Great Uprising of 1934 and established the precedent that without workers, industry could not move forward. In 1936, the United Rubber Workers staged the first **sit-down strike** where instead of walking off the job, they stayed at their posts but refused to work. The United Auto Workers used the sit-down strike against General Motors in 1936.

Strikes were met with varying degrees of resistance by the companies. Sometimes, "**scabs**" were brought in to replace the striking workers. In 1936, the Anti-Strikebreaker Act (the Byrnes Act) made it illegal to transport or aid strikebreakers in interstate or foreign trade. During a 1937 strike of the Steel Workers Organizing Committee against Republic Steel, police attacked a crowd gathered in support of the strike, killing ten and injuring eighty. This came to be called **The Memorial Day Massacre**.

A number of acts were passed to provide fair compensation and other benefits to workers. The Davis-Bacon Act provided that employers of contractors and subcontractors on public construction should be paid the prevailing wages. Wisconsin created the first unemployment insurance act in the country in 1932. The Public Contracts Act (the **Walsh-Healey Act**) of 1936 established labor standards, including minimum wages, overtime pay, child and convict labor provisions and safety standards on federal contracts. The **Fair Labor Standards**

Act created a minimum wage, stipulated time-and-a-half pay for hours over 40 per week. The Social Security Act was passed in 1935.

There were also efforts to unionize particular industries. The Supreme Court upheld the **Railway Labor Act** in 1930, including its prohibition of employer interference or coercion in the choice of bargaining representatives. This was later applied to other labor unions. The **Guffey Act** stabilized the coal industry and improved labor conditions, though a year later it was declared unconstitutional. General Motors recognized the **United Auto Workers** and US Steel recognized the **Steel Workers Organizing Committee**. The Merchant Marine Act created a Federal Maritime Labor Board.

One of labor's biggest unions was formed in 1935. The Committee for Industrial Organization (**CIO**) was formed within the AFL to carry unionism to the industrial sector. Two years later the CIO was expelled from the AFL over charges of dual unionism or competition. It then became known as the Congress of Industrial Organizations.

Federal labor efforts included:

- The Anti-Injunction Act that prohibited federal injunctions in most labor disputes
- The Wagner-Peyser Act that created the United States Employment Service within the Department of Labor
- The Secretary of Labor calling for the first National Labor Legislation Conference to obtain better cooperation between the federal government and the States in defining a national labor legislation program
- The U.S. joining the International Labor Organization
- The National Apprenticeship Act establishing the Bureau of Apprenticeship within the Department of Labor

COMPETENCY 2.9   WORLD WAR II

Skill 2.9a   Explain the origins of American involvement in World War II, including reactions to events in Europe, Africa, and Asia.

After war began in Europe in 1939, **President Franklin D. Roosevelt** announced that the United States was neutral. President Roosevelt and his supporters, called interventionists, favored all aid except war to the Allied nations fighting Axis aggression. They feared that an Axis victory would seriously threaten and endanger all democracies. The isolationists were against any U.S. aid to the warring nations. Isolationists believed that any aid would lead the U.S. into a war the country was unprepared to fight. Roosevelt's plan was to defeat the Axis nations by sending the Allied nations the equipment needed to fight: ships, aircraft, tanks, and other war materials.

In Asia, the U.S. had opposed Japan's invasion of Southeast Asia, an effort to gain Japanese control of that region's rich resources. Consequently, the U.S. stopped all important exports to Japan, whose industries depended heavily on petroleum, scrap metal, and other raw materials. Later Roosevelt refused to allow the withdrawal of Japanese funds from American banks. General Tojo became the Japanese premier in October 1941 and quickly realized that the U.S. Navy was powerful enough to block Japanese expansion into Asia. In an attempt to cripple the U.S. Pacific Fleet Japan launched a surprise attack on December 7, 1941. The Japanese did immense damage to the fleet while at anchor in **Pearl Harbor**, Hawaii. The attack quickly motivated America to join the war.

Skill 2.9b   Analyze American foreign policy before and during WWII.

By the 1930s, the U.S. and the rest of the world entered a period of economic decline known as the Depression. Roosevelt tried to pursue peace and cooperation, especially in regards to the American continent and the nations of Central and South America. His policy was called the **Good Neighbor Policy**. In Europe matters became more difficult because the worldwide economic downturn had more serious effects there.

Because of the problems in Europe, the isolationist mood in the United States gained support well into the late 1930s. With the rise of fascism in Germany and Italy war became inevitable.

After the outbreak of war in 1939, the American government proclaimed a public stance of neutrality, while covertly and carefully doing what it could to aid its friends and allies. This involved the process that came to be known as **Lend-Lease**, in which the United States would give, on what was presumed a temporary basis, certain war supplies to the forces fighting Germany and its allies. At first, Lend-Lease went only to Great Britain. When Germany attacked the Soviet Union in June 1941, it went there, as well.

Skill 2.9c   Evaluate and analyze significant events, issues, and experiences during World War II, including Internment of people of Japanese ancestry; Allied response to the Holocaust; the experiences and contributions of American fighting forces, including the role of minorities (e.g. the Tuskegee Airmen, the 442nd Regimental Combat Unit, Navajo Code Talkers); the role of women and minority groups at home; major developments in aviation, weaponry, communications, and medicine; the significance and ramifications of the decision to drop the atomic bomb.

Military strategy in the European theater of war was developed by **Roosevelt, Churchill, and Stalin** and concentrated on Germany's defeat first, then Japan's. Fighting in North Africa began in 1942 and the German and Italian armies were pushed off the continent in May, 1943. Before the war, Hitler and Stalin had signed a non-aggression pact in 1939, which Hitler violated in 1941 when he invaded the Soviet Union. The German defeat at Stalingrad, in the Soviet Union, marked a turning point in the war and was brought about by a combination of entrapment of German troops by Soviet troops and the death of many more Germans by starvation and freezing due to the horrendous winter conditions. All of this occurred at the same time the Allies drove the Axis out of North Africa.

The liberation of Italy began in July 1943 and ended in May 1945. The third part of the strategy began with **D-Day, June 6, 1944,** and the Allied invasion of France on the beaches of Normandy. The Soviets began to push German troops back into Europe in January, 1943. The Soviet Union's effort was greatly assisted by supplies from Britain and the United States. By April, 1945, the Allies occupied positions beyond the Rhine River in Germany and the Soviets moved on to Berlin, surrounding it by April 25. Germany surrendered May 7, 1945.

The **Yalta Conference** took place at Yalta in the Crimea in February 1945. The Allied leaders—Winston Churchill, Franklin Roosevelt and Joseph Stalin—met to determine the shape of post-war Europe. Germany would be divided into four zones of occupation, as was the capital city of Berlin. Germany was also to undergo demilitarization and to make reparations for the war. Poland was to remain under control of Soviet Russia. Roosevelt also received a promise from Stalin that the Soviet Union would join the new United Nations.

After the surrender of Germany the Allies met in Potsdam, Germany, in July, 1945. At the **Potsdam Conference**, Prime Minister Clement Attlee, President Harry Truman and Marshal Stalin addressed the administration of post-war Germany and provided for the forced migration of millions of Germans from previously occupied regions.

In the six months after the attack on Pearl Harbor, Japanese forces moved across Southeast Asia and the western Pacific Ocean. By August 1942, the Japanese Empire was at its largest size and stretched northeast to Alaska's Aleutian Islands, west to Burma, and south to what is now Indonesia. Conquered areas included Hong Kong, Guam, Wake Island, Thailand, part of Malaysia, Singapore, and the Philippines. The Japanese even bombed Darwin on the north coast of Australia.

General Doolittle's bombers flew raids over Japanese cities. The American naval victory at **Midway** and the fighting in the **Battle of the Coral Sea** helped turn the tide against Japan. **Island-hopping** by U.S. Seabees and Marines and the grueling bloody battles fought resulted in gradually pushing the Japanese back toward Japan. It took dropping two atomic bombs on the Japanese cities of **Hiroshima** and **Nagasaki** to finally end the war in the Pacific. Japan formally surrendered on September 2, 1945, aboard the U.S. battleship Missouri, anchored in Tokyo Bay.

After Japan's defeat, the Allies began a military occupation of Japan directed by American **General Douglas MacArthur**, who introduced a number of reforms and eventually rid Japan of its military institutions. A constitution was drawn up in 1947, transferring all political rights from the emperor to the people, granting women the right to vote, and denying Japan the right to declare war. War crimes trials of twenty-five war leaders and government officials were also conducted. The U.S. did not sign a peace treaty until 1951. The treaty permitted Japan to rearm but took away its overseas empire.

Internment of people of Japanese ancestry. From the turn of the twentieth century, there was tension between Caucasians and Japanese in California. A series of laws had been passed discouraging Japanese immigration and prohibiting land ownership by Japanese. The Alien Registration Act of 1940 (the **Smith Act**) required the fingerprinting and registration of all aliens over the age of fourteen. Aliens were required to report any change of address within five days. Almost five million aliens registered under the provisions of this act. The Japanese attack on Pearl Harbor (December 7, 1941) raised suspicion that Japan was planning a full-scale attack on the West Coast. Many believed that American citizenship did not necessarily imply loyalty. Some authorities feared sabotage of both civilian and military facilities within the country. In early 1942, Presidential Executive Orders authorized the arrest of all aliens suspected of subversive activities and the creation of exclusion zones where people could be isolated from the remainder of the population and kept where they could not damage national infrastructure. These War Relocation Camps were used to isolate about 120,000 Japanese and Japanese Americans (62% were citizens) during World War II.

Allied response to the Holocaust. International organizations received sharp criticism during WWII for their failure to act to save European Jews. The Allied Powers, in particular, were accused of gross negligence. Many organizations and individuals did not believe reports of the abuse and mass genocide that occurred in Europe. Many nations did not want to accept Jewish refugees. The International Red Cross was one of the organizations that discounted reports of atrocities. One particular point of criticism was the failure of the Allied Powers to bomb the death camp at **Auschwitz-Birkenau** or the railroad tracks that led there. Military leaders argued that their planes did not have the range to reach the camp and that they could not provide sufficiently precise targeting to safeguard the inmates. Critics have claimed that even if Allied bombs killed all inmates at Auschwitz at the time, the destruction of the camp would have saved thousands of other Jews.

The word **genocide** was invented by lawyer Raphael Lemkin to describe the crimes of the Second World War. . In 1948, three years after its founding, the UN unanimously passed the **Universal Declaration of Human Rights**. The **Nuremberg Trials** redefined morality on a global scale. The phrase "crimes against humanity" attained popular currency, and individuals, rather than governments, were held accountable for war crimes.

Women and minorities accepted remarkable new roles and served them with great distinction during WWII, both in the theater of military operations and at home.

Women served in the military as drivers, nurses, communications operators, and clerks. The Flight Nurses corps was created at the beginning of the war. Among the most notable minority groups in the military were:

The Tuskegee Airmen - a group of African American aviators who made a major contribution to the war effort. Although they were not considered eligible for the gold wings of an Army Pilot until 1948, they completed standard Army flight classroom instruction and the required flight time. They were the first blacks permitted to fly for the military. They flew more than 15,000 missions, destroyed over 1,000 German aircraft, and earned more than 150 Distinguished Flying Crosses and hundreds of Air Medals.

The 442nd Regimental Combat Team - a unit composed of Japanese Americans who fought in Europe. This unit was the most highly decorated unit of its size and in its length of service in the history of the U.S. Army. This self-sufficient force served with great distinction in North Africa, Italy, southern France, and Germany. The medals earned by the group include 21 Congressional Medals of Honor (the highest award given). The unit was awarded 9,486 purple hearts (for being wounded in battle). The casualty rate, combining those killed in action, missing in action, and wounded and removed from action, was 93%.

The Navajo Code Talkers have been credited with saving countless lives and accelerating the end of the war. There were more than 400 Navajo Indians who served in all six Marine divisions from 1942 to 1945. At the time of WWII, less than 30 non-Navajos understood the Navajo language, a complex language. Because it was not a code, it was unbreakable by the Germans or the Japanese. The Code Talkers transmitted information about tactics, troop movements, orders and other vital military information. It is generally accepted that without the Navajo Code Talkers, Iwo Jima could not have been taken.

Several minorities, including blacks, Chinese, Japanese, Hawaiians, American Indians, Filipinos, and Puerto Ricans represented the U.S. military during WWII.

The role of women and minority groups at home overturned many expectations and assumptions. To a greater extent than any previous war, WWII required industrial production. Those who remained at home were needed to build the planes, tanks, ships, bombs, torpedoes, etc. A call went out to women to join the effort and enter the industrial work force. A vast campaign was launched to recruit women to these tasks that combined emotional appeals and patriotism. One of the most famous recruitment campaigns featured "**Rosie the Riveter**." By the middle of 1944, more than 19 million women had entered the work force. Women worked all manufacturing shifts making everything from clothing to fighter jets. Most women and their families tended **Victory Gardens** at home to produce food items that were in short supply.

There were major **developments in aviation, weaponry, communications, and medicine** during the war. Major developments included flight-based weapon delivery systems such as the long-range bomber, jet fighters, cruise missiles, and ballistic missiles. Glider planes were heavily used in WWII because they were silent upon approach. Another significant development was the broad use of paratrooper units. Hospital planes came into use to move the seriously wounded from the front and transport them to hospitals for treatment. Used for the first time were: radar, electronic computers, nuclear weapons, and new tank designs.

Materiel first used in World War II included

aircraft carriers	Higgins boats	light tanks
armored vehicles	bazookas	mine-clearing flail tanks
tank destroyers	guided weapons	flame tanks
anti-tank weapons	napalm	rockets
assault rifles	cruise missiles	submersible tanks

The significance and ramifications of the decision to drop the atomic bomb. The development of the atomic bomb was the most profound military development of the war years. This invention made it possible for a single plane to carry a single bomb that could destroy an entire city. It was believed that possession of the bomb would serve as a deterrent to any nation because it would make aggression against a nation with a bomb mass suicide. The development and use of nuclear weapons marked the beginning of a new age in warfare that created greater distance from the act of killing and eliminated the ability to minimize the effect of war on non-combatants.

Two nuclear bombs were dropped in 1945 on the Japanese cities of Nagasaki and Hiroshima. They caused the immediate deaths of 100,000 to 200,000 people, and far more deaths over time. Dropping the bomb was (and still is) a controversial decision.

Skill 2.9d   Assess American foreign policy in the aftermath of World War II, using geographic, political, and economic perspectives.

The American isolationist mood was given a shocking and lasting blow in 1941 with the Japanese attack on Pearl Harbor. Declaring itself "the arsenal of democracy", it entered the Second World War and emerged not only victorious, but also as the *strongest power* on Earth.

At the end of the Second World War, the United States perceived its greatest threat to be the expansion of Communism. To that end, it devoted a large share of its foreign policy, diplomacy, and both economic and military might to combating it.

In the aftermath of the Second World War, the Soviet Union emerged as the *second* strongest power on Earth. The United States embarked on a policy known as **Containment**. Its purpose was to stop communism from spreading. The **Marshall Plan** and the "**Truman Doctrine**" were implemented to assist in this policy. The Marshall Plan sent economic aid to Europe after the war.

The Truman Doctrine offered military aid to countries, such as Greece, that were in danger of communist upheaval. This led to the era known as the **Cold War** in which the United States took the lead along with the Western European nations against the Soviet Union and the Eastern Bloc countries. It was also at this time that the United States joined the **North Atlantic Treaty Organization** or **NATO**, an organization formed in 1949 for the purpose of opposing communist aggression.

The **United Nations** was formed in 1945 to replace the defunct League of Nations to ensure world peace. In the 1950s, the United States implemented the **Eisenhower Doctrine** to maintain peace in a troubled Middle East.

The possession of nuclear weapons by the United States quickly led to the development of similar weapons by other nations and massive fear of the effects of the use of these weapons, including radiation poisoning and **nuclear winter**.

The United States became involved in a number of world conflicts. Each had at the core the struggle against communist expansion. Among these were the **Korean War** (1950–1953), the **Vietnam War** (1965-1975), and various continuing entanglements in Central America, South America, and the Middle East. By the early 1970s, under Secretary of State, Henry Kissinger, the United States and its allies embarked on the policy that came to be known as **Détente.** This policy's goal was to tensions between the United States and the Soviet Union.

By the 1980s, the U. S. embarked on what some saw as a renewal of the Cold War. The U.S. became more involved in trying to prevent communist insurgency in Central America and expanded its armed forces and the development of space-based weapons systems. As this occurred, the Soviet Union found itself unable to compete. In 1989 the breakdown of the Communist Bloc began, with the collapse occurring in the early 1990s.

COMPETENCY 2.10 **POST-WORLD WAR II AMERICA**

Skill 2.10a **Describe and evaluate the significance of changes in international migration patterns and their impact on society and the economy.**

Until the middle of the twentieth century, voluntary migrations to America were primarily European. The United Nations created the **International Refugee Organization** in 1946. In the next three years this organization relocated over a million European refugees. The impact of the Cold War on migration patterns was significant. American policies toward immigration became more open to political escapees from communist countries and the number of immigrants from third-world nations increased dramatically. The end of the Cold War marked a shift in migration patterns. South to north migrations began to dominate global migration.

U.S. immigration policy was carefully aligned with foreign policy. President Truman introduced the **Displaced Persons Act** in 1948 that facilitated the admission of more than 400,000 persons from Europe. During the 1950s, the immigration policy became restrictive. The **McCarran-Walter Immigration Nationality Act** of 1952 established a quota system that was clearly anti-Asian. The number of refugees from Eastern Europe far exceeded these quotas. Presidents Truman and Eisenhower urged extension of the quotas, and in time they were abandoned. Refugees from communist Europe were admitted under the **President's Escapee Program** of 1952 and the **Refugee Relief Act** of 1953.

Asian immigration policies did not change after WWII.

Skill 2.10b **Describe the increased role of the federal government in response to World War II and the Cold War and assess the impact of this increased role on regional economic structures, society, and the political system.**

During World War II Americans found it advisable to cede to the federal government a greater degree of control over the economy, key institutions and services to ensure their personal welfare and their security. This led to significant growth in both the reach and size of the federal government. This marked the culmination of a major change in the role of the federal government that many have called **the rise of the welfare state**.

New challenges led to the growth of the power and control of the federal government. The attempts to bring the nation through both the Depression and the war saw much experimentation. Roosevelt's use of the radio to speak to the American people in his **fireside chats** permitted him to rally the populace and convince the public to consider new ideas and new approaches to the problems of the day. Essentially, Roosevelt convinced the nation that a more active role for the federal government, internationally and at home, would prevent another Depression and world war.

In many ways, the period from 1945 to 1972 was a time of unprecedented prosperity for everyone in the nation. Wages increased, car and home ownership increased, average educational levels increased when the veterans of the war took the opportunity to receive a college education paid for by their G.I benefits. People gave the government this major role in perpetuating this prosperous society. Just as WWII had united the people in a common commitment to support the troops and win the war, they again rallied together to support the government in the Cold War.

Skill 2.10c   Describe the effects of technological developments on society, politics, and the economy since 1945.

Post-WWII was a time of great hope and economic prosperity in America. Europe had been redefined and began to recover from the devastating effects of the war. However, the threat of the spread of communism and the Cold War was a palpable feature of everyday life.

The discoveries and innovations of the war years in science and technology were simultaneously directed to: peaceful and life-enhancing uses of technology, and the buildup of a sufficient military to ensure the security of the nation against future aggression.

Significant advances in science and medicine made it possible to treat and prevent deadly and crippling diseases. Life expectancy and quality of life with such discoveries as the **polio vaccine.**

Major technological developments since 1945 include
  - discovery of penicillin
  - manufacture of atomic bombs
  - supersonic airplanes
  - the transistor
  - long-playing records (LPs)
  - reflecting telescope
  - launched guided missile
  - separation of plutonium
  - nuclear-powered submarines.

Skill 2.10d   Analyze the major domestic policies of presidential administrations from Harry S Truman to the present.

Harry S. Truman became president near the end of WWII. When Japan refused to surrender, Truman authorized the use of atomic bombs on Japanese cities. He took to the Congress a plan that came to be known as the **Fair Deal**. It included: expansion of Social Security, a full-employment program, public housing and slum clearance, and a permanent **Fair Employment Practices Act**.

The **Truman Doctrine** provided support for Greece and Turkey when they were threatened by the Soviet Union. The **Marshall Plan** stimulated economic recovery for Western Europe. Truman participated in the negotiations that resulted in the formation of NATO. He and his administration believed it necessary to support South Korea when it was invaded by the communist government of North Korea. Truman contained American involvement in Korea so as not to risk conflict with China or Russia.

Dwight David Eisenhower succeeded Truman. Eisenhower obtained a truce in Korea and worked during his two terms to mitigate the tension of the Cold War. . He continued most of the programs introduced under both the New Deal and the Fair Deal. He enforced school desegregation by sending federal troops to Little Rock, Arkansas. Eisenhower enforced President Truman's ordered to completely **desegregate** the military. Eisenhower's administration created the Departments of Health, Education and Welfare and the National Aeronautics and Space Administration.

John F. Kennedy's Inaugural Address is remembered for his statement, "Ask not what your country can do for you — ask what you can do for your country." He pledged to get America moving again. During his brief presidency, his economic programs created the longest period of continuous expansion in the country since WWII. He wanted the U.S. to again take up the mission of being committed to the spread of human rights. Through the Alliance for Progress and the **Peace Corps**, the nation reached out to assist developing nations. He believed the arts were critical to a society and instituted programs to support the arts.

Lyndon B. Johnson assumed the presidency after the assassination of Kennedy. His vision for America was called **The Great Society**. He won support in Congress for the largest group of legislative programs in the history of the nation. These included a new civil rights bill and a tax cut. He defined the Great Society as "a place where the meaning of man's life matches the marvels of man's labor."

The legislation enacted during the Johnson administration included:

- an attack on disease
- urban renewal
- Medicare
- aid to education
- conservation and beautification
- development of economically depressed areas

- a war on poverty
- voting rights for all
- and control of crime and delinquency

President Johnson managed an unpopular war in Vietnam and encouraged the exploration of space. His administration created the Department of Transportation and appointed the first black Supreme Court Justice, Thurgood Marshall.

Richard Nixon inherited racial unrest and the Vietnam War. Nixon expanded the war to include Cambodia and Laos. His administration improved relations with China and the USSR. President Nixon is best known for the **Watergate** scandal that led to his resignation. His major domestic achievements were: the appointment of conservative justices to the Supreme Court, passage of new anti-crime legislation, a broad environmental program, creation of the **Environmental Protection Agency**, revenue sharing legislation, and ending the draft. Do you want a paragraph on Watergate?

Gerald Ford was the first Vice President selected under the 25th Amendment. His administration faced a depressed economy, inflation, and energy shortages. Once inflation slowed and recession was the major economic problem, he instituted measures that would stimulate the economy. He tried to reduce the role of the federal government. He reduced business taxes and lessened the controls on business. His international focus was on preventing a major war in the Middle East. He negotiated with Russia for limitations on nuclear weapons.

Jimmy Carter strove to make the government "competent and compassionate" in response to the expectations of the American people. His administration made significant strides in job creation and decreased the budget deficit but inflation and interest rates were at record highs. His administration established a national energy policy to deal with the energy shortage, controlled petroleum prices to stimulate production, implemented civil service reform, deregulated the trucking and airline industries, and created the Department of Education. He expanded the national park system, supported the Social Security system, and appointed a record number of women and minorities to government jobs. During the last year of his presidency, fifty-two American hostages were held in Iran.

Ronald Reagan's program came to be known as the Reagan Revolution. The goal was to reduce the reliance of the American people upon government. His legislative accomplishments include economic growth stimulation, lower inflation, increased employment, and strengthening the national defense. He won Congressional support for a complete overhaul of the income tax code in 1986. When he left office there was prosperity and peace. His foreign policy was "peace through strength." Reagan nominated Sandra Day O'Connor as the first female justice on the Supreme Court.

George H. W. Bush was committed to traditional American values and to make America a kinder and gentler nation. He dealt with defense of the Panama Canal and Iraq's invasion of Kuwait, which led to the first Gulf War, known as **Operation Desert Storm**. His international affairs record was strong but he could not turn around the struggling economy or increased violence in the inner cities.

Bill Clinton's domestic accomplishments include: the lowest inflation in thirty years, the lowest unemployment rate in modern days, the highest home ownership rate in history, lower crime rates, and smaller welfare rolls. He proposed and achieved a balanced budget and achieved a budget surplus.

George W. Bush's presidency was radically altered by the 9/11 attacks. George W. Bush campaigned, was elected and inaugurated in the pre-9/11 world. After the attacks President Bush created the **Department of Homeland Security** and presided over the invasions of Afghanistan (2001) and Iraq (2003). The Bush Administration's domestic goals were overshadowed by **The War on Terror**. President Bush passed a large tax cut, attempted to move Social Security to greater privatization and passed some Medicare reform. In 2007–2008 The American economy suffered through **The Great Recession.** It was the worst economic downturn since the Great Depression.

Barack Obama was elected in 2008 and is America's first African-American president. President Obama presided over the longest streak of peacetime job growth in American history. President Obama is most well-known for the **Obamacare** initiative. This was a large scale reform of America's health insurance sector. Obamacare provides subsidies so people can afford health insurance and made sure that no one could be turned down due to pre-existing conditions. In 2011 American forces found and killed Osama bin Laden.

COMPETENCY 2.11   POST-WORLD WAR II U.S. FOREIGN POLICY

Skill 2.11a   Trace the origins of the Cold War.

The major thrust of U.S. foreign policy from the end of World War II to 1990 was the post-war struggle between non-Communist nations (led by the United States) and Communist nations (led by the Soviet Union). It was referred to as the Cold War because its conflicts did not lead to a major war, or hot war. The Soviet Union and the United States embarked on a buildup of atomic and hydrogen bombs as well as other nuclear weapons. Both nations had the capability of destroying each other but because of the continuous threat of nuclear war and accidents, extreme caution was practiced on both sides. The efforts of both sides to serve and protect their political philosophies and to support and assist their allies resulted in a number of events during this 45-year period.

In 1946, Josef Stalin stated publicly that the presence of capitalism and its development of the world's economy made international peace impossible.

George F. Kennan, future American ambassador to the Soviet Union, proposed the foreign policy known as **containment**.

Skill 2.11b **Analyze the roles of the Truman Doctrine, the Marshall Plan and military alliances, including the North American Treaty Organization (NATO), the South East Asian Treaty Organization (SEATO), and the Warsaw Pact.**

The Soviet Union emerged from World War II as the *second* strongest power on Earth. The United States embarked on a policy known as **Containment** to confront the expansion of Soviet power. This included the **Marshall Plan** and the **Truman Doctrine**. The Marshall Plan provided economic aid for Europe and the Truman Doctrine provided financial aid to prevent the spread of communism. The Marshall Plan was also known as the European Recovery Program. In February 1948, Britain and the U.S. combined their two zones in Germany, with France joining in June.

These actions led to the **Cold War**. The U.S. joined the **North Atlantic Treaty Organization (NATO)** that had been formed in 1949 to oppose communist aggression.

The **Southeast Treaty Organization (SEATO)** is a defense pact for Southeast Asia. When it originated in 1954, it had eight member nations. It is similar to NATO and was created as part of the Truman Doctrine, to stop the spread of communism.

The **Warsaw Pact** was the Soviet response to NATO. It was a military alliance but also a "treaty of friendship, cooperation and mutual assistance." It was a treaty among Eastern European nations and the Soviet Union. It was signed in 1955 in Warsaw, Poland.

Skill 2.11c **Trace the origins and consequences of the Korean War.**

The first "hot war" in the post-World War II era was the Korean War (1950–53). Communist North Korean troops invaded South Korea in an effort to unite both sections under Communist control. Member countries of the United Nations furnished peacekeeping troops. It was the first war in which a world organization played a major military role. President Truman sent American troops to help South Korea. The war ended with a truce, and Korea remains divided.

Korea had been under control of Japan from 1895 to the end of the Second World War in 1945. At war's end, the Soviet and U.S. military troops moved into Korea with the U.S. troops in the southern half and the Soviet troops in the northern half with the **38th degree North Latitude** line as the boundary.

In 1947, the UN General Assembly ordered elections in Korea to select one government for the entire country. The Soviet Union did not allow the North Koreans to vote and set up a Communist government there. The South Koreans set up a democratic government but both claimed the entire country. The U.S. removed its troops in 1949 and announced in early 1950 that Korea was not part of its defense line in Asia. The Communists then invaded.

Skill 2.11d   Explain and analyze the relationship between domestic and foreign policy during the Cold War.

After 1945, social and economic chaos continued in Western Europe, especially in Germany. Secretary of State George C. Marshall proposed a program known as the European Recovery Program or the **Marshall Plan**. Although the Soviet Union withdrew from any participation, the U.S. continued to assist Europe to regain economic stability. In Germany the situation was critical, with the American Army shouldering the staggering burden of relieving the serious problems of the German economy. In February 1948, Britain and the U.S. combined their two zones. France joined in June.

The Soviets were opposed to German unification and in 1948 blocked all road traffic access to West Berlin from West Germany. To avoid any armed conflict, it was decided to airlift needed supplies into West Berlin. From June 1948 to mid-May 1949 during the **Berlin Airlift** Allied air forces flew needed items into the city. The Soviets lifted the blockade and permitted vehicle access to the city.

In 1954, the French were forced to give up their colonial claims in Indochina, the present-day countries of Vietnam, Laos, and Cambodia. The Communist North fought with South Vietnam for control of the entire country. In the late 1950s and early 1960s Presidents Eisenhower and Kennedy sent military advisers and aid to assist and support South Vietnam's non-Communist government.

During Lyndon Johnson's presidency, the war escalated with hundreds of thousands of American troops sent into combat against the North Vietnamese. The war was unpopular in America and caused such serious divisiveness among its citizens that Johnson decided not to seek reelection in 1968. In 1973, during Richard Nixon's second term in office the U.S. signed an agreement that ended the Vietnam War. American troops would complete the withdrawal from Vietnam in 1975, during the presidency of Gerald Ford.

Skill 2.11e   Analyze the foreign policies of post-World War II presidential administrations and their effect on the Cold War.

In 1962 **Premier Khrushchev** of the Soviet Union decided to install nuclear missiles on the Cuba. American U-2 spy planes identified missile bases under construction, touching off the **Cuban Missile Crisis**. **President John F. Kennedy** announced that the U.S. would blockade Cuba and stop any Soviet ships from reaching the island.

The Soviets were concerned about American missiles in Turkey aimed at the Soviet Union and about a possible invasion of Cuba. Khrushchev wanted to demonstrate to the Russian and Chinese critics of his policy of peaceful coexistence that he was tough. A week of incredible tension and anxiety gripped the entire world until Khrushchev capitulated. Soviet ships carrying missiles for the Cuban bases turned back and the crisis eased. America agreed to remove its missiles in Turkey and a telephone "hot line" was set up between Moscow and Washington to allow the two heads of government to have instant contact with each other. The U.S. agreed to sell its surplus wheat to the Soviets.

During **Lyndon Johnson**'s presidency, the war in Vietnam escalated with hundreds of thousands of American troops sent to fight alongside the South Vietnamese against the **Vietcong** or North Vietnamese army. The war was unpopular in America and caused such divisiveness that Johnson decided not to seek reelection in 1968.

Probably the highlight of the foreign policy of **President Richard Nixon** was his 1972 trip to **China**. Since 1949 America had refused to recognize the communist government of China. For more than two decades official American policy regarded the legitimate government of China to be that of Chiang Kai-shek, who was exiled on the island of Taiwan.

In 1971, Nixon sent Secretary of State **Henry Kissinger** on a secret trip to Peking to investigate whether it would be possible for America to give recognition to Communist or **Red China**. In 1972, President and Mrs. Nixon spent a number of days in China and met with the two leaders, Mao Zedong and Zhou Enlai. Agreements were made for cultural and scientific exchanges, eventual resumption of trade, and future unification of the mainland with Taiwan. In 1979, formal diplomatic recognition was achieved. With this one visit, the pattern of the Cold War shifted.

Under the administration of **President Jimmy Carter,** Egyptian President Anwar el-Sadat and Israeli Prime Minister Menachem Begin met at presidential retreat **Camp David** and agreed to sign a formal treaty of peace between the two countries. In 1979, the Soviets invaded Afghanistan. The Carter administration perceived the action as a threat to the rich oil fields in the Persian Gulf but did not take action. The last year of Carter's presidential term was taken up with the 52 American hostages held in Iran. The Shah was deposed and control of the government and the country was in the hands of Muslim leader, Ayatollah Ruhollah Khomeini.

President Carter froze all Iranian assets in the U.S., set up trade restrictions, and approved a risky rescue attempt, which failed. He appealed to the UN for aid in gaining release for the hostages and to European allies to join the trade embargo on Iran. Khomeini ignored UN requests to release the Americans and Europeans refused to support the embargo so as not to risk losing access to Iran's oil.

American prestige was damaged and Carter's chances for reelection were doomed. The hostages were released on the day of Ronald Reagan's inauguration as President when Iranian assets were released as ransom.

President Ronald Reagan's foreign policy focused primarily on the Western Hemisphere, particularly in Central America and the West Indies during his first term. U.S. involvement in the domestic revolutions of El Salvador and Nicaragua continued into Reagan's second term when Congress held televised hearings on what came to be known as the **Iran-Contra Affair**. A cover-up was exposed showing that profits from secretly selling military hardware to Iran had been used to give support to rebels, called Contras, who fought in Nicaragua.

In 1983, more than 200 American Marines were killed in Lebanon when an Islamic suicide bomber drove an explosive-laden truck into the United States Marines headquarters in Beirut. This tragic event came as part of the unrest and violence between the Israelis and the Palestinian Liberation Organization (PLO) forces in southern Lebanon. American Marines landed on the island of **Grenada** in the same year to rescue a small group of American medical students and depose the leftist government.

A pivotal event of Reagan's second term was the arms-reduction agreement Reagan reached with Soviet General Secretary **Mikhail Gorbachev**. Gorbachev began to relax East-West tensions by stressing the importance of cooperation with the West and easing the harsh and restrictive life of the people in the Soviet Union. Reagan regarded Gorbachev as a fierce Cold Warrior and compared the Soviet Union to an evil empire but was willing to talk repeatedly with the Soviets to reach a new level of accord.

Since this standard is about the Cold War should the Bush and Clinton paragraphs be deleted?

President George H.W. Bush sent U.S. troops to invade **Panama** and arrest the Panamanian dictator Manuel Noriega in 1989. Noriega had laundered money from drug smuggling and gunrunning through Panama's banks. When a political associate tried unsuccessfully to depose him and an off-duty U.S. Marine was shot and killed at a roadblock, Bush acted. Noriega was brought to the U.S. where he stood trial on charges of drug distribution and racketeering.

Iraq and Iran fought a war in which the U.S. and most of Iraq's neighbors supported Iraq. In a five-year period, **Saddam Hussein** received from the U.S. $500 million worth of American technology, including lasers, advanced computers, and special machine tools used in missile development. The Iraq-Iran war resulted in a stalemate and a UN truce ended the war. Deeply in debt from the war and totally dependent on oil revenues, Saddam invaded and occupied Kuwait. The U.S. successfully liberated Kuwait in four days in **Operation Desert**

Storm. Iraq was defeated. Saddam remained in power although Iraq's economy was seriously damaged.

President William Clinton sent U.S. troops to Haiti to reinstall Jean-Bertrand Aristide as the democratically elected president of Haiti.. Clinton deployed troops to assist U.N. peacekeeping forces in an effort to end the ethnic cleansing in Bosnia. He inherited from the Bush administration the problem of Somalia in East Africa, where U.S. troops had been sent in December 1992 to support U.N. efforts to end the starvation of the Somalis and restore peace. The efforts were successful at first, but eventually failed due to the severity of the intricate political problems within the country. American troops were eventually withdrawn and returned home.

Skill 2.11f   Trace the causes, controversies, and consequences of the Vietnam War, its effects on American combatants and civilians, and its continued impact on American society.

U.S. involvement in the **Vietnam War** from 1957 to 1973 was the second of three phases in Vietnam's modern history.

Since 1861 Vietnam, Laos and Cambodia had been part of the French colony of Indochina. The first phase of Vietnam's modern history began in 1946 when the Vietnamese fought French troops for control of the country.

The French-Indochina War (1946–1954) involved France, which had ruled Vietnam as its colony (French Indochina), and the newly independent Democratic Republic of Vietnam under **Ho Chi Minh**. On May 7, 1954, at a French military base known as **Dien Bien Phu**, Vietnamese troops emerged victorious after a 56-day siege. Dien Bien Phu led directly to the end of France's involvement in Indochina. The defeated French left and the country was divided into communist North and capitalist South. The United States' aid and influence continued as part of the U.S. Cold War foreign policy to help any nation threatened by Communism.

The second phase involved a much more direct U.S. commitment. The Communist North Vietnamese considered the war one of national liberation, a struggle to avoid continual dominance of a foreign power. Participants were the United States of America, Australia, New Zealand, South and North Vietnam, South Korea, Thailand, and the Philippines. With active U.S. involvement from 1957 to 1973, it was the longest war participated in by the U.S. to that date.

The Vietnam War divided the Democratic Party, and the **1968 Democratic National Convention** in Chicago turned out to be a highly contentious and bitterly fought over event. Outside the convention thousands had gathered to protest the Vietnam War. Vice President Hubert H. Humphrey became the party's nominee, but he led a divided party.

In Vietnam, the forces of the **Viet Cong** and the **North Vietnamese Army (NVA)** launched a coordinated and devastating offensive on the eve of Tet (the Lunar New Year), 1968. **The Tet Offensive** disproved the Johnson Administration officials who claimed that the Vietnamese Communists were no longer a viable military force. Although the Tet Offensive was a tactical defeat for the Viet Cong, it was a strategic defeat for the Americans. America lost the political will to continue in a seemingly endless conflict. A cease-fire was arranged five years later in January 1973 and by 1975 U.S. troops left for good.

The third and final phase consisted of fighting between the North and South Vietnamese but ended April 30, 1975, with the surrender of South Vietnam. The entire country was united under Communist rule.

Poverty remained a serious problem in the inner cities resulting in riots and soaring crime rates. The escalation of the war in Vietnam and the social conflict and upheaval of support vs. opposition to U.S. involvement led to antiwar demonstrations, escalation of drug abuse, weakening of the family unit, homelessness, poverty, mental illness, along with increased social, mental, and physical problems experienced by the Vietnam veterans returning to families, marriages, and a country torn apart.

Returning veterans faced not only readjustment to civilian life but also bitterness, anger, rejection, and no heroes' welcomes. Many suffered severe physical and deep psychological problems. The war set a precedent where both Congress and the American people actively challenged U.S. military and foreign policy.

COMPETENCY 2.12   CIVIL RIGHTS MOVEMENT

Skill 2.12a   Examine and analyze the key people, events, policies, and court cases in the field of civil rights from varying perspectives.

The economic boom that followed WW II led to prosperity for many Americans in the 1950s. This prosperity did not extend to the poor blacks of the South, and the economic disparities between the races became more pronounced. Efforts began to end discrimination in education, housing, and jobs.

A civil rights movement began to gain momentum under such leaders as **Dr. Martin Luther King, Jr**. The phrase the **"Civil Rights Movement"** generally refers to the nation-wide effort made by black people and those who supported them to gain equal rights and to eliminate segregation. Discussion of this movement is generally understood in terms of the period of the 1950s and 1960s.

Key people in the civil rights movement include:

Rosa Parks – A black seamstress from Montgomery Alabama who, in 1955, refused to give up her seat on the bus to a white man. This event is generally understood as the spark that lit the fire of the Civil Rights Movement. She has been generally regarded as the "mother of the Civil Rights Movement."

Martin Luther King, Jr. – the most prominent member of the Civil Rights movement. King promoted nonviolent methods of opposition to segregation. The **Letter from Birmingham Jail** explained the purpose of nonviolent action as a way to make people notice injustice. He led the march on Washington in 1963, at which he delivered the "**I Have a Dream**" speech. He received the 1964 Nobel Prize for Peace.

James Meredith – the first African American to enroll at the University of Mississippi.

Emmett Till – a teenage boy who was murdered in Mississippi while visiting from Chicago. He was accused was "whistling at a white woman in a store." He was beaten and murdered, and his body was dumped in a river. His two white abductors were apprehended and tried but acquitted by an all-white jury. After the acquittal, they admitted their guilt, but remained free because of double jeopardy laws.

Ralph Abernathy – successor to Martin Luther King, Jr. as head of the Southern Christian Leadership Conference

Malcolm X – a political leader, Black Muslim, and part of the Civil Rights Movement who did not take a pacifist stance. He maintained the view that African Americans should do everything that was necessary to secure their rights.

Stokeley Carmichael – a leader of the Black Power movement who called for independent development of political and social institutions for blacks. He called for black pride and maintenance of black culture. He was head of the Student Nonviolent Coordinating Committee.

Key events of the Civil Rights Movement include:

Brown vs. Board of Education, 1954 – U.S. Supreme Court case that ended the separate but equal doctrine in public education.

The Montgomery Bus Boycott, 1955–56 – After refusing to give up her seat on a bus in Montgomery, Alabama, Parks was arrested, tried, and convicted of disorderly conduct and violating a local ordinance. When word reached the black community a bus boycott was organized to protest the segregation of blacks and whites on public buses. The boycott lasted 381 days, until the ordinance was lifted.

Direct action (1955–65) – nonviolent resistance and civil disobedience, consisting mostly of bus boycotts, sit-ins, freedom rides.

Formation of the Southern Christian Leadership Conference, 1957. - by Martin Luther King, Jr., John Duffy, Rev. C. D. Steele, Rev. T. J. Jemison, Rev. Fred Shuttlesworth, Ella Baker, A. Philip Randolph, Bayard Rustin and Stanley Levison to provide training and assistance to local efforts to fight segregation with non-violent methods.

Desegregation of Central High School, Little Rock, Arkansas, 1957. Following the decision of the Supreme Court in *Brown vs. Board of Education*, the school board voted to integrate the school system. However, Governor Orville Faubus called up the National Guard to prevent nine black students from attending Little Rock's Central High School. President Eisenhower sent federal troops to enforce integration of the school.

Sit-ins – In 1960, students began to stage "sit-ins" at local lunch counters and stores as a means of protesting the refusal of those businesses to desegregate. The first was in Greensboro, NC. This led to a rash of similar campaigns throughout the South. Demonstrators began to protest parks, beaches, theaters, museums, and libraries. When arrested, the protesters made "jail-no-bail" pledges.

Freedom Rides – Activists traveled by bus throughout the Deep South to desegregate bus terminals (required by federal law). Many buses were firebombed, and protestors were attacked by the KKK and beaten. Key figures in this effort included John Lewis, James Lawson, Diane Nash, Bob Moses, James Bevel, Charles McDew, Bernard Lafayette, Charles Jones, Lonnie King, Julian Bond, Hosea Williams, and Stokeley Carmichael.

The Birmingham Campaign, 1963–64. A campaign to use sit-ins, kneel-ins in churches, and a march to the county building to launch a voter registration campaign. The City obtained an injunction to forbid all such protests. The protesters, including Martin Luther King, Jr., believed the injunction was unconstitutional, and defied it. They were arrested. While in jail, King wrote his famous "Letter from Birmingham Jail." When the campaign began to falter, the "Children's Crusade" called students to leave school and join the protests. The events became news when more than 600 students were jailed.

Media coverage resulted in public outrage. The Kennedy administration intervened and formed a committee to end hiring discrimination, arrange for the release of jailed protesters, and establish communication between blacks and whites. The KKK bombed the **Sixteenth Street Baptist Church**, killing four girls.

The March on Washington, 1963. – A march on Washington for jobs and freedom. A combined effort of all major civil rights organizations, the march had the goals of civil rights laws, a federal works program, full and fair employment, decent housing, the right to vote, and adequate integrated education. Here, Martin Luther King, Jr. made the famous "I Have a Dream" speech.

Mississippi Freedom Summer, 1964. Students from various states assisted local activists in registering voters, teaching in **Freedom Schools** and in forming the Mississippi Freedom Democratic Party. Three of the workers, James Chaney, Michael Schwerner Andrew Goodman disappeared – murdered by the KKK. President Johnson sent in the FBI and effected passage of the 1964 Civil Rights Act by Congress.

Selma to Montgomery marches, 1965. Marches led by Martin Luther King to obtain voting rights for blacks. Marches were met with violent resistance by police. National broadcast of police action provoked a nation-wide response and passage of the Voting Rights Act of 1965.

Key policies, legislation and court cases:

***Brown v. Board of Education*, 1954** – U.S. Supreme Court overturned the separate but equal doctrine set forth in *Plessy v. Ferguson*. The Court ordered immediate desegregation of public schools.

Civil Rights Act of 1964 – bars discrimination in public accommodations, employment and education.

Voting Rights Act of 1965 – suspended poll taxes, literacy tests and other tests for voter registration.

Skill 2.12b   Describe the civil rights movements of African Americans and other minority groups and their impacts on government, society, and the economy.

"**Minority rights**" encompasses two ideas: individual rights for members of ethnic, racial, class, religious or sexual minorities and collective rights of minority groups.

Anti-discrimination laws that protect minority rights include: Fair Employment Act; Civil Rights Acts of 1964, 1968, and 1991; Immigration and Nationality Services Act; Voting Rights Act; Age Discrimination in Employment Act; Age Discrimination Act of 1975; Pregnancy Discrimination Act; Americans with Disabilities Act; and Employment Non-Discrimination Act.

The **disability rights** movement was a successful effort to guarantee access to public buildings and transportation, equal access to education and employment, and equal protection under the law in terms of access to insurance, and other basic rights of American citizens. As a result of these efforts, public buildings and public transportation must be accessible to persons with disabilities. Discrimination in hiring and housing on the basis of disability is also illegal.

A **prisoners' rights** movement works to ensure protections of rights for the incarcerated. Immigrant rights movements have provided for employment and housing rights, as well as preventing abuse of immigrants through hate crimes. In some states, **immigrant rights** movements have led to bi-lingual education and public information access. Another group movement to obtain equal rights is the lesbian, gay, bisexual and transgender social movement. This movement seeks equal housing, freedom from social and employment discrimination, and equal recognition of relationships under the law.

Skill 2.12c Analyze the development of the women's rights movement and its connections to other social and political movements.

The **women's rights** movement is concerned with the freedoms of women as separate from other groups. These issues are generally different from those that affect men and boys because of biological conditions or social constructs. The rights the movement has sought to protect throughout history include the right to: vote, to work, fair wages, bodily integrity and autonomy, own property, education, and hold public office. Rights also include: marital, parental, religious, and the right to serve in the military and to enter into legal contracts.

Some of the most famous leaders in the women's movement throughout American history include: Abigail Adams, Susan B. Anthony, Gloria E. Anzaldua, Betty Friedan, Olympe de Gouges, Gloria Steinem, Harriet Tubman, Mary Wollstonecraft, Virginia Woolf, and Germaine Greer.

DOMAIN 3   CALIFORNIA HISTORY

COMPETENCY 3.1   PRE-COLUMBIAN PERIOD THROUGH THE END OF MEXICAN RULE

Skill 3.1a   Describe the geography, economic life, and culture of California's American Indian peoples, as well as their relationship with the environment.

Geographically California can be understood in terms of four primary sections: the coast, the mountains, the central valley, and the deserts. California offers a wide variety of habitats and many species of plants and animals, as well as climates. As a result, there was great cultural diversity among the early people of California. These differences included housing, dress, kinship systems, political organizations, and religious beliefs and practices.

Each culture has its own story of creation. But most anthropologists believe that the early native population was descended from ancient people who crossed the **Bering Land Bridge** that once connected Asia and North America. There is no certainty about when the first people reached California, but there is widespread belief that Native Americans lived in this region for 15,000 years before the first European explorers visited the California coast.

Most California Native Americans subsisted by hunting and gathering, but they also managed the natural resources. Tribes pruned plants and trees, culled animal populations, and periodically burned groundcover to enrich the earth. The **Cahuilla** dug wells in the deserts and created pools by building up the sand around the wells. They cultivated melons, squash, beans and corn. The **Yumas,** who lived near the lower Colorado River, planted corn, pumpkins and beans in the mud after the annual floods of the river. The primary food for most tribes was the acorn. Hunters had access to deer, antelope, elk, sheep and bears. Fish were plentiful in the lakes, rivers, streams and ocean.

The number of tribes, cultures and languages of the early Native Californians was vast. There were seven groups of languages: Penutian, Hokan, Utian, Yukian, Algic, Uto-Aztecan, and Na-Dene. More than 100 tribes have been identified and they have been further subdivided into tribelets or groups of villages. It is believed that there were as many as 500 of these tribelets.

Due to the great diversity of the native communities, the state is generally divided into six culture areas.

The Southern Culture Area was home to some of the most populous tribes. Some of these communities had as many as 2,000 residents. The **Kumeyaay** migrated each year as plants in their territory ripened. The **Cahuilla** hunted with bows and arrows, nets, traps, or by throwing sticks at small animals. The women gathered nuts and fruits. They also planted corn, squash, beans and melons when there was sufficient water. The **Tongva** tribe had a structured society that was divided into distinct classes. The villages of the **Chumash** sometimes included as many as 2,000 people and generally included a storehouse, sweathouse, cemetery, ceremonial enclosure and playing field. The Chumash were skilled fishermen and navigators who made canoes of planks caulked with asphaltum. They harpooned seals, sea otters, and porpoises and traveled between the coast and the many islands off shore. They also produced spectacular colorful rock paintings.

The Central Culture Area included about 60% of all of the Native people of California. The climate was mild, and hunting and gathering was easy. Their tools and weapons were unsophisticated, but their basketry was quite advanced. These groups were organized into tribelets and small villages. The people of the villages were quite territorial and did forbid trespassing. However, clashes between tribes were minor. The **Yokuts** were hunters and gatherers, as well as fishermen. They are notable for the development of hunting strategies such as wearing animal disguises and for building traps for quail. The **Miwok** groups were spread over a large area and constructed dwellings differently in these areas that ranged from earth-covered homes that were partly underground to thatched huts, to bark slab structures. Each of the triblets was autonomous. The **Pomo**, actually several groups of native peoples, were particularly known for their basketry.

The Northwestern Culture Area was notable for tribes that valued material wealth. The possession of certain prized items determined social status. Political leadership belonged to the wealthiest. The **Yurok** lived along the Klamath River in permanent villages of distinctive dwellings built of split planks. Their proximity to the redwood forests provided the wood which was made into numerous household items and dugout canoes. The **Hupa** lived near the Trinity River. Wealth determined social rank. They subsisted primarily on salmon and acorns. Their religion included the "world-renewal rituals" of the White Deerskin and Jumping Dances. The **Shasta** lived in the mountain area of northwestern California. They settled in river valleys or at the mouths of rivers. In the villages, individual families owned hunting and fishing grounds, tobacco plots, and oak trees. They traded with their neighbors.

The Northeastern Culture Area was sparsely settled. Some of the tribes in this area occupied rich lands and lived much like tribes in other areas. Other tribes, however, lived in more desolate areas and subsisted on small game and gathered seeds and roots. The **Achumawi** lived along the Pit River. They dug pits to trap deer and other animals. Deer skins were used to make caps, capes, belts, moccasins, leggings, skirts and quivers. They had elaborate puberty rituals for girls, extensive mourning rites, and respected their Shamans. About half of their shamans were women. The **Atsugewi** lived in rugged valleys and barren plains. They valued and respected hard work. They fished with baskets and nets, hunted small game in groups, and individually hunted large game, which they shared with the community. They set aside every sixth day for rest, and held an annual celebration to which they invited people of neighboring villages.

The Great Basic Culture Area included the areas along the current eastern border and the eastern deserts of the southern part of the state. Food and water are scarce in this area. The **Tubatulabal** lived in the southern foothills of the Sierra Nevada. They were divided into three groups, each spoke a different dialect. These tribes were led by a headman (timiwal) who was elected for life by a council of elders. His function was primarily dispute resolution and representation of the tribe when dealing with other groups. They subsisted by hunting, fishing and gathering. The **Owens Valley Paiute** lived in an area that received very little rainfall and had little vegetation. Small groups tended to migrate frequently to seek food and water. The men hunted and the women gathered. This group was notable for its development of a system of agriculture that utilized communal labor. They built dams and ditches to irrigate wild plants.

The Colorado River Culture Area was on the western edge of the Southwest Culture Area. These Native Americans hunted and gathered and grew beans, corn, and pumpkins. They considered themselves more unified than the tribes that divided themselves into tribelets. They traveled extensively outside their own regions. The people of this area include the **Quechan (Yuma)**, the **Halchidhoma**, and the **Mohave**.

Skill 3.1b   Define and assess the impact of Spanish exploration and colonization, including the establishment of the mission system, ranchos, and pueblos, and their influences on the development of the agricultural economy of early California.

The first explorers visited California in search of riches and a route to Asia. **Hernan Cortes** led an expedition north from Acapulco to the Baja peninsula in 1535. He established a colonial outpost on the coast of the Bay of La Paz, but it was abandoned in 1536. The coastal areas of California were first explored by Portuguese explorer Jouan Rodriguez Cabrillo in 1542 who was working for the Spaniard Cortes. Cabrillo's expedition resulted in the discovery of Alta California. **Francis Drake**, an Englishman, was the first to explore the entire coast and claim possession of the territory.

The strategy of the Spanish empire in California was to exploit, transform, and include the native people of the Americas in the new settlements called missions. **Missions** were the key to transplanting the empire and converting the native people to Roman Catholicism. Beginning in 1769, California missions were established along the coast by Spanish Catholic missionaries in a program called the **Sacred Expedition**. The first mission was at San Diego. By 1823, there were 21 missions. The Franciscan leader of the San Diego mission was Father

Junipero Serra. After Serra's death, Fermin Francisco de Lasuen became the leader of the missionary effort.

Missions were generally established with the distance of a day's walk between them. Native people were brought to the missions, given religious instruction, and taught various practical skills. The secondary goal of the missions was to thoroughly transition the native people to life under the Spanish empire. This included language, work habits, social organization, and attire.

The missions were surrounded by orange groves, grape plantations and cattle ranches. Some of the native people cooperated with the missionaries and some chose a course of passive or active resistance. Revolts were quickly and violently put down.

The missions were intended to be temporary schools that would convert the native people and acculturate them as Spaniards. Once this was accomplished, the missions were to be disbanded. When Mexico declared independence from Spain, the missions became possessions of the Mexican government. By 1832 they were essentially abandoned.

The impact of the missions on the native people of California is a matter of considerable debate. It is clear that the change in lifestyle, the compression of the people in a small area, and the introduction of new diseases resulted in an exceptionally high death rate. The life of the native people at the missions was harsh.

In the 1820s, trappers and settlers from Canada and the United States began to reach California. They brought tremendous change. Russia made a weak attempt to claim part of California. The territory was sparsely settled during this period due to frequent endemic outbreaks of malaria, plague and yellow fever.

Spanish colonial officials built four military forts, **presidios**, along the coast of California. They were built near the best ports so the harbors could be defended against attack. Presidios were built in close proximity to the missions so soldiers could be dispatched quickly in the event of an uprising. To ensure an adequate food supply for the soldiers, civilian towns, called **pueblos,** were founded. Settlers were attracted to these settlements with offers of free land, farming equipment, livestock, and an annual stipend. In return they had to sell their surplus agricultural products to the presidios.

Cattle and horses were introduced in the late eighteenth century. Their numbers doubled about every five years, giving rise to cattle ranches (**ranchos**) that became the primary expressions of the lifestyle of Mexican California. Families that owned and operated these ranches were the elite of Mexican California. The ranches relied on native labor. This resulted in the creation of a feudal state in

California. One where the natives were held on the land and received food and shelter in return for their labor.

Skill 3.1c Describe the causes of the Mexican-American War and assess its impact on California.

The immediate cause of the **Mexican-American War** was the annexation of Texas by the United States in 1845. In 1836, Texas had revolted from Mexico and established itself as an independent republic. The **Republic of Texas** was recognized by the U.S. in 1837. Mexico never acknowledged Texan independence. Mexico warned the U.S. that Mexico would consider an attempt to annex Texas to the American Union a declaration of war.

The Texas issue was a major consideration in the Presidential election of 1844. Democrats favored annexation; the Whigs opposed it. Democrat **James K. Polk** was elected President and made the annexation of Texas the first major action of his administration. He ordered General Zachary Taylor to lead troops to the Rio Grande. Taylor was met by a Mexican army counter-offensive. The war bagan on April 25, 1846. On May 13, Congress formally declared war.

Although the annexation of Texas was the direct cause of the Mexican-American War, there were also indirect causes. By the terms of the **Missouri Compromise,** slavery was banned north of the boundary 36° 30'. Texas was the last potential slave-holding state that could be admitted to the Union. The balance of power in the Senate on the slavery debate was at stake.

Lt. **John C. Fremont** (an officer with the Army Corps of Topographical Engineers) and a troop of about sixty armed men arrived in California. All of the men were expert marksmen. Mexican officials ordered them out of California. After initially refusing to leave, Fremont relented and started moving north toward Oregon. He later returned to California and helped instigate what the **Bear Flag Revolt.** Fremont joined forces with a group of Anglo-American settlers in northern California who seized Colonel Mariano Guadalupe Vallejo and other Mexicans in Sonoma on June 14, 1846. The combined force (called the **California Battalion**) declared California an independent republic. They raised a flag that showed a crude drawing of a bear, a single star, and the words "California Republic." The flag raising came to be known as the Bear Flag Revolt. The Revolt created tension and bitterness between the Anglo-Americans and the Spanish-speaking **Californios**.

U.S. naval forces landed on the coast of California in July 1846 and proclaimed California part of the United States. Mexico responded with military force that included the Californios. Fighting in California ended on January 13, 1847 when Andres Pico surrendered to John C. Fremont.

The Mexican-American War officially ended with the signing of the **Treaty of Guadalupe Hidalgo** on February 2, 1848. The U.S. agreed to pay Mexico $15 million and to assume unpaid claims against Mexico. Mexico agreed to transfer to the United States more than 525,000 square miles of land, an area that includes the present-day states of California, Nevada and Utah, most of Arizona and New Mexico, and parts of Colorado and Wyoming. Mexico lost half of its land, and the American people believed they had achieved their Manifest Destiny. A small strip of land north of the Rio Grande remained in Mexican control. It was later purchased by the U.S. in the **Gadsden Purchase**. Slavery was prohibited in this area.

The major results of the Mexican-American War were the addition of more than 525,000 square miles of territory to the United States and the reorganization of the political parties along the lines of anti-slavery and pro-slavery. Indirect results included an increase in the prestige of the United States with the acquisition of an extended coastline on the Pacific. In addition, the settlement of California was facilitated by the discovery of gold. The doctrine of **squatter sovereignty** or **popular sovereignty** (the idea that the people of a territory should decide whether they would be free or slave) was introduced and became an underlying cause of the Civil War.

COMPETENCY 3.2   FROM THE GOLD RUSH TO THE PRESENT

Skill 3.2a   Describe the discovery of gold and assess its consequences on the cultures, societies, politics, and economies of California, including its impact on California Indians and Californios.

In January 1848, James Marshall, an employee of Captain John A. Sutter, observed the glitter of gold in sands he had picked up in a mill race (the water that turns a water wheel) at Sutter's Coloma sawmill. By August, word of the discovery of gold had reached the East. In December, more than 300 ounces of pure gold reached Washington, D.C. Gold fever swept the nation. Men left farms, businesses, and families to become part of the **Gold Rush**. The population of California rose from 14,000 to more than 100,000 within a year and to more than 220,000 by 1852. **Mark Twain** and **Bret Harte** wrote of the Gold Rush and the roughness, sentiment and unexpected heroism of the **Forty-Niners**.

People came from all over the world to seek gold. Those who came from the East traveled by **prairie schooner** (covered wagon), and proclaimed the motto "**California or bust.**" Many made the journey in ships and endured the dangers of rounding Cape Horn.

Most who came were men without families. Widespread disorder was the result of this influx of men who experienced the sudden rise to wealth or the dark despair of failure. The land had just been ceded from Mexico and had no established government or laws. What law there was varied from camp to camp. Nugget stealing and horse stealing were considered worse than murder and were punished accordingly.

The early settlers had the important task of establishing communication with the rest of the world. Steamship lines began to make the 19,000-mile trip around Cape Horn. Overland routes carried mail and freight from Missouri to San Francisco. The most notable overland routes were:

- The Merchant's Express, with 2,000 wagons and 20,000 yoke of oxen to move freight across the continent
- The **Pony Express** that relayed mail from Missouri to San Francisco in just ten days.
- Stage lines that traveled twice a week from Saint Louis to San Francisco and made it possible to travel from coast to coast in only three weeks.
- The **Union Pacific Railroad** was completed in 1869, eliminating the need for stage travel.

The successful miners built fabulous homes along the crest of **Nob Hill** in San Francisco. Those who provided supplies and services for the minors also amassed great wealth. The unsuccessful drifted down into the valley and filled land with wheat fields and orchards and began the remarkable agricultural development that would define California well into the future. To a large extent, California's economic and social character can be traced to both the successful and unsuccessful miners of the Gold Rush.

The Gold Rush gave rise to several notable **boom towns**. The largest in the central part of the state were Sacramento and Stockton. Sacramento was the gateway to the mines in the central and northern part of the state, and Stockton was the supply center for the southern mines. **San Francisco** was the greatest of the boom towns. It was the port through which those who sailed to California entered the state and was the center of banking and manufacturing.

The earliest mining methods (panning, rockers, "long tom") were essentially innocuous in environmental terms. But as the supply of readily available gold was exhausted, miners turned to more destructive methods to find and extract gold from the earth. Some dug deep shafts or tunnels into the earth. Most destructive was **hydraulicking**, a method that used high-pressure water to erode banks and hills. This uniquely California innovation was the predominant type of mining for about 30 years.

Skill 3.2b **Describe the international migration to California in the 19th century, the social, economic, and political responses to this migration, and the contributions of immigrants to the development of California.**

Regional mining districts were established that paid lip service to democratic principles. But they were discriminatory. These mining districts generally excluded **African Americans, Asians,** and **Latinos,** and resorted to **vigilante justice** when people were suspected of wrongdoing.

The discrimination practiced by the Anglo-American settlers had far-reaching effects on an increasingly and uniquely diverse and predominantly immigrant society. There were frequent ethnic conflicts because the lure of gold had attracted people from America, Mexico, Chile, Peru, and other South and Central American countries, from Europe, and from China and the Pacific islands.

The **Native people** of California responded in several ways. Some simply got out of the way and moved into the central part of the state. Some, particularly the Miwok and Yokuts, raided the settlements for horses and livestock. Some became miners, or worked for white miners, and some mined gold and traded it to white merchants for goods.

Within four years of the beginning of the gold rush, the Native American population declined from about 150,000 to 30,000. Much of this was due to malnutrition and **disease** introduced by the white men. Thousands of Native people died in campaigns of **extermination** carried out by the whites. Miners and ranchers joined forces, with the support of locals, to carry out raids on native villages. Some frontier communities even paid **bounties** for Indian scalps and heads.

The Treaty of Guadalupe Hidalgo ended the Mexican American War and provided for the property rights of **Mexicans** who owned property in the lands claimed by the United States. At the time, the ranchos covered about 13 million acres but the gold frenzy had ignored the property rights of the rancho owners. Miners settled on rancho lands as "**squatters.**" There was vast confusion about ownership of the land. In 1851 Congress passed a land law that outlined an extensive process by which rancho owners could prove their title to the land and have the squatters removed. Resolution of these claims took about seventeen years. About 200 of the claim owners lost land amounting to nearly four million acres. About 600 of the claim owners demonstrated their ownership of about nine million acres. But by the time the claims were won, the owners were usually bankrupt and lost the land, anyway.

African Americans accounted for about one percent of the non-Indian population during the Gold Rush. These were both escaped slaves and free persons. The free blacks came to mine for themselves. Slaves were brought by their southern owners, despite the fact that California was a free state. African Americans were victims of discrimination. The state constitution restricted voting rights to "free white males." Membership in the state militia was also restricted to whites. California enacted a harsh fugitive slave law and the state passed a law that made it illegal for "blacks, negroes, mulattoes" and Indians from testifying either for or against a "white man."

Latin American immigrants made up the largest group of foreign miners. There was great hostility between the Latino miners and the Anglo miners. Some of this hostility was a residual effect of the recent war. But a large part of the animosity was due to economic competition. Most of the Latino miners were more experienced and more knowledgeable in mining.

In 1850, the state legislature passed the **Foreign Miners License Tax**. All miners who were not U.S. citizens were required to pay a monthly tax of $20. After the tax was passed, about two-thirds of the Mexican miners returned to Mexico.

In 1853, a newspaper estimated there were 32,000 French gold miners in the state. The French also suffered discrimination from U.S. citizens. The Americans called the French "Keskydees", a derogatory imitation of the question frequently asked by the French miners, "Qu'est-ce qu'il dit?" (What does he say?). The French miners objected to paying the monthly tax of $20 to mine gold in California. Some of the French miners joined forces with Germans and Mexicans and staged a peaceful protest at Sonora. This came to be called **The French Revolution**.

Natives of the **Hawaiian Islands** (called Kanakas) began to immigrate to California fifty years earlier to hunt sea otter and work in other coastal areas. Hundreds more came to work in the gold mines. They were treated no better.

Thousands of **Chinese** came during the gold rush. Anglo-American miners feared that they, too, would take too much of the gold. Others hated them because they were willing to work for very low wages. The state legislature enacted another Foreign Miners License Tax of $3 per month in 1852 that was particularly directed against the Chinese. For 18 years this tax generated almost 25% of the California's annual revenue. It was not until 1870 that it was declared unconstitutional.

Despite discrimination and hostility, California's development resulted to a great extent from the labor and struggle of immigrants. The Chinese, in particular, who worked in the mines had superior knowledge of explosives. They were also the major source of labor for the railroads.

The completion of the **transcontinental railroad** in 1869 ended California's isolation from the rest of the country. The four men who provided the vision and much of the initial financial backing for the construction of the railroad were known as the **Big Four (Leland Stanford, Collis P. Huntington, Mark Hopkins, and Charles Crocker)**. They became the wealthiest and most powerful men of their generation. Construction took more than six years. There was a great celebration when the tracks of the **Central Pacific Railroad** met the tracks of the **Union Pacific Railroad**. The track was attached to the final tie with three commemorative spikes—one was silver and two were gold.

The immediate benefit of the completion of the railroad and the invention of the refrigerated car was that the cars could deliver California produce to the East quickly, and the produce could be kept ripe and cool during shipment.

Yet the first ten years after the completion of the railroad were disappointing. The expected new prosperity did not arrive. What followed completion were ten years of economic depression. Merchants overextended themselves in expectation of a large influx of new settlers. When new settlers did not arrive, the market was over-supplied and the prices of the goods declined. Land prices rose as the railroad neared completion, also in anticipation of new settlers. Completion of the railroad actually resulted in decreases in land prices. The completion of the work also returned thousands of workers back to the California labor pool, reducing wages and caused extensive unemployment.

The expected boom did come in the 1880s, partly due to the railroad. The owners of the railroad advertised California throughout the nation. A second railroad line (the Atchison, Topeka, and Santa Fe) reached Los Angeles in the middle of the decade. A rate war between the two railroads ensued. More than 200,000 new residents came to California in 1887 alone.

The railroad recruited Chinese laborers because they were willing to work for low wages (usually a dollar a day) and to do dangerous work. More than 10,000 Chinese laborers, and many Irish immigrants, built the railroad. When construction ended and the Chinese returned to California, the resulting depression was blamed on them. Anti-Chinese activities included riots and the looting and burning of Chinese settlements. Several cities passed laws that were intended to drive out the Chinese. Unemployed whites frequently destroyed Chinese businesses. In 1877, unemployed white men of San Francisco formed a new political party called **The Workingmen's Party** and demanded the expulsion of Chinese immigrants.

California voters adopted a new state constitution in 1879, during the height of anti-Chinese hostility. The new constitution included anti-Chinese provisions that prohibited the Chinese being employed by government except as punishment for crimes. Chinese were required to live outside of city or town limits if they did not live in designated parts of towns. Chinese immigrants were ineligible for U.S. citizenship and further Chinese immigration was discouraged.

The **Chinese Exclusion Act** was passed by the U.S. Congress in 1882. It prohibited Chinese immigration for ten years. In 1892, it was extended for another ten years. In 1902, it became permanent. It was not repealed until China and the U.S. became allies against the Japanese in World War II. This law produced further difficulties for the Chinese, including boycotts of Chinese-produced goods.

Skill 3.2c   **Analyze key principles in California's constitutional and political development (including the Progressive Era reforms of initiative, referendum, and recall), and compare and contrast the California and U.S. Constitutions.**

Between the end of the Mexican American War and California's admission to the Union in 1850, the political situation was unstable. The U.S. Congress was consumed with the issue of slavery in the areas ceded to the U.S. by the treaty that ended the war. For this reason, no formal government was established for California until 1850.

In 1849, a constitution was drafted but the most pressing issue was whether to petition for admission as a state. Due to the great influx of new settlers and gold fever, the delegates decided to apply for statehood immediately. The second major issue was the question of slavery. California requested to be admitted as a free state. The constitution included a provision that permitted **married women** to own property independently of their husbands. Any property owned by a woman prior to marriage or during marriage would remain her personal property. This was the first such provision in the nation. This provision was included because Mexican California had the same law. The eastern boundary of the state was established as the eastern slope of the Sierra Nevada.

The admission of California as a free state would upset the balance between slave and free states in the Congress. The issue was resolved when Congress passed a strict new fugitive slave law. California became a state on September 9, 1850, during the presidency of Millard Fillmore.

One of the critical issues not addressed in the original state constitution was the location of the state capital. The location was to be determined on the basis of bids from the various towns. For about six years, the capital moved between San Jose, Vallejo, and Benicia. **Sacramento** was selected as the permanent capital in 1854.

The pre-statehood constitution was superseded by the current California Constitution, which was ratified in 1879. Unlike most constitutions, it is long—110 pages. It has been amended more than 425 times.

Executive power is vested in a **governor, lieutenant-governor, secretary of state, controller, treasurer, attorney-general** and **surveyor-general,** each elected to four-year terms. The governor and lieutenant governor are elected separately. The governor may use a **line-item veto** for legislation. A line-item veto gives the executive the power to veto certain sections of a bill without vetoing the whole bill.

The California legislature is **bi-cameral** and both houses are based on population. Members are term limited. The senate is made up of a representative of each county, elected for four years, and an assembly made up of representatives of districts of equal population, elected for two years. The judiciary consists of a **supreme court** (a chief justice and six associates) elected for twelve-year terms, a **superior court** for each county, and **inferior courts** established by the legislature. In civil cases, a finding may be established by agreement of three-fourths of the jury.

California's constitution includes provisions for the **initiative** that allows voters to directly create laws or constitutional amendments, the **referendum** that allows voters to veto acts of the legislature, and the **recall** that permits voters to remove from office any elected official.

Skill 3.2d   Describe 20th century migration to California from the rest of the U.S. and the world, and analyze its impact on the cultural, economic, social, and political evolution of the state.

In the late nineteenth and twentieth centuries, California experienced dramatic growth. The climate of the central valley is perfect for growing wheat. This agricultural industry fostered the development of new approaches to agriculture and the development of new technology. The first was the **Stockton gang plow** that was made up of a beam to which was attached several plowshares. This was mounted on wheels and was pulled by a team of horses or mules. New machines were developed for planting seeds and for cutting and threshing grain. Steam-powered **combined harvesters** and steam-powered tractors were invented. The first internal combustion tractor was invented in Stockton, California.

Luther Burbank, a horticulturist, arrived in California from Massachusetts in the latter part of the nineteenth century. He created hundreds of new varieties of plants, including new types of plums, lilies, berries, apples, rhubarb, and quince. Although the Spanish missionaries had first introduced oranges to California, it was not until 1870 that **John Wesley North** planted orange trees into sandy soil of riverbanks and irrigating the groves with water from the river. He produced winter-ripening Riverside navel oranges and shipped them across the country in refrigerated rail cars. A few years later California produced summer-ripening Valencia oranges. The state was then able to provide fresh **oranges** year-round. It was the source of more than 65% of the nation's oranges and 90% of its lemons.

The discovery of extensive **oil deposits** in the late nineteenth century created California's petroleum industry. The deposits were located in the San Joaquin Valley, the Los Angeles basin, and Santa Barbara County. New discoveries of oil in the 1920s led to a second major economic boom for California. Petroleum refinement became the state's major manufacturing industry and the Los Angeles harbor became the leading oil-exporting port in the world.

At about the same time as the discovery of oil in California the **automobile** was became more popular in California than anywhere else in the nation. By the middle of the 1920s the car was a mainstay of the California lifestyle. It also facilitated numerous other changes. The suburbs grew and were connected to the cities by networks of new roads. The suburbs began to experience the rise of shopping centers, supermarkets and single-family homes. And tourism became a major industry for California, which in turn gave rise to motels, auto camps, tourist cabins, and even drive-ins.

Soon after this, the **motion picture industry** made its home in southern California. In 1913, Samuel Goldfish and Archibald Selwyn formed the feature motion picture company Goldwyn. They then partnered with Louis B. Mayer to form **Metro-Goldwyn Mayer**, the leading studio in Hollywood for more than a quarter of a century.

Of particular significance in the early twentieth century were the labor struggles and the growth of **labor unions**. This struggle was very intense, particularly in San Francisco. Throughout the first two decades of the twentieth century, San Francisco was a **closed-shop** city (i.e., one in which employers hired only union members). In Los Angeles, largely through the efforts of Harrison Gray Otis and the *Los Angeles Times*, the **open shop** (employers refuse to hire union members) prevailed.

California agriculture depended on migratory farm workers. Most of them were foreign-born, not unionized, and non-white. They became organized in the early part of the century (**Industrial Workers of the World**). Farm owners tended to regard the union as dangerous to the American way of life. Many local governments tried to pass laws that banned the activities of the union.

In 1916, a bomb exploded during a parade near the San Francisco waterfront area. **Thomas J. Mooney** was blamed, tried, and convicted of murder. He was sentenced to hang. Labor leaders throughout the nation believed Mooney had been framed by an anti-labor conspiracy. The governor commuted his sentence to life in prison. Twenty-three years later, Mooney was pardoned and released from prison. Is this paragraph necessary?

The number of **Japanese immigrants** steadily increased in the early twentieth century. Anti-Japanese sentiment also grew. A series of actions were taken against Japanese immigrants. Labor leaders in San Francisco formed the

Asiatic Exclusion League in 1905 and demanded public policies against the Japanese. They pressured the city into requiring that Japanese children attend segregated schools with other Asian children. Protests from Japan led to intervention by President Theodore Roosevelt. The city agreed to suspend the segregation act in exchange for a law that would limit Japanese immigration. Japan agreed in 1907 to prohibit its workers from immigrating to the U.S.

Japanese immigrants were capable farmers. White farmers tried to eliminate the competition. In 1913 the state legislature passed a law prohibiting anyone who was not eligible for citizenship to own land in the state. Asians were ineligible for naturalization under federal law. In 1924, U.S. Congress passed the **National Origins Quota Act** that prohibited all further immigration from Japan.

This period of rapid economic growth and industrial expansion in California came to an abrupt end with the **Stock Market crash of 1929**. With 20–25% of the population unemployed and losing everything, nativism and a fear of foreigners rose quickly. White workers complained that **Filipino** immigrants posed an economic threat to native-born workers. Numerous riots broke out. Congress passed the **Filipino Repatriation Act** in 1935. The government offered to pay transportation expenses for any Filipinos who wished to return home.

Mexican immigrants then became targets. The U.S. government created a repatriation program. Up to 100,000 people were deported to Mexico.

In the 1930s **Dust Bowl refugees** came by the hundreds of thousands in search of a better life in California. These refugees held on to the culture of the Southwest, created their own subculture in California, and were called **Okies** because many came from Oklahoma, although they came from several states.

California hosted the **Olympics in 1932** and constructed the **San Francisco-Oakland Bay Bridge**. Coit Tower in San Francisco and the murals that present California history were completed in the 1930s, and in 1939, San Francisco hosted the **Golden Gate International Exposition** on an island built specifically for the fair.

Skill 3.2e Identify major environmental issues in California history and their economic, social, and political implications (e.g., water supply and delivery, air/water/soil quality, transportation).

Environmental issues have always been part of the history of California. The early native tribes in parts of the state subsisted by moving around constantly in search of water and food.

Hydraulicking caused problems because it eroded hills and banks as miners searched for gold. The runoff deposited tons of mud, gravel, rock and sand into the rivers, burying farms, depositing silt in the rivers, and causing more frequent flooding. Farmers banded together to create the **Anti-Debris Association**, to urge the government to outlaw the dumping of mining debris into rivers. The **California Debris Commission**, a federal regulatory agency, was created to enforce the law.

John Muir was responsible for the establishment of Yosemite National Park in 1890. A few years later he founded the Sierra Club.

California's water issue results from the majority of the precipitation in the state occurring in the northern third of the state while 80% of the need for water is in the southern two-thirds of the state. As Los Angeles grew, its water supply proved to be inadequate. Water from the melting snows in the Sierra Nevada was diverted with an **aqueduct** to provide water for Los Angeles. This project was completed in 1913, but it deprived a farming community in the Owens Valley of much-needed water.

The most aggressive approach to moving water in California was the **Central Valley Project.** Construction of the Central Valley Project began in 1937. The original phase of the plan called for the construction of three dams, five canals, and two power transmission lines. This program provides flood control and water for agriculture throughout the Central Valley.

DOMAIN 4   **PRINCIPLES OF AMERICAN DEMOCRACY**

COMPETENCY 4.1   **PRINCIPLES OF AMERICAN DEMOCRACY**

Skill 4.1a   Analyze the influence of ancient Classical and Enlightenment political thinkers and the pre-Revolutionary colonial and indigenous peoples' experience on the development of the American government, and consider the historical contexts in which democratic theories emerged.

(See Skill 2.2a)

Skill 4.1b   Explain and analyze the principles of the Declaration of Independence and how the U.S. Constitution reflects a balance between classical republican and classical liberal thinking.

The terms **civil liberties** and **civil rights** are often used interchangeably, but there are some distinctions between the terms. **Civil liberties** implies that the state has a positive role to play in assuring that all citizens have equal protection and justice under the law with equal opportunities to exercise their privileges of citizenship and to participate fully in the life of the nation, regardless of race, religion, sex, color, or creed. **Civil rights** refers to rights that may be described as guarantees against the state authority, implying limitations on the actions of the state to interfere with citizens' liberties. The two concepts are really inseparable and interacting. Equality implies the proper order of liberty in a society so that an individual's freedom does not infringe on the rights of others.

The beginnings of civil liberties and the idea of civil rights in the United States go back to the ideas of the ancient Greeks. American colonists struggled for civil rights against the British. Religious freedom, political freedom, and the right to live one's life as one sees fit are basic to the American ideal. These were embodied in the ideas expressed in the Declaration of Independence and the Constitution.

All these ideas found their final expression in the United States Constitution's first ten amendments, known as the **Bill of Rights**. The Bill of Rights protects certain liberties and basic rights. James Madison, who wrote the amendments, said that the Bill of Rights does not give Americans these rights. People, Madison said, already have these rights. They are natural rights that belong to all human beings. The Bill of Rights simply prevents the government from taking away these rights.

Skill 4.1c **Evaluate the Founding Fathers' contribution to the establishment of a constitutional system as articulated in the Federalist Papers, constitutional debates, and the U.S. Constitution.**

It quickly became apparent that there were serious defects with the Articles of Confederation. In 1786, the **Annapolis Convention** made an effort to regulate commerce. Because only five states were represented, this Convention was unable to accomplish anything. The debates, however, made it clear that foreign and interstate commerce could not be regulated by a government with as little authority as the Articles of Confederation allowed. Congress called a convention to provide changes that would address the needs of the new nation.

The convention met in Philadelphia with fifty-five of the sixty-five appointed members present. A constitution was written in four months. The **Constitution of the United States** is the fundamental law of the republic. It is the **supreme law of the land.** Amendments to the Constitution must be ratified by two-thirds of Congress and three-fourths of the states. The compromises that resolved the conflicts are reflected in the final document. The first point of disagreement and compromise was related to the Presidency. The compromise was to give the President broad powers but to limit the president to a four year term, subject to re-election. Appointments and treaties made by the president must be consented to by the Senate.

The second conflict was between populous and non-populous states over representation in Congress. The populous states wanted power proportionate to their voting strength; the non-populous states opposed this plan. The compromise was that all states should have equal voting power in the Senate, but linked membership in the House of Representatives to a state's population.

The third conflict was about slavery. One compromise was that (a) fugitive slaves should be returned to their owners (b) that no law would be passed for 20 years (1808) prohibiting the importation of slaves. Another was that 3/5 of the slaves would be counted toward the population for deciding the number of representatives a state would have in the House of Representatives.

The fourth major area of conflict was how the president would be chosen. The Compromise was the **Electoral College. Do you want a paragraph here on how the Electoral College works?**

A system of **checks and balances** was created to ensure that no branch of government became too powerful. **Separation of powers** was also an important concept provided for in the Constitution. Each branch of government had its own duties/functions.

The **Federalist Papers** were written to win popular support for the newly proposed Constitution. The papers provide an explanation of the underlying philosophies of the Constitution. The Federalist Papers are still an important resource to understand the Constitution.

Skill 4.1d **Describe the significance of the Bill of Rights and the 14th Amendment as limits on government in the American constitutional process as compared to English Common Law.**

Bill of Rights - The first ten amendments to the United States Constitution deal with civil liberties and civil rights.

1. Freedom of speech, press, assembly, religion, and the right to petition the government for redress of grievances
2. A well-regulated militia, being necessary for the security of a free state, the right to keep and bear arms shall not be infringed
3. The government cannot quarter troops in private homes during peacetime
4. Right against unreasonable search and seizures
5. Right to due process and protection from self-incrimination
6. Right to trial by jury and legal counsel
7. Right to jury trial for civil actions
8. No cruel or unusual punishment
9. The rights listed in the Constitution are not the only rights the people enjoy
10. Powers not mentioned in the Constitution shall be retained by the states or the people

The Magna Carta is considered the basis of English constitutional liberties. In 1215 the noblemen forced King John to define their rights. The nobles refused to pay any taxes until King John granted the noble class certain inalienable property rights. The Magna Carta is considered to be the first modern document that sought to limit the powers of state authority. The Magna Carta only dealt with the rights of the nobility and all of its provisions excluded the rights of common people. It would take more than seven centuries before the rights won by the nobles were given to other English people.

The Great Council in England grew into a representative assembly called **Parliament**. By the 1600s, Parliament was divided into the House of Lords, made up of nobles, and the House of Commons. Members of the House of Commons were elected. In the beginning, only a few wealthy men could vote. Still English people firmly believed that the ruler must consult Parliament on money matters and obey the law. Thus, it did set a precedent that there was a limit to the power of the state.

The Petition of Right was addressed to the King **Charles I,** by the British parliament in 1628. Parliament demanded the King stop proclaiming new taxes without its consent. Parliament demanded that he cease housing soldiers and sailors in the homes of private citizens, proclaiming martial law in times of peace, and imprisoning people without good cause. These demands were echoed American colonists 150 years later, as these were some of the rights that, as Englishmen, they felt were denied to them.

The **British Bill of Rights** was known as the **Declaration of Rights.** It spelled out the rights that were considered to belong to Englishmen. It was granted by **King William III** in 1689. It had previously been passed by Parliament and it came out of the struggle for power that took place in Great Britain that was known as **The Glorious Revolution**, a revolution that was accomplished with virtually no bloodshed and led to King William III and Queen Mary II becoming joint sovereigns.

The Declaration of Rights is similar to the American Bill of Rights. It protects the rights of individuals and gives anyone accused of a crime the right to trial by jury. It outlaws cruel punishments and states that a ruler could not raise taxes or an army without the consent of Parliament.

All of these events and the principles that arose from them are of the utmost importance in understanding the process that eventually led to the ideals that are inherent in the Constitution of the United States. The fact is that all of these ideals are universal in nature and have become the basis for the idea of human freedoms throughout the world.

The British settlers in the American colonies brought with them the form of law they had known in England, the **Common Law.** Common law is judge-made law and is based on the concept of precedent. Case decisions follow earlier case decisions, when possible, common law is different from statutory law, which is law made by a legislative body.

Skill 4.1e   Describe the nature and importance of law in U.S. political theory, including the democratic procedures of law making, the rule of adherence to the law, and the role of civil disobedience.

The **rule of law** recognizes that the authority of the government is to be exercised only within the context and boundaries established by laws that are enacted according to established procedure and publicly disclosed. As a Constitutional government and political system, the basis of all laws, decisions and enforcement of laws is the U.S. Constitution. The Constitution establishes the process by which law can be written and enacted and the means of interpretation and enforcement of those laws by the courts.

The Constitution grants Congress the power to enact laws. Congressional statutes are gathered and published in the **United States Code**. Agencies of the executive branch have the power to create regulations that carry the force of law.

When these regulations are challenged, courts interpret the meaning of the regulations.

Laws are introduced, debated, and passed by Congress. When both houses of Congress pass the same version of the law the law must then be signed by the president. Once signed, the law is considered enacted. Challenges to the constitutionality of the federal law and questions of interpretation of federal law are decided by the federal courts. Each state has the authority to make laws covering anything not reserved to the federal government. State laws cannot negate or be contrary to federal laws.

Civil disobedience is the refusal to obey certain laws, regulations, or requirements of a government because those laws are believed to be unjust. Civil disobedience is a **nonviolent** protest against unjust laws.

Notable examples of civil disobedience have included Henry David Thoreau's refusal to pay taxes in protest against slavery and the Mexican-American War. Dr. Martin Luther King, Jr. led the Civil Rights Movement on the principle and practices of peaceable civil disobedience.

Skill 4.1f   Analyze the significance and evolving meaning of the principles of American democracy; autonomy/liberty, equality, basic opportunity, debate and deliberation, and representation.

The American nation was founded on the idea that the people would have a large degree of autonomy and liberty. The famous maxim "no taxation without representation" was a rallying cry for the Revolution, not only because people felt unfairly taxed, but also because the people could not influence Parliament in regard to those taxes.

The American colonists had become used to doing things their way and solving their own problems. Especially during the French and Indian War, when a large number of soldiers who served and died for the British Army called America home. The colonists were allowed to choose some of the people who governed them, although colonial governors were chosen in England. When the French and Indian War ended, the British government attempted to levy heavy taxes on the American colonists. The colonists believed the taxes were an infringement on their autonomy.

One of the most famous words in the Declaration of Independence is "**liberty**," the pursuit of which all people should be free to attempt. That idea, that a people should be free to pursue their own course, even to the extent of making their own mistakes, has dominated political thought in the 200-plus years of the American republic.

Representation is the idea that a people can vote for individuals to represent them in government. Representation was not a new idea in Britain, but was in the colonies because residents of other British colonies did not have these rights. When individuals and groups (such as the Sons of Liberty) objected to a lack of representation, they were asking to stand on an equal footing with the mother country. Along with the idea of representation comes the idea that issues should be debated, discussed, and deliberated. Taxation without representation ran counter to that idea.

Another key concept in the American ideal is **equality**, the idea that every person has the same rights and responsibilities under the law. The goals of the Declaration of Independence and the Constitution were to provide equality for all who read those documents. The reality was vastly different for large sectors of society, including women and non-white Americans.

The so-called **American Dream** is that every individual has an equal chance to make his or her fortune and that the initiative will be welcomed and even encouraged. For many, who were not white males that basic opportunity has been difficult to achieve.

Skill 4.1g   Describe the meaning and importance of each of the rights guaranteed in the Bill of Rights and analyze the reciprocal nature of citizenship, including the obligation to obey the law, serve as a juror, vote, pay taxes, and pursue various avenues of participation open to citizens.

The First Amendment provides for **freedom of religion**. The policy of the government has been guided by the premise that church and state should be separate. However, when religious practices have been at cross-purposes with attitudes prevailing in the nation at particular times, there have been restrictions placed on these practices. Some of these have been restrictions against the practice of polygamy and the prohibition of animal sacrifice that is promoted by some religious groups. The use of mind altering illegal substances that some use in religious rituals has been restricted. In the United States, all recognized religious institutions are tax-exempt, following the idea of separation of church and state. **Freedom of speech, press, and assembly** are rights that have historically have been given wide latitude; however, there have been instances when they have been limited for various reasons. The classic limitation, for instance, in regards to freedom of speech, has been the famous precept that an individual is prohibited from yelling 'fire!' in a crowded theater. This prohibition is an example of the state saying that freedom of speech does not extend to speech that might endanger other people. There is also a prohibition against **slander,** or the knowing statement of a deliberate falsehood about a person. Regulations regarding freedom of the press include **libel**, which is the printing of a known falsehood. In times of national emergency, various restrictions have been placed on the rights of press, speech and sometimes assembly.

The next three amendments were the result of the colonists' struggle with Great Britain. The Second Amendment guarantees the right to bear arms and the Third Amendment prevents the government from forcing citizens to keep troops in their homes during peacetime.

The Fourth Amendment protects from unreasonable searches and seizures. The prohibition is against unreasonable searches and seizures. There are established procedures where searches can be conducted with a warrant and seizures can take place if the search is valid.

Amendments five through eight protect citizens who are accused of crimes and are brought to trial. Every citizen has the right to due process of law. Although due process has not been precisely defined, the term means a process that is fair. What is "fair" depends on the facts and circumstances of a case. A person cannot be compelled to testify against him/herself. The Fifth Amendment guarantee against self-incrimination is a criminal defendant's right.

If a citizen is accused of a crime, they are, pursuant to the Sixth Amendment, entitled to a speedy, public trial, the right to an attorney, and an impartial jury of their peers. Individuals may not be subject to cruel or unusual punishment, according to the Eighth Amendment.

The last two amendments in the Bill of Rights limit the powers of the federal government to those that are expressly granted in the Constitution and provide that any rights not expressly mentioned in the Constitution belong to the states or to the people.

The protections guaranteed in the Bill of Rights apply to actions of the federal government. It was not until the Fourteenth Amendment (1868) that these guarantees and prohibitions were extended to the states. However, it was not until the 1960s that this interpretation of the Fourteenth Amendment was put into practice.

The nature of citizenship carries with it responsibilities such as obeying the law, paying taxes, and serving as a juror. Voting is another responsibility of citizens.

Skill 4.1h   Explain the basis and practice of acquiring American citizenship.

A citizen of the United States may either be native-born or a **naturalized** citizen. **Naturalization** is the process by which one acquires citizenship. In certain circumstances a person may have dual-citizenship that is citizenship in the United States as well as in another country.

In order to become a citizen the applicant must be least 18 years old and lawfully admitted into the U.S. as a permanent resident. There is a residency requirement in most situations and the applicant must be of good moral character and believe in the principles of the Constitution of the United States of America. The applicant must have an understanding of American history and government and be able to read, write, speak, and understand basic English. An oath giving up foreign allegiance and promising to obey the Constitution and U.S. laws is also required. Successful candidates become American citizens at a ceremony presided over by a judge.

Once a person is naturalized, it is expected the person will vote, serve on a jury, participate in military service, if appropriate, and participate in the government as responsible citizens do.

COMPETENCY 4.2   FUNDAMENTAL VALUES AND PRINCIPLES OF CIVIL SOCIETY

Skill 4.2a   Explain and analyze the historical role of religion, religious diversity, and religious discrimination and conflict in American life.

The second set of English settlers who built a colony in North America are commonly known as the **Pilgrims**. They fled religious persecution in their homeland. As more people settled on the East Coast of what is now America, they brought more religions. Puritans (the largest group of Protestants to immigrate to America) targeted people who didn't share their strict religious views for expulsion from the community. Two examples of such discrimination involved **Anne Hutchison** and **Roger Williams.** Both were dynamic preachers who were forced to leave Massachusetts for having views different than the Puritan majority (even though they were both Puritans themselves). Williams founded the neighboring colony of Rhode Island and Hutchinson followed him there before settling in New York.

Another religion to suffer at the hands of Puritans was the Society of Friends, or the **Quakers**. In 1660 Massachusetts Puritans hanged Quaker leader Mary Dyer for refusing to convert to Puritanism. The Pennsylvania colony was later founded, among other things, as a refuge for Quakers.

Maryland was founded in large part as a colony for **Catholics**, supporters of Mary Stuart, the embattled queen for whom the colony was named. The language of the colony's charter contained absolutely no reference to religion, a significant departure from the charter language of other colonies.

The Church of England, or **Anglicanism**, was founded by Henry VIII and preferred by his daughter Elizabeth. It became an established religion in Virginia but the Virginia Anglicans wanted all Virginians to be Anglicans and went out of their way to convince new settlers to embrace the religion.

The **First Great Awakening** (1730–1740s) was a time of intense religious revival in America. It made religion a main part of everyday lives. Dynamic sermons by George Whitefield, Cotton Mather, and Jonathan Edwards made settlers in America think about their souls and how to better their chances of going to heaven.

The zealots were the **Deists.** They believed in the general idea of a supreme being but didn't think he took any active part in human lives. Famous Deists included George Washington and Thomas Jefferson.

Government documents of the newly formed United States sanction no religion. Rather, the First Amendment to the Constitution states that Congress will not sanction *any* religion. The First Amendment guarantees freedom for religion and freedom from religion. This was certainly a departure from the colonial charters that demanded that their citizens believe and behave in certain ways.

Baptists, were on the wrong end of religious arguments in many states. Violence often flared up as the result of religious disagreements. Age-old debates between Catholics and Protestants continued.

Skill 4.2b   Analyze citizen participation in governmental decision-making in a large modern society and the challenges Americans faced historically to their political participation.

Most Americans don't play a large role in governmental decision-making, except perhaps at the local level. Only there, in the towns and cities in which they live, can they afford the time and money to personally lobby their lawmakers in the name of passage or defeat of laws. Where people make a difference at the higher levels is in joining political parties and, more importantly, **citizen action groups** or **political action committees**. Only in the larger numbers that make up these groups can individual people make a difference in government.

However, the avenues of lobbying lawmakers are not closed to the average American. Letters are still read, phone calls are still taken, and donations are still appreciated. Emails, hashtag campaigns and other social media outlets have proven effective in moving the needle with lawmakers. Personal office visits are definitely appreciated as well. If enough people write or call or visit their lawmakers and say the same thing, those lawmakers will listen. That's why it's still important for people to speak out, not only to their neighbors but also their elected officials. And of course, the ultimate way of expressing one's political views is to elect or oust a lawmaker on Election Day.

The colonies weren't totally devoid of representative government. In 1619, Virginia's **House of Burgesses** was established. There, Patrick Henry introduced the resolutions (1765) that ultimately resulted in the repeal of the Stamp Act.

Fifteen of the 22 members of the House of Burgesses were elected by the people of Virginia. The governor (who was appointed by the king) and six of his appointees were the seven unelected members. The Burgesses could make laws, and the governor could veto them. The Burgesses met once a year but the elements of representative government were there.

Generally, each colony had a legislature. They had various names; most were called the **Assembly**. They dealt with financial matters, like taxes and budgets. The governor had the power to dissolve the Assembly, which was done frequently during the months leading up to the Revolutionary War.

Representation was limited to free, white, property-owning males. Women couldn't vote or own property. The cry for representation was a key rallying point of the Revolution. The Constitution was a blueprint of a representative government. Senators, who made up the upper house of government, were appointed by the Legislature of each state. This practice lasted until 1913 when the Seventeenth Amendment allowed for the direct election of senators. African-American men had to wait to vote until the Fifteenth Amendment was ratified after the Civil War, and women had to wait until the twentieth century (1920) to vote in national elections.

Skill 4.2c Analyze the evolving practices of citizen collaboration and deliberation, and special interest influence in American democratic decision-making.

From the earliest days of political expression in America, efforts were a collaborative affair. One of the first of the democratic movements was the **Sons of Liberty**, an organization that made its actions known but kept the identity of its members a secret. Famous members of this group included John and Samuel Adams.

American political discussion built on the example of the British Parliament, the legislative branch of government that had two houses. The assemblies of the American colonies inherited this tradition and enjoyed spirited debate, even though they met just once or a few times a year. One of the most famous examples of both collaboration and deliberation was the **Stamp Act Congress**, a gathering of Americans who demanded that Great Britain repeal the unpopular tax on paper and documents. The Americans who met at both the Continental Congresses and the Constitutional Convention built on this tradition, as well.

James Madison took voluminous notes at the Constitutional Convention and as a result, we have a clear record of just how contentious the debate over the shape and scope of the American federal government was. The result was a blueprint for government approved by the vast majority of the delegates and eventually approved by people in all of the American colonies. This ratification process has continued to modern times.

The nation's first **political parties**, the Federalists and the Democratic-Republicans, were formed for people to see their political interests protected.

As the nation grew, so did the number of political parties and so did the number of people who pursued so-called **special interests**. A special interest is nothing more than a subject that a person or people pursue. Special interests can be found today. We can draw a straight line from the deliberative-collaborative traditions of today to the secret meetings and political conventions of colonial days.

Skill 4.2d **Compare and contrast the role of the individual in democratic and authoritarian societies.**

A person who lives in a democratic society has rights guaranteed to him or her by the government. Some of the important rights are

- the right to speak out in public
- the right to pursue any religion
- the right for a group of people to gather in public for *any* reason that doesn't fall under a national security cloud
- the right *not* to have soldiers stationed in your home
- the right *not* to be forced to testify against yourself in a court of law
- the right to a speedy and public trial by a jury of your peers
- the right *not* to the victim of cruel and unusual punishment
- and the right to avoid unreasonable search and seizure of your person, your house, and your vehicle

Citizens of authoritarian countries have few, if any, of these rights and must watch his or her words and actions to avoid the appearance of disobeying the law.

Citizens in both types of society can serve in government. They can run for office and can be voted in by their peers. One large difference exists. In an authoritarian society, the members of government will most likely be of the same political party. China is an example of an authoritarian society. Citizens in democratic societies can vote for whomever they want and can run for any office they choose. Democratic countries have more than one political party. American citizens can have political party meetings, fund-raisers, and even conventions without fear of reprisals from the Government.

Skill 4.2e **Explain how civil society provides opportunities for individuals to promote private or public interests.**

In a **civil society** people are free to pursue business interests, both private and public. Private activities are less regulated than public ones, but public activities are not discouraged or dissuaded, as long as they don't violate laws or invade other people's rights.

In America, a person has the right to pursue any kind of legal business strategy he or she wants. The age of Internet advertising and marketing has created opportunities for new and different businesses. State and federal governments encourage businesses to succeed and provide loans and grants to start-ups.

Americans are also encouraged to join non-business organizations, both public and private. America is a land full of groups: religious, political, social, and economic. All these groups meet in public and in private, and the people who belong to these groups are free to associate with any groups that they choose, again as long as the practices of those groups are not illegal or harmful to other people.

Religious participation finds extraordinary protection under the law. The First Amendment guarantees every American the right to worship as he or she sees fit, without fear of reprisal by the government. Religious organizations do not, for the most part, receive funding from governments to support their efforts. The First Amendment denies the government the right to establish a religion, meaning that it can favor no one religion over another. Entities such as parochial schools, which provide both education and religious training, routinely have to seek funding in places other than the federal or state governments.

Social groups are encouraged. The First Amendment gives Americans people the right to peaceable assembly. This describes the meetings of most social organizations in America, from clubs to interest groups to veterans organizations.

One public interest that many people pursue is politics. Theoretically, anyone who is a U.S. citizen can get on a ballot somewhere and run for something. Participation in politics is encouraged in America, and more and more people are getting involved at the local, state, and federal levels.

COMPETENCY 4.3 THE THREE BRANCHES OF GOVERNMENT

Skill 4.3a Analyze Articles I, II, and III as they relate to the legislative, executive, and judicial branches of government.

The three branches of government, **Executive**, **Legislative**, and **Judicial,** that make up the federal government each have specific powers.

Legislative – Article I of the Constitution establishes the legislative, or law-making, branch of the government called the Congress. Congress is a **bicameral** legislature, meaning that it is made up of two houses, the House of Representatives and the Senate. Voters in each state elect the members who serve in each chamber of Congress. The legislative branch is responsible for making laws, raising and printing money, regulating trade, establishing the postal service and federal courts, approving the president's appointments, declaring war and supporting the armed forces. Congress also has the power to **amend** (change) the Constitution. The House of Representatives can **impeach** (bring charges against) the President or other federal officials. The Senate tries cases of impeachment.

Executive – Article II of the Constitution creates the Executive branch of the government, which is headed by the president. The president can recommend (though Congress is under no obligation to consider) new laws and can veto bills passed by the legislative branch. As the head of state, the president is responsible for executing (carrying out) the laws of the country and the treaties and declarations of war passed by the Legislative branch. The President appoints federal judges (who must be confirmed by the Senate) and is commander-in-chief of the military. Other members of the Executive branch include the elected Vice-President, and various cabinet members the president might appoint. Ambassadors, presidential advisors, and civil servants must be confirmed by the Senate.

Judicial – Article III of the Constitution establishes the Judicial branch of government. It creates the Supreme Court and provides that Congress may create lower (inferior) federal courts as needed. The Supreme Court's function is to interpret the law. It has the power to declare acts of Congress unconstitutional. Most cases heard before the Supreme Court are brought to it on appeal but the Court has **original jurisdiction** (hearing a case for the first time) in certain types of cases, such as cases between states.

Powers delegated to the federal government:

1. To tax
2. To borrow and coin money
3. To establish postal service
4. To grant patents and copyrights
5. To regulate interstate and foreign commerce
6. To establish courts
7. To declare war
8. To raise and support the armed forces
9. To govern territories
10. To define and punish felonies and piracy on the high seas
11. To fix standards of weights and measures
12. To conduct foreign affairs

Powers reserved to the states:

1. To regulate intrastate trade
2. To establish local governments
3. To protect the general welfare
4. To protect life and property
5. To ratify amendments
6. To conduct elections
7. To make state and local laws

Concurrent powers of the federal government and states.

1. Both Congress and the states may tax.
2. Both may borrow money.
3. Both may charter banks and corporations.
4. Both may establish courts.
5. Both may make and enforce laws.
6. Both may take property for public purposes.
7. Both may spend money to provide for the public welfare.

Implied powers of the federal government.

1. To establish banks or other corporations, implied from delegated powers to tax, borrow, and to regulate commerce
2. To spend money for roads, schools, health, insurance, etc. implied from powers to establish post roads, to tax to provide for general welfare and defense, and to regulate commerce
3. To create military academies, implied from powers to raise and support an armed force.
4. To locate and generate sources of power and sell surplus, implied from powers to dispose of government property, commerce, and war powers
5. To assist and regulate agriculture, implied from power to tax and spend for general welfare and regulate commerce

Skill 4.3b   Analyze how and why the existing roles and practices of the three branches of government have evolved.

(See Skill 4.3a)

Skill 4.3c   Describe and analyze the issues that arise as a result of the checks and balances system.

In the United States, **checks and balances** refers to the ability of each branch of government to limit the actions of the others. Examples of checks and balances: The Executive branch limits the Legislature through its veto power. The Judicial branch limits the power of the Legislature through **judicial review**. Judicial review is the power to declare acts of Congress or the president unconstitutional and to force those actions to stop. The Legislature checks the Executive by power of impeachment and denial of appointments.

Issues arise when a branch of government uses its powers to become stronger than the other branches. For example, recently a person was appointed by President Obama to fill a Supreme Court vacancy but Congress did not hold confirmation hearings because of pending elections in which members of Congress believed the new president should make the appointment..

Skill 4.3d   **Explain the process by which the Constitution is amended.**

An **amendment** is a change or addition to the United States Constitution. Amending the United States Constitution is difficult. Two-thirds of each house of Congress must approve proposed amendments. If the amendment is proposed by state legislatures, then two-thirds of the state legislatures must call a convention to propose the amendment. Constitutional amendments must be ratified by three-fourths of the state legislatures. To date there are only twenty-seven amendments to the Constitution. An amendment may be used to cancel out a previous one. For example, the 18th Amendment (1919) created Prohibition but the 21st Amendment (1933) canceled Prohibition.

COMPETENCY 4.4   LANDMARK U.S. SUPREME COURT CASES

Skill 4.4a   **Analyze the changing interpretations of the Bill of Rights and later constitutional amendments.**

The Bill of Rights comprises the first ten Amendments to the U.S. Constitution. These amendments were passed almost immediately upon ratification of the Constitution by the states. They reflect the concerns that were raised throughout the country and by the Founding Fathers during the ratification process. People believed that the power and authority of the government must be restricted from denying or limiting the rights of the people of the nation. The experiences of the founders of the nation as colonists formed the foundation of the concern to limit the power of government.

The Bill of Rights has been interpreted in different ways at different times by different interpreters. These, and other, constitutional amendments may be interpreted very strictly or very loosely. The terms of the amendments may be defined in different way to enfranchise or to disenfranchise individuals or groups of persons. For example, until the passage of the Thirteenth, Fourteenth, and Fifteenth Amendments, the Constitution interpreted blacks as property — not people. The Fourteenth Amendment's provision of "equal protection under the law" made the Constitution applicable to minority groups. The doctrine of "separate but equal" pronounced in the *Plessey* case in 1896 was reversed as to education 50 years later in the case of *Brown v. Board of Education*. During times of war, limitations have been placed on the freedom of speech and the meaning of what constitutes an unreasonable search or seizure has changed over the years.

Skill 4.4b   Evaluate the effects of the Court's interpretations of the Constitution in Marbury v. Madison, McCullough v. Maryland, and United States v. Nixon.

Marbury v. Madison is the Supreme Court case that established the doctrine of **judicial review**. Judicial review is the theory that the courts can declare laws or acts unconstitutional. John Adams was a Federalist president. Thomas Jefferson was a Democratic-Republican. Jefferson was elected in November 1800. At that time, the new president didn't take office until March of the following year. Shortly before Adams left office, he appointed several Federalist judges. Those judges were known as the "**Midnight Judges**." One of these "Midnight Judges" was **William Marbury**, who was appointed to be justice of the peace for the District of Columbia.

The Secretary of State had the duty of notifying the appointed person by delivering a **"commission**," or notice, of appointment. President Jefferson told his Secretary of State **James Madison** not to deliver the commissions that were still waiting to be delivered. Marbury sued Madison and asked the Supreme Court to force the delivery of the commission. The Supreme Court decided that the power to deliver commissions to judges was provided for in the Judiciary Act of 1789. Because the power was not provided for in the Constitution, it was in conflict with the Constitution and, therefore subject to review by the Supreme Court. The Court held that the law was unconstitutional, but did not order Madison to deliver Marbury's commission.

McCulloch v. Maryland involved Maryland's attempt to tax the Bank of the United States. Maryland voted to tax all bank business not done with state banks. Andrew McCulloch, who worked in the Baltimore branch of the Bank of the United States, refused to pay the tax. The State of Maryland sued, and the Supreme Court accepted the case. **Chief Justice John Marshall** wrote the opinion of the Court. The decision was that the federal government had the right and power to set up a federal bank and that a state did not have the power to tax the federal government.

In *United States v. Nixon*, the Supreme Court was asked whether the tape recordings in President Richard Nixon's possession were required to be turned over to the Watergate prosecutor. The recordings were thought to implicate Nixon in the cover-up of the Watergate break-in, an attempt by a team of thieves to gain information on the activities of George McGovern, Nixon's opponent in the 1972 election. Nixon claimed that the tapes were the property of the Executive Branch and, more to the point, of Nixon himself. Nixon claimed an "executive privilege" that would keep him from having to relinquish the recordings. In this case, the court ordered President Nixon to over the tapes.

Skill 4.4c   **Describe and analyze the controversies that have resulted over the changing interpretations of civil rights, including, but not limited to, those in Plessy v. Ferguson; Brown v. Board of Education; Miranda v. Arizona; Roe v. Wade; Regents of the University of California v. Bakke; Adarand Constructors, Inc. v. Pena; United States v. Virginia (VMI) and Bush v. Palm Beach County Canvassing Board.**

In ***Dred Scott v. Sanford*** the Supreme Court had to decide whether a slave taken to a free state and then returned to a slave state was a free person. The court ruled that Scott had no right to sue because he was not a citizen. This ensured that Scott remained a slave.

The *Civil Rights Cases* involved five separate cases where private individuals or companies were sued for violations of equal protection. The Supreme Court ruled that the newly minted Fourteenth Amendment and its equal protection clause didn't apply to private individuals or their companies. This 1883 ruling opened the floodgates to Jim Crow laws and the enshrinement of segregation into American life.

Little more than a decade later, the Court expanded its denial of the equal protection clause in ***Plessy v. Ferguson*** (1896) when it decided "separate but equal" railway cars were legal.

In ***Brown v. Board of Education*** the Supreme Court's unanimous decision overturned the *Plessy* separate but equal doctrine in the realm of education.

The ***Heart of Atlanta*** case involved interstate travel. It was a landmark case and the court's decision held that Congress could, pursuant to the Civil Rights Act of 1964 and the Commerce Clause of the U.S. Constitution, force businesses to comply with Civil Rights legislation

In ***Miranda v. Arizona*** *(1966)* the Supreme Court ruled that arresting officers were required to provide an arrested person with information about their rights: such as the right to an attorney, the right to avoid self-incrimination, and the right to a trial by jury.

Roe v. Wade was a landmark **right to privacy** case that was decided in 1973. The Supreme Court ruled that the Fourteenth Amendment's Due Process clause extended to a woman's right to have an abortion. The court balanced that right against the state's interest in protecting health and the potential human life. The court limited the state's regulation of abortions to the third trimester of a woman's pregnancy.

The phrase **race-neutral** has been used by the Supreme Court in decisions about affirmative action programs, which attempted to grant preferences to

African-Americans. In *Regents of the University of California* v. *Bakke* (1978) the Supreme Court invalidated the denial of a white student from law school because the school had to meet its mandated quota of minority applicants.

In the 1995 case of *Adarand Constructors, Inc.* v. *Pena*, the Court mandated that race neutrality be examined in federal agencies under **strict scrutiny**; in effect, the Court validated the idea of race neutrality and ended the raft of affirmative action programs in the federal government's departments and agencies.

United States v. Virginia (VMI) was a 1996 case that struck down the Virginia Military Institute policy against the admission of females. The high court ruled that the all-male admission policy violated the Equal Protection clause of the Fourteenth Amendment.

In *Bush* v. *Palm Beach County Canvassing Board* (2000), presidential candidate George W. Bush sued to invalidate the recount that had begun in the wake of Bush's narrow victory over Al Gore in Florida. Bush claimed, among other things, that his Fifth Amendment due process rights were violated by the various court orders since Election Day. The Court stopped all recounts and declared Bush the winner of the 2000 presidential election. This was not a classical civil rights case, per se, but it was one that involved the sort of protections that had been argued under previous Fifth and Fourteenth Amendment cases.

COMPETENCY 4.5   **ISSUES REGARDING CAMPAIGNS FOR NATIONAL, STATE, AND LOCAL ELECTIVE OFFICES**

Skill 4.5a   **Analyze the origin, development, and role of political parties.**

(See Skill 2.3a)

Skill 4.5b   **Describe the means that citizens use to participate in the political process.**

The most basic way for citizens to participate in the political process is to **vote**. Since the passing of the 23rd Amendment in 1965, U.S. citizens who are at least 18 years old are eligible to vote.

Citizens who wish to engage in the political process to a greater degree have several paths open, such as **participating in local government**. Counties, states, and sometimes even neighborhoods are governed by locally-elected boards or councils which meet publicly. Citizens are usually able to address these boards: to bring their concerns and express their opinions on matters being considered. Citizens may even wish to stand for local election and join a governing board, or seek support for higher office.

Supporting a political party is another means by which citizens can participate in the political process. Political parties endorse certain platforms that express general social and political goals, and support candidates in elections. Political parties make use of volunteer labor, with supporters making telephone calls, distributing printed material and campaigning for the party's causes and candidates. Political parties solicit donations to support their efforts as well. Contributing money to a political party is another form of participation citizens can undertake.

Another form of political activity is to **support an issue-related political group**. Several political groups work to sway public opinion on various issues or on behalf of a segment of American society. These groups may have representatives who meet with state and federal legislators to **lobby** them. To lobby is to provide information on an issue and persuade lawmakers to take favorable action.

Skill 4.5c   Explain the function and evolution of the College of Electors and analyze its role in contemporary American politics.

The College of Electors, or the **Electoral College** as it is more commonly known, was provided for in the Constitution.

Article II of the Constitution lists the specifics of the Electoral College. The Founding Fathers included the Electoral College as one of the checks and balances for two reasons. To give states with small populations more weight in the presidential election.   To have informed voters make the decision for president because the Founders didn't trust the common man to make a proper decision on which candidate would make the best president.

Individuals from each state are chosen as Electors. The Electoral College meets a few weeks after the presidential election. When all the electoral votes are counted, the candidate with the most votes wins. In most cases, the candidate who wins the popular vote also wins in the Electoral College. However, this has not always been the case.

In 1800, **Thomas Jefferson** and **Aaron Burr**, both candidates of the Democratic-Republican Party, received the same number of electoral votes. The election went to the House of Representatives to break the tie. Federalist leader Alexander Hamilton who hated both Jefferson and Burr, had a clear preference for Thomas Jefferson. Hamilton worked behind the scenes to ensure that Burr would never become president. The House of Representatives chose Jefferson on the 36th ballot. Aaron Burr became Jefferson's vice-president.

In 1824, all of the candidates were members of the Democratic-Republican Party. **John Quincy Adams**, son of President John Adams, was the most experienced. **Andrew Jackson** was a war hero. **Henry Clay** was the Speaker of the House. When the votes were counted, Jackson had the most, but not enough to win. The decision was then made by the House of Representatives. Clay, as Speaker of the House, had control over the proceedings and, when it became clear that something had to be done, he agreed to withdraw from the race if his supporters would support Adams. Each state had one vote in the House of Representatives. The country had 24 states at the time, and 13 of them voted for Adams. Clay, in turn, was named Secretary of State. Jackson and his supporters, along with many other neutral observers, deemed this turn of events the **Corrupt Bargain.**

The third election decided by the House of Representatives was that of 1876. By then, the concept of a popular vote was well established and the electoral vote had become a reflection of that popular vote. In 1876, however, that wasn't the case. The country was still healing from the wounds of the Civil War. Federal troops were still in Southern states, sometimes in large numbers, enforcing the Thirteenth, Fourteenth, and Fifteenth Amendments. Reconstruction was still in effect and many people in the South resented what they saw as the continuation of an occupation by the victorious North.

The two presidential terms of Ulysses S. Grant were marred by political scandal. Samuel J. Tilden, the governor of New York, was the Democratic candidate, and the Republicans had nominated Ohio governor **Rutherford B. Hayes**. When the popular votes were counted, Tilden had 280,000 more than Hayes. But he didn't have enough electoral votes to win. Hayes gained enough Democratic support from the House to win the presidency when he promised to withdraw federal troops from the South if elected.

The 2000 presidential election came down to Florida and Florida's method of counting votes. The election was eventually decided by the Supreme Court. The Democratic Party's nominee was Vice-President **Al Gore**. Gore had served as vice-president for both of President Bill Clinton's terms. As such, he was both a champion of Clinton's successes and a reflection of his failures. The Republican Party's nominee was **George W. Bush**, governor of Texas and son of former President George Bush. He campaigned on a platform of a strong national defense and an end to questionable ethics in the White House. The election was hotly contested, and many states were decided by only a handful of votes. Gore won the popular vote, by nearly 540,000 votes. But he didn't win the electoral vote. The vote was so close in Florida that a recount was necessary under federal law. Eventually, the Supreme Court stopped all the recounts. Florida's electoral votes went to Bush, and he became president.

Sixteen years later **Donald Trump** won the presidency without the popular vote. The 2016 presidential election was between Republican nominee Donald Trump and Democratic nominee **Hillary Clinton**. Hillary Clinton, First Lady, Senator and Secretary of State, was the first woman to lead a major party's ticket. Donald Trump ran as a Washington outsider who would bring his business experience to government. Secretary Clinton won the popular vote by almost 3,000,000 votes. Mr. Trump captured the swing states of Ohio and Florida along with Michigan, Wisconsin and Pennsylvania and with them the presidency.

Many argue that the Electoral College, should be abolished. Proponents of the Electoral College point to reasons why the College was provided for in the Constitution.

Skill 4.5d   Describe and evaluate issues of state redistricting and the political nature of reapportionment.

Equal political representation for all of the people in the United States is important. Problems include trying to ensure proper racial and minority representation. Various civil rights acts, notably the Voting Rights Act of 1965, sought to eliminate the remaining features of unequal suffrage in the United States.

Questions can involve the issue of **gerrymandering**, which involves the adjustment of various electoral districts in order to achieve a predetermined goal. This may be to affect minority political representation or the strength of a political party within a voting district. Gerrymandering sometimes creates odd and unusual looking districts.

State redistricting takes place when a state's population changes and there is a reapportionment of Congressional districts. Population changes are noted as the result of the census that is taken every ten years. When a state loses, or gains, population it must adjust the number of people elected to the U.S. House of Representatives. Therefore, it is necessary to redraw the boundary lines for the Congressional districts. The party in power in the state government can have an effect on the final boundary lines that are drawn.

COMPETENCY 4.6   POWERS AND PROCEDURES OF THE NATIONAL, STATE, LOCAL AND TRIBAL GOVERNMENTS

Skill 4.6a   Identify the various ways in which federal, state, local, and tribal governments are organized.

The various governments of the United States and of Native American tribes have many similarities and a few notable differences.

The United States Government has three distinct branches: the Executive, the Legislative, and the Judicial. Each has its own function and its own "check" on the other two.

The Legislative Branch consists of the House of Representatives and the Senate. The House has 435 members and the Senate has 100 (two for each state). House members serve two-year terms; Senators serve six-year terms. Each house can initiate a bill, but that bill must be passed by a majority of both houses in order to become a law. The House is primarily responsible for initiating spending bills; the Senate is responsible for ratifying treaties that the president might sign with other countries.

The Executive Branch is headed by the president. The president is the commander-in-chief of the armed forces and the person who can approve or veto any bill from Congress. (Vetoed bills can become law if two-thirds of each house of Congress vote to override the veto) The president is elected to a four-year term by the Electoral College and can serve a total of two terms. Advisors to the president form the cabinet. These departments include State, Defense, Education, Treasury, and Commerce, among others. Members of these departments are appointed by the President and approved by the Senate.

The Judicial Branch consists of courts, with the highest court being the Supreme Court. The Court decides whether laws are constitutional. Any law invalidated by the Supreme Court is no longer in effect. Cases make their way to the Supreme Court from federal Appeals Courts, which hear appeals of decisions made by federal trial courts called District Courts. Federal court judges are appointed by the president and confirmed by the Senate. They serve during good behavior, which usually means for life.

State governments are generally organized in the same manner as the federal government. State Supreme Court decisions that involve a constitutional question can be appealed to federal courts.

Local governments vary widely across the country, although none of them have a judicial branch per se. Some local governments consist of a city council, of which the mayor is a member and has limited powers. In other cities, the mayor is the head of the government and the city council are the chief lawmakers. Local governments also have looser requirements for people running for office than the state and federal governments.

The format of the governments of the Native American tribes varies, as well. Most tribes have governments along the lines of the U.S. federal or state governments. An example is the Cherokee Nation, which has a 15-member **Tribal Council** as the head of the Legislative branch, a Principal Chief and Deputy Chief who head up the Executive branch and carry out the laws passed by the Tribal Council. They have judicial branch made up of the Judicial Appeals Tribunal and the Cherokee Nation District Court. Members of the Tribunal are appointed by the Principal Chief. Members of the other two branches are elected by popular vote of the Cherokee Nation.

Skill 4.6b **Analyze the issues that arise out of the divisions of jurisdiction among federal, state, local, and tribal governments at each level of government; consider their impacts on those different levels of government.**

America operates on a system of **federalism**. This means that while the states are subordinate to the federal government they still retain a great deal of power over their own affairs. Criminal matters are handled by states. Unless the crime crosses state lines, in which case the federal government has jurisdiction. States control their election laws and practices. That is why North Carolina has early voting but New York does not.

State governments are sometimes called the "laboratories of democracy" because they can experiment to find the best way to govern. What works best in Montana may not fit Texas and vice versa. Sometimes the federal government needs to step in to ensure a basic minimum of fairness.

In 1963 The Supreme Court heard *Gideon v Wainwright*. The case hinged on the question of whether a man could get a fair trial without counsel. **Clarence Gideon** was tried for the burglary of a Florida pool hall. He asked the local court for a lawyer and was told that it was not the responsibility of the court to provide Gideon with a lawyer. Gideon was convicted and sentenced to prison.

From prison Gideon appealed to the Supreme Court. Florida argued that as a sovereign state they have the right to structure their criminal courts as they see fit. Florida further argued that because the crime occurred solely within Florida the Sixth and Fourteenth Amendments do not apply to Gideon. Had Gideon been charged with a federal crime he would be entitled to a lawyer, however, because the matter falls entirely within Florida's jurisdiction only Florida's rules apply. Gideon argued that it is impossible to get a fair trial without an advocate. That a man with no legal training cannot hope to defend himself against a professional prosecutor and a legal system that is for all intents and purposes conducted in another language.

The Court agreed with Gideon and ruled that every criminal defendant in America had the absolute right to an attorney. The Court ruled that if a defendant could not afford an attorney then the state must provide that attorney. *Gideon v Wainwright* is an example of **federalism**. The states are allowed structure their systems as they see fit; however, when things become unconstitutional it is the responsibility of the federal government to correct the abuse of power.

Skill 4.6c **Analyze the sources of power and influence in democratic politics, such as access to and use of the mass media, money, economic interests, and the ability to mobilize groups.**

Money is a source of power and influence in politics. It is needed to pay the people who will run a candidate's campaign and to buy or rent all of the tangible and intangible *things* that are needed to power a political campaign: office supplies, meeting places, and transportation vehicles, for example. Media advertising is the most expensive kind of advertising, but it also has the potential to reach the widest audience.

The sources of money can be personal funds of the candidate, outside donations and personal interest groups.

Money is important to a campaign, but so is the ability to mobilize groups who support a candidate. That is why a good volunteer base is important. Volunteers generate interest in a campaign and bring on supporters and voters for the candidate.

Another powerful source of support for a political campaign is the **special interest group**. These are groups that want to effect political change (or make sure that such change doesn't take place). Anti-abortion groups, environmental groups and labor groups are examples.

COMPETENCY 4.7 **THE MEDIA IN AMERICAN POLITICAL LIFE**

Skill 4.7a **Describe the significance of a free press, including the role of the broadcast, print, and electronic media in American society and government.**

A **free press** is essential to maintaining responsibility and civic-mindedness in government and in society. The broadcast, print, and electronic media in America serve as societal and governmental **watchdogs**, who show America and the world what elected officials are doing.

Media reports on policy debates, discussions on controversial issues, struggles against foreign powers in economic and wartime endeavors. The First Amendment guarantees media in America the right to report on these things.

Reporting is covered by newspapers, radio stations, magazines, and websites. Today, mass media is an important method of communicating news. The Internet carries out functions that the magazines and newspapers did in the past. A free press can sway public opinion. For that reason, the role of the press is an important one.

In other countries that do not have a free press, the government controls what is published and the press does little to sway voters and/or the public

Skill 4.7b   Analyze the interaction between public officials and the media to communicate and influence public opinion.

Public officials need to communicate to the public to explain how they are carrying out duties as elected officials. The press can help elected officials convey those ideas. Good communications between public officials and the media can help mold public opinion. When the press or the public official is resistant to cover government events in a non-partisan way, or in a way the public understands, the results can be negative either for the press or the official.

Public officials often employ individuals who are good at **public relations**. These individuals write press releases, arrange media events (like tours of schools or soup kitchens), and keep their employer's name in the public eye. This includes making the lawmaker's position on important issues known to the public.

COMPETENCY 4.8   POLITICAL SYSTEMS

Skill 4.8a   Explain and analyze different political systems and the philosophies that underlie them, including the parliamentary system.

Anarchism - Political movement believing in the elimination of all government and its replacement by a cooperative community of individuals. Sometimes it has involved political violence such as assassinations of important political or governmental figures. The historical banner of the movement is a black flag.

Communism - A belief as well as a political system, characterized by the ideology of class conflict and revolution, one party state and dictatorship, repressive police apparatus, and government ownership of the means of production and distribution of goods and services. A revolutionary ideology preaching the eventual overthrow of all other political orders and the establishment of one world Communist government. Same as Marxism. The historical banner of the movement is a red flag and variation of stars, hammer and sickles, representing the various types of workers.

Dictatorship - The rule by an individual or small group of individuals (Oligarchy) that centralizes all political control in itself and enforces its will with a terrorist police force.

Fascism - A belief as well as a political system, opposed ideologically to Communism, though similar in basic structure, with a one-party state, centralized political control and a repressive police system. It however tolerates private ownership of the means of production, though it maintains tight overall control. Central to its belief is the idolization of the Leader, a "Cult of the Personality," and most often an expansionist ideology. Examples have been German Nazism and Italian Fascism.

Monarchy - The rule of a nation by a monarch, (a non-elected usually hereditary leader), most often a king or queen. There may or may not be some measure of democratic open institutions and elections at various levels. A modern example is Saudi Arabia.

Parliamentary System - A system of government with a legislature and usually involves a multiplicity of political parties, and often coalition politics. There is division between the head of state and head of government. The head of government is usually known as a prime minister who is also usually the head of the largest party. The head of government and cabinet usually both sit and vote in the parliament. The head of state is most often an elected president, (though in the case of a constitutional monarchy, like Great Britain, the sovereign may take the place of a president as head of state). A government may fall when a majority in parliament votes "no confidence" in the government. When that happens, a new prime minister or party head is chosen.

Presidential System - A system of government with a legislature that can involve few or many political parties. There is no division between head of state and head of government. The president serves both capacities. The president is elected either by direct or indirect election. A president and cabinet usually do not sit or vote in the legislature and the president may or may not be the head of the largest political party. A President can only be removed from office before an election for major infractions of the law.

Socialism - Political belief and system in which the state takes a guiding role in the national economy and provides extensive social services to its population. It may or may not own outright means of production, but even where it does not, it exercises regulatory control. It usually promotes democracy, (Democratic-Socialism), though the heavy state involvement produces excessive bureaucracy and usually inefficiency. Socialism is a variant of Marxism. It also has used a red flag as a symbol.

Skill 4.8b   Analyze problems of new democracies in the 19th and 20th centuries and their internal struggles.

Most countries in **South America** and the **Caribbean** region gained their independence in the nineteenth century. In some cases, countries replaced one colonial governor with another authoritarian figure. To varying degrees, these countries suffered internal strife, most notably in the twentieth century as the Cold War and horrendous debt threatened to engulf countries.

Two of the most notable conversions to democracy in the twentieth century were **India** and **Japan**. India, one of the most ancient of societies, was most recently a colony of Great Britain. Thanks largely to the efforts of **Mohandas Gandhi** and other activists, India achieved its independence by the mid-twentieth century. The country became a democracy, with a parliamentary system. The change in political theory, however, didn't mean an end to internal strife.

At the heart of the country's political identity is a religious dichotomy — the struggle between Muslims and Hindus. This religious conflict has continued for centuries and has not been diminished by the fact that the Indian people elect their own leaders. Shortly after India gained independence the country was split into Muslim Pakistan and Hindu India. In the seventy years since independence India and Pakistan have fought several wars. There is a continued conflict over the Kashmir region, an area that was known as India at various times under various masters, including Great Britain, but was partitioned when it was freed. Another main source of internal strife in India is an economic one. India is the world's second most populous country, and a huge number of its people have little or no resources of their own.

Japan, by contrast, has suffered much less religious and political strife since becoming a democracy after its defeat in World War II. The occupying American army instituted a new constitution, which provided for a representative government, and also led efforts to rebuild the country. The result has been an economic powerhouse that is now one of the world's strongest and most wide-ranging economies. Japan has had its periods of economic weakness, of course, but has bounced back each time stronger than ever.

The end of World War II was the beginning of the end of African colonization. In many cases, African countries embraced the idea of representative government, with mixed results

Political divisions on the **Korean Peninsula** and in Southeast Asia have created intense internal strife of a mostly economic and political nature. North Korea, an authoritarian state, has lived in relative isolation from the rest of the world and has suffered economically from that isolation. South Korea became a democracy and has prospered economically, although the specter of war with North Korea has loomed large for more than 50 years. The two countries did go to war in 1950. The resulting three-year conflict involved forces from a handful of other countries, most notably China and the United States, and resulted in the status quo geographically. The most notable facet of life in either Korean country is the idea that another war could begin tomorrow. An intensely patrolled area known as the **Demilitarized Zone** (DMZ) serves as the border between the countries.

Southeast Asia has also seen its share of strife since the 1950s, most notably in Vietnam, which was once two countries. It is similar to Korea because the North is Communist and the South was an American ally. Those two countries began to fight not long after the end of WWII, and the United Nations became involved. The war consumed the two countries and most of their neighbors for many years, resulting in horrible economic and social conditions throughout the region for many years afterward. North Vietnam ended up winning the war, absorbing all of South Vietnam into one country. The country, which continues under an authoritarian government, is becoming more economically important.

COMPETENCY 4.9   TENSIONS WITHIN OUR CONSTITUTIONAL DEMOCRACY

Skill 4.9a   Analyze the constitutional interpretations of the First Amendment's statement about the separation of church and state.

The First Amendment to the Constitution prohibits a state-sponsored religion while also prohibiting the government from interfering with people's exercise of their religions. These have been two of the most fundamental tenets and faithfully upheld provisions of the Constitution since their inception.

The First Amendment builds the wall of **separation between church and state** and means there will not be an entanglement between government and religion.

Funding for parochial schools has raised the issue of separation of church and state in the courts. In *Cochran* v. *Louisiana State Board of Educators* (1930), the Supreme Court ruled that a law that provided textbook funds for students of secular and parochial schools did not violate the First Amendment because the funds were intended to benefit the students, not the religious entities that sponsored the schools. The effectiveness of that decision has weakened in the seventy years since it was issued, as subsequent court decisions have found fault with it to one degree or another.

Engle v. *Vitale* (1962) is a landmark case in which the Supreme Court invalidated a school policy of beginning each class day with a school wide prayer. This principle was reaffirmed in *Wallace* v. *Jaffree* (1985), when the Court invalidated a day-opening moment of silence because the law that mandated it made clear that it was intended as a time for prayer.

Universities allow religious groups to meet on university property, provided that secular groups have the same meeting opportunity.

The **Free Exercise Clause** of the First Amendment means a person has the ability to practice their religion as he/she sees fit. Many businesses in America close on Sunday, the traditional day of worship for Christians. This practice is enforced by laws in many states, called **Blue Laws**, laws that require certain types of businesses to close on Sunday. Some Jewish businessmen challenged the Blue Laws but in *Braunfeld* v. *Brown* (1961), the Supreme Court ruled in favor of the Blue Laws, deciding that the loss of business that Jewish owners suffered by closing Sunday in addition to Saturday (which they did because of *their* religious beliefs) was not a state-mandated restriction of their religious beliefs but, rather, a secular policy.

Other famous religious beliefs-government mandated cases have involved the Amish religion's prohibition of education beyond eighth grade (*Wisconsin* v. *Yoder*, 1972 and *United States* v. *Lee*, 1982). A particularly contentious issue involves the Native American use of **peyote**, a narcotic in religious ceremonies. According to American law, the use of such a drug is illegal. Native Americans, however, claim that they use it as part of sacred practices that supersede the laws of the land. The result has been a federal law that protects such practices, extending to the growth and cultivation of said substance but only for religious purposes.

Public displays of religious images on state-owned property have also been issues resolved by the courts. Various groups have tried to prevent such displays. Generally secular decorations may be used to celebrate holidays and in narrow circumstances religious symbols may be used. Whether the displays are constitutional depends upon the facts of the case and courts decide each case on its own facts.

Skill 4.9b   Debate the adequacy of the solution of majority rule and the role of minority rights in a majority-rules system.

A **majority-rules system** is one that places the responsibility for governing and policy-making in the hands of the group that has at least more than 50 percent of the members. Those in the minority may be ignored, passed over, or disenfranchised in favor of the majority. The role of a minority is important because a minority may become a majority. The winning side may be victorious by a small majority. With a few changes in the next election, the majority may lose its strength. The minority role is important because minority views may take hold and eventually cause members of the majority to change position on an issue.

DOMAIN 5   **PRINCIPLES OF ECONOMICS**

COMPETENCY 5.1   **ECONOMIC TERMS AND CONCEPTS AND ECONOMIC REASONING**

Skill 5.1a   **Describe the causal relationship between scarcity and choices, and explain opportunity cost and marginal benefit and marginal cost.**

Economics is defined as a study of how scarce resources are allocated to satisfy unlimited wants. Resources refer to the four factors of production: **labor, capital, land and entrepreneurship**. The fact that the supply of these resources is finite means that society cannot have as much of everything that it wants. There is a constraint on production and consumption and on the kinds of goods and services that can be produced and consumed.

Scarcity means that choices have to be made. If society decides to produce more of one good, this means that there are fewer resources available for the production of other goods. Assume a society can produce two goods, good A and good B. The society uses resources in the production of each good. If producing one unit of good A results in an amount of resources used to produce three units of good B then producing one more unit of good A results in a decrease in three units of good B. In effect, one unit of good A costs three units of good B. This cost is referred to as opportunity cost.

Opportunity cost is the value of the sacrificed alternative, the value of what had to be given up in order to have the output of good A. Opportunity cost does not just refer to production. Your opportunity cost of studying the content in this guide is the value of what you are not doing because you are studying and not watching TV, spending time with family or working. Every choice has an opportunity cost.

Marginal analysis is used in the study of economics. The term marginal always means "the change in". There are benefits and costs associated with every decision. The benefits are the gains or the advantages of a decision or action. If we are talking about production, the gains are the increases in output. If we are talking about an additional hour of study, the gains are the amount of material covered. There are also costs associated with each. The **production costs** involve the cost of the resources involved and the cost of their alternative uses. The costs of studying are the **opportunity costs** of what you have to give up, whether it is sleep, socializing, or working.

In terms of marginal analysis, the **marginal benefit** of the additional unit of output is the change in total benefits from a one unit change in output. The marginal benefit is the benefit weighed against the status quo. This can be expressed mathematically as the change in total benefits divided by the change in the quantity of output. The same is true for marginal cost.

Marginal cost is the increase in costs from producing one more unit of output, or the change in total cost divided by the change in quantity of output. The marginal cost is the cost weighed against the status quo. Looking at costs and benefits in this way is referred to as making decisions at the margin, and this is the method used in the study of economics.

Skill 5.1b Identify the difference between monetary and non-monetary incentives and how changes in incentives cause changes in behavior.

Economics differs from other disciplines in that it considers both monetary and non-monetary factors in decision making. Monetary factors are those that have a dollar value attached, like the cost of a unit of input. These are referred to as explicit costs or accounting costs. **Non-monetary** factors are referred to as **implicit costs**. These include opportunity costs or the value of the sacrificed alternative.

If we talk about entrepreneurial activities, then we have to include the value of what that factor could earn in its next best activity, because this is the minimum amount of return that is required to keep that factor performing its present function. If a factory can earn X dollars in its next best **alternative activity**, then X dollars is the minimum amount required to keep that factor performing its present activity. If it doesn't earn those X dollars, it will shift into its next best alternative activity. In calculating the total cost of a decision, both monetary and non-monetary factors have to be considered.

The economic costs of a decision will always be greater than the accounting costs of the same decision, because economics includes the non-monetary aspects of that decision. For example, using this study guide has monetary and non-monetary costs associated with it. The **monetary cost** is the cost of the book. The **non-monetary costs** are the value of what you are not doing because you are studying. If there is a change in the cost of any of these monetary or non-monetary factors or incentives, there will be a change in behavior.

For example, if teacher salaries double, obtaining that teaching certificate becomes more important because it represents greater future income. Therefore, the student will work harder to obtain it. On the other hand, if your present salary doubles, then you are not willing to sacrifice hours of work to study and the teaching certificate is not as valuable as it was before.

The same thing is true for other factors of production. If the rate of return in widget production is higher than the rate of return in other industries in the economy, you will see an expansion of the widget industry as factors of production shift into widget production. This shift is caused by a change in monetary incentives in the widget and other industries. This change in a monetary incentive causes a realignment of resources throughout the economy as resources shift out of the relatively lower return industries into the relatively higher return industry.

Skill 5.1c   Debate the role of private property as an incentive in conserving and improving scarce resources, including renewable and nonrenewable natural resources.

Private property rights play an important role in the conservation of resources and the improvement in the allocation of scarce resources. We have problems in our society that result from the lack of ownership of resources, whether they are renewable or non-renewable. An example of this is pollution. Why does air and water pollution occur? Why do firms emit noxious emissions into the air, if they are not restrained from doing so? Nobody owns the air; therefore the air is treated as a free input into the production process. It doesn't cost the firm anything to use the air, in terms of monetary costs. The firm, for the most part, just opens the doors and windows and expels the obnoxious emission.

If the firm couldn't do this, it would have to devise and pay for a technology that would eliminate noxious emissions. This represents a change in the production process because of the increased equipment and labor activities required to deal with the emissions that the firm no longer can just emit into the air. If the firm had to pay for the air, it would have higher costs of production. It wouldn't waste the air because it would have to pay for it, as it pays for any other input. It is the lack of ownership of the air that leads to its use as a free good and its waste. Since nobody owns the air and property rights can't be assigned, there is inefficiency and a misallocation of resources associated with the pollution.

What can government do in this situation to try to correct for the misallocation of resources? Since they can't assign property rights for air, they can do things to put a penalty on the creation of pollution. This is the theory behind fines for pollution and the sale of pollution permits. They can also require the installation of new technology to prevent the pollution. Each of these remedies is an attempt to put a price on air. Air no longer is a free input into the production process and the misallocation of resources is somewhat corrected for.

Private property rights play an important role in **resource allocation** in our economy. If the pond next door to you is owned by your neighbor, you won't dump garbage in the pond without compensating your neighbor. Since the owner of a resource must be compensated, private ownership results in prices being assigned to resources. These prices, based on scarcity, result in an efficient allocation of resources. Without these prices, there is inefficiency and waste of scarce resources whether they are widgets or water. Without private ownership of resources there is no incentive to be efficient and to conserve scarce resources, as shown in the pollution examples. This is where a role is defined for government to somehow correct for the misallocation and inefficiency caused by the lack of ownership rights.

Skill 5.1d   Describe and analyze the debate concerning the role of a market economy versus a planned economy in establishing and preserving political and personal liberty.

The roles of political and personal liberty differ greatly depending on the economic role of the government. The cause of the difference is the role of incentives. A **market economy** functions on the basis of the financial incentive. Firms use society's scarce resources to produce the goods that consumers want. Firms know they have a good that society wants when they earn profit. Firms have a good that consumers don't want when they consistently incur losses. Firms with consistent losses eventually go out of business and those resources shift into other industries, producing goods that consumers do want.

Consumers vote for the goods and services they want with their dollars. Technological progress is advanced because of the financial incentives, whether they are personal or corporate. Firms invest in research and development to find newer and more efficient technologies that result in greater output at lower prices. Individuals risk their own time and money on inventions because of the potential financial rewards. They live in the structure of a market economy that allows them the liberty of choosing what to do with their own resources within the confines of the law. Students study whatever it is that they want to major in. There are more scholarships available for certain occupations than others, but the student can still obtain an education whether or not he wants to be in one of those needed areas.

In a **planned economy**, particularly one based on public ownership of the means of production, a planning entity substitutes for the market, to varying degrees from partial to total. Instead of consumers voting with their dollars, they have a bureaucratic entity trying to substitute for the functions of supply and demand in making production decisions. This is why planned economies are often plagued by a misallocation of resources that result in shortages and surpluses. In most cases, the incentive for technological progress and innovation is absent because of the lack of financial rewards. There is no financial incentive for the firm to engage in research and development activities, even if they have the authorization to do so.

Many planned economies have less personal and political freedom than do market economies. The economy needs resources for a particular area. The labor force is directed into that area by assignment, not by financial incentives. They attract more engineers not by offering a higher salary and more perks for engineers, but by assigning people to be engineers. Their schooling isn't financed if they don't study the required disciplines.

It is obvious why there is a differing degree of political freedom in each of the above paradigms. The lack of freedom of choice in a planned economy carries over to the political area. Most planned economies are usually headed by dictators whereas market economies have elected officials. A populace does not vote for and elect those officials who suppress them. A market economy allows for more political and personal freedoms than a planned economy.

COMPETENCY 5.2   ELEMENTS OF AMERICA'S MARKET ECONOMY IN A GLOBAL SETTING

Skill 5.2a   Describe and analyze the relationship of the concepts of incentives and substitutes to the law of supply and demand.

Supply and demand perform important functions in a market economy. Supply and demand make markets function efficiently. **Supply** is defined as the quantity of a good or service that a producer is willing to make available. **Demand** is defined as the quantity of goods and services that a buyer is willing and able to buy.

The consumers' decisions are based on both income and preferences. If you want a Ferrari, but cannot afford one you are not a part of the relevant market demand. You may need to substitute a Toyota for the Ferrari. On the other hand, you may be able to afford a Ferrari, but don't want one. Again, you are not part of the relevant market demand.

A **market equilibrium** occurs where the selling decisions of producers are equal to the buying decisions of consumers, or where the supply and demand curves intersect. This gives us the market equilibrium price and quantity and results in an efficient allocation of resources in accordance with consumer preferences. In other words, producers use society's resources to produce the goods and services that society wants. Producers know this because they have a profitable business.

Incentives and **substitutes** affect the market situation. Incentives for consumers are things like sales, coupons, rebates, etc. The incentives results in increased sales for the firm, even though there is a cost to the incentives. There is a change in the market equilibrium situation and possibly market shares. The increased demand coupled with brand loyalty means the firm will be able to raise prices at some point and not lose their customers. On the production side, incentives to innovate result in increased output at lower costs, or more profit and greater market share for the innovating firm. The individual inventor also experiences financial rewards. Many firms reward employees who propose time or money saving suggestions.

Many of these effects are absent without the use of markets. Supply and demand serve the function of registering the wishes and decisions of producers and consumers with the market tabulating these results. This leads to efficiency. Using a bureaucrat to substitute for the role of supply and demand, leads to inefficiency in both production and consumption. Consumers are no longer directing the allocation of resources with their dollars. They may not be getting the goods and services that they want their society's resources used for. Prices are not efficient because they don't have their allocation function. Incentives don't function in the same way. Most consumers don't buy what they don't want even if it's on sale.

The result in trying to substitute in some way for the supply and demand functions of the market is inefficiency in both production and consumption.

This means higher production costs and more waste.

Skill 5.2b   Describe the effects of changes in supply and/or demand on the relative scarcity, price, and quantity of particular products.

The **supply curve** represents the selling and production decisions of the seller and is based on the costs of production. The costs of production of a product are based on the costs of the resources used in its production. The costs of resources are based on the scarcity of the resource. The scarcer a resource is, relatively speaking, the higher its price. A diamond costs more than paper because diamonds are scarcer than paper. All of these concepts are embodied in the seller's supply curve. The same thing is true on the buying side of the market. The buyer's preferences, tastes, income are embodied in the **demand curve**. Where the demand and supply curves intersect is where the buying decisions of buyers are equal to the selling decisions of sellers. The quantity that buyers want to buy at a particular price is equal to the quantity that sellers want to sell at that particular price. The market is in **equilibrium**.

What happens when there is a change? Suppose a new big oil field is found. Also suppose there is a technology that allows its recovery and refining at a fraction of the present costs. The result is a big increase in the supply of oil at lower costs, as reflected by a rightward shifting oil supply curve. Oil is used as an input into almost all production. Firms now have lower costs. This means that the firm can produce the same amount of output at a lower cost. The result is a rightward shift of the industry supply curve. This means that sellers are willing and able to offer for sale larger quantities of output at each price. Assuming buyers' buying decisions stay the same, there is a new market equilibrium, or new point of intersection of the shifted supply curve with the buyers' demand curve. The result is a lower price with a larger quantity of output. The market has achieved a new equilibrium based on the increase in the quantity of a resource.

If consumer preferences change in favor of widgets there is an increase or rightward shift of the demand curve for widgets. The immediate effects of this change in preference is a shortage of widgets at the given price level.

Consumers want to buy more widgets at the original price than sellers want to sell at that price. Consumers who want the widgets will pay a higher price for them, or they will bid up the price of widgets. As a result, there will be a higher price for widgets. The higher price calls forth increased production of widgets to meet the increased demand.

Producing more widgets requires the use of more resources, so there is an increase in the demand for the factors used in widget production and a higher price commanded by these resources. The end result of the consumer change in preferences in favor of widgets is increased widget production and a higher cost and price. The price of the output will be affected whenever there is a change in demand or a change in the supply of the resources used to produce the product. Those changes will result in higher or lower costs to the consumer as the markets adjust to reflect the changes.

Skill 5.2c   Explain and analyze the roles of property rights, competition, and profit in a market economy.

Property rights, competition and profit are all factors involved in the efficient allocation of resources in a market economy. The assignment of property rights prevents waste and inefficient use of resources. An example of this is an industrial firm dumping waste into a river, causing water pollution. The river is a free input to the firm because there is no assignment of property rights with an owner demanding compensation for the use of his property. If the firm had to pay for the use of the river, its production costs would be higher and the firm would produce less output for the given level of costs and charge a higher price for its item. The lack of property rights' assignment results in overproduction of the item – too many resources are being used in the production of that item. This may give the firm an undue edge in the market because the firm can charge a lower price than competitors who have to pay for a way to deal with their wastes. The misallocation of resources must be corrected for in some way with fines, requiring pollution abatement technologies, the sale of pollution permits, or other methods the community deems fit. The result is higher costs for the firm who now lowers its production levels. This somewhat corrects for the over allocation of resources and forces the firm to be more competitive.

Competition guarantees a more efficient use of society's resources. Firms have to compete with other firms for the available supply of resources to use in production. They have to compete with other firms to win the consumer's dollar. Competition means that they have to be efficient in order to survive. If they aren't using an efficient production process, they will have higher costs than their competitors. This means they will have to charge a higher price for their product than their competitors do. Consumers who shop around will buy the product at the lowest possible price. Eventually the higher cost, more inefficient firm will be forced out of business. Consumers, who vote with their dollars, are buying the same product at a lower price from the competitors of the higher priced firm. The lower priced, more efficient firms will have higher sales and profits while the inefficient, higher cost firms will experience losses. Lack of profits result in the inefficient firms leaving the industry as the owner's resources are shifted into industries where they earn a better rate of return.

Markets function on the basis of competition and competition leads to efficiency in the use of resources. Resource owners want to get the best price for their resource. Producers want to get the best price for their output. Buyers want to get the best deal for the product they are purchasing. All of these factors combine to result in an efficient allocation of resources or resources that are used in accordance with the preferences of society. Inefficiency is eliminated by competition in the market place and the inefficient firm goes out of business due to lack of profit.

Skill 5.2d   Explain and analyze how prices reflect the relative scarcity of goods and services and perform the function of allocation in a market economy.

Prices serve an important function in a market economy. Prices are determined by the interaction of demand and supply in the market place. Relatively speaking, the scarcer the supply is, the higher the price of the resource is: the more abundant the supply is, the lower the price of the resource. Diamonds cost more than water. Water is more abundant than diamonds and water is easier to obtain.

Prices function to allocate the supply of a resource or good to those who are willing and able to pay for it. The supply curve is based on the production costs of sellers and embodies the sellers selling decisions. If his production costs increase, he will sell fewer units of the good at each price. This is reflected by a leftward shift in his supply curve. If his production costs decrease, he will sell more units of the good at each price. This is represented by a rightward shift of his supply curve. This is the **supply side** of the market.

On the **buying side** of the market, the consumers buying decisions are given by the demand curve. This curve represents the quantities of the good the consumer is willing and able to purchase. If a consumer will buy more at each price, there is a rightward shift of his demand curve. A leftward shift of the demand curve represents a decrease in demand. Putting the demand and supply side together, we have the market equilibrium at the intersection of demand and supply. The equilibrium price equates the buying and selling decisions of each side.

Those buyers and sellers who are willing and able to transact at the equilibrium price are included in the market. Those who can't or won't transact at the market price are excluded from the market. This is true whether the good is a resource or an output. Both input and output markets function on the basis of supply and demand. Both markets arrive at equilibrium prices that allocate the resource or good to those who are willing to transact at that price. If the resource market is labor, the wage rate is the equilibrium price for occupations like clerks.

The firm can hire all of the clerks it wants at the market rate. If the firm won't pay the market wage, the clerk will find employment someplace else. The owner has little incentive to pay higher than the market rate, because of the supply of clerks available at the market rate. If the employer wants to hire a professional, such as an engineer, he has to pay a higher rate because of the greater amount of education and skills involved in the job. If he won't pay the higher rate, he likely will not find an engineer to employ. Again, price performs its allocation function that results in an efficient allocation of resources. If prices weren't based on scarcity, they couldn't perform this allocation function and there wouldn't be an efficient allocation of resources.

Skill 5.2e   Explain the process by which competition among buyers and sellers determines a market price.

Market prices are the result of the competition between buyers and sellers in the market place. Prices are determined by supply and demand. The supply side of the market represents the scarcity of resources that determines the price the producer pays for his inputs. The firm has to compete with other firms for the available supply of inputs. The firm has to be able to pay the market price or better in order to attract the inputs that it needs. The supply curve is calculated from the firm's cost curves. A change in the firm's costs results in a change in the supply curve. The lower the firm's costs are at any given price level, the greater the amount of output the firm can produce. Firms want to be cost efficient in order to be competitive because the firm also has to compete for the consumer's dollar in the output market. If the firm's production costs are higher than its competitors, then its competitors will be able to charge a lower price for their product and still be profitable. The cost inefficient firm will experience losses at that price and eventually be forced out of business.

On the buying side of the market, the consumers' **demand curve** is based on their preferences, tastes, income and the price of other goods. The consumer has numerous goods that he wants to buy but is constrained by his income. The demand curve indicates what consumers are willing and able to do subject to their income **constraint**. An increase in the consumer's income, results in an increase in demand for most goods. These goods are referred to as normal goods. A decrease in income means that consumer demands smaller quantities of goods. The consumer's income comes from the input market where he sells whatever skills he has at the best rate. He has to compete with other laborers for the available income he receives that he can spend on goods and services.

Putting the demand side together with the supply side, we arrive at a market price. The intersection of demand and supply represents the market equilibrium price and quantity at which buyers and sellers and willing to transact. Buyers who want the product bid up the price for the available supply. A higher price will result in a larger quantity supplied because it is more profitable for the firm.

All of these markets function on the basis of competition and it is this competition that results in market prices that reflect an efficient allocation of resources. If prices do not accurately reflect the scarcity of an input, then there is a distortion in production costs (as in the case of pollution) that carries through to the output market and the price of the product. In this case the output price does not accurately reflect the production costs or the scarcity of the factors of production used in its production. The result is an under allocation or over allocation of resources, depending on the situation. This means that society is not getting exactly what it wants for its dollar.

Skill 5.2f   Describe the effect of price controls on buyers and sellers.

Price controls interfere with the market's ability to arrive at an equilibrium price that equates supply and demand. Price controls rob the market of what is called the rationing function of prices, the ability to adjust to equate demand and supply. Price controls are administratively imposed prices above or below the market equilibrium.

A price imposed above the market equilibrium price is called a **price floor**. It represents the lowest price that can be charged for the good. The price of the good cannot fall below the price floor. At the imposed floor price, the market cannot equate supply and demand. The higher legally mandated price results in a larger quantity supplied as sellers are willing to supply larger quantities at higher prices than they are at lower prices. The higher price also means that buyers don't want as many units of output. Buyers are willing and able to buy larger quantities at lower prices than at higher prices. The legally imposed floor price results in a situation where quantity supplied is greater than quantity demanded, or there is a surplus of the good and there is no way that the market can function to eliminate the surplus because it can't lower prices to attract more buyers. This has been the situation in agriculture for years. Price supports needed for the farmer's survival result in overproduction and surpluses in agricultural goods.

A **price ceiling** is a legally imposed price below the market equilibrium. Its purpose is to keep prices from rising, as in periods of severe inflation. With a price ceiling, the lower price results in a smaller quantity supplied by sellers. The lower price means an increase in quantity demanded by buyers, who want to buy larger quantities at lower prices than at higher prices. The result is a situation where quantity demanded exceeds quantity supplied, or a shortage. There is no way for the market to eliminate the shortage with buyers bidding up the price for the available quantity.

The legally imposed price means that the price can't rise to eliminate the shortage and the shortage will remain as long as the price controls are in effect. When the price ceilings are lifted, prices usually shoot upwards as buyers and sellers try to make up for lost time.

Price controls, whether they are ceilings or floors, are never a good way to deal with economic problems. They result in misallocations of resources. Price floors, as in agriculture, result in an over allocation of resources to that industry and an overproduction of output that the market cannot eliminate by lowering prices. The resources used in agriculture are not used elsewhere where they might be more productive. The price ceiling causes the opposite: an under allocation of resources and underproduction of output. Consumers don't get enough of the output that they want and resources are used inefficiently. Any interference with the market results in a misallocation.

Skill 5.2g Analyze how domestic and international competition in a market economy affects the quality, quantity, and price of goods and services produced.

The introduction of international competition results in greater efficiency in the allocation of resources. International trade that takes place on the basis of comparative advantage results in lower output prices and higher resource prices. According to trade theory, nations or regions should specialize in the production of the good which they can produce at a relatively lower cost than another country can.

In other words, if in country A one unit of X costs one unit of Y, and in country B one unit of X costs three units of Y, X is cheaper in country A. If country B can produce one unit of W for one unit of Y and country A can produce one unit of W for three units of Y, then W is cheaper in country B. This does not take into account shipping costs. Therefore, country A has the **comparative advantage** in the production of X. Country B has the comparative advantage in the production of good W.

Theory says that each country should specialize in the production of the good in which it has the comparative advantage and trade for the other good. This means country B should use all of its resources to produce good W and trade for good X. Country A should do the opposite and specialize in the production of good X and trade for good W. Specialization and trade on this basis results in lower prices in both countries, or regions, and greater efficiency in the use of resources. Each country will also experience increased consumption since it is getting the maximum amount of output from its given inputs by specializing according to comparative advantage. Each country, or region, can consume its own goods and the goods it has traded for.

The introduction of national or international competition into a market can result in greater efficiency if the trade is without restrictions, like **tariffs** or quotas. A tariff is a tax placed on imported goods. Consumers in both countries have more output at lower prices. The introduction of competition forces existing firms to be more efficient as they strive to be more competitive. If they can't compete with the new competition and they don't have any form of protection, they will eventually go out of business. If they go out of business, there will be unemployment until the workers find new jobs.

Adjustments take place in both economies, as with NAFTA, as input and output markets adjust to the new conditions. But the end results, whether free trade is introduced into a new region or trade barriers are removed between existing trading partners, is that consumers have a wider variety of products, usually of better quality and at lower prices than they had before. There is greater efficiency in the allocation of resources because each resource is being employed in its most productive capacity. The long run result is increased benefits for both of the trading partners. Even if the short run effect of trade is unemployment as resources shift into more productive uses, both countries will benefit in the end.

Skill 5.2h Explain the role of profit as the incentive to entrepreneurs in a market economy.

Financial incentives are the key to the functioning of a market economy. All market participants are willing to take a risk for the opportunity of being a financial success. **Entrepreneurs** are willing to undertake the risk of new business ventures for monetary gain. Resources move into higher than normal rate of return industries because they are attracted by the profit potential. Inventors are willing to take the **risk** of spending time and money to come up with new products in the hope of monetary gain. All of these represent the ways financial incentives operate in a market economy.

The existence of economic profits in an industry functions as a market signal to firms to enter the industry. **Economic profits** means there is an above normal rate of return in this industry. As the number of firms increase, the market supply curve shifts to the right. Assuming cost curves stay the same, the expansion continues until the economic profits are eliminated and the industry earns a normal rate of return. Depending on the level of capital intensity, this process might take a few years or it might take many years. The easier it is to shift resources from one industry to another, the faster the process will be. But the expansion will continue as long as there are economic profits to attract firms. Resources will go where they earn the highest rate of return especially if they earned a lower than normal rate of return.

Without a profit incentive there would be no reason for firms to spend millions and billions on research and development and technological progress would be almost nonexistent. This was a problem in the planned economies in the Soviet era. There were little or no financial incentives to innovate. Firms met their quotas and targets, workers received their paychecks and that was that. Since the means of production were owned by the state, there was no incentive to improve technology or to develop new production processes. The individual had no reason to take the risks involved in entrepreneurial activities because there was nothing in it for him but a letter of commendation. The results were a slow, inefficient production processes.

The entrepreneur is willing to take the risks. He knows there is a good probability that his business will fail, but there is also a chance that it will succeed and there is a remote chance that it will be another Microsoft. Given this, entrepreneurs risk their own money and investors risk money on the chance that the business venture will succeed. If the venture isn't successful, the consumers are telling that business that they don't want their scarce resources used in that way. Profits are the market signal that indicate the proper allocation of resources in accordance with consumer preferences. Excess profits, or an above normal rate of return, signal an expansion as resources are attracted into the industry.

Skill 5.2i   Describe the functions of the financial markets.

All markets function to affect an efficient allocation of resources, even financial markets. These markets also function on the basis of supply and demand and serve to allocate loanable funds to those who are willing to transact at the market price. The market price of loanable funds is the interest rate. The supply of loanable funds come from savings. Since savings represent dollars of postponed spending, households have to have some form of inducement to save. They have to be compensated in some way to postpone their spending and holding dollars in the form of savings. This inducement or payment for savings dollars is the interest rate. The higher the interest rate is the more dollars households will save. The interest rate is an **opportunity cost**. At higher interest rates, the opportunity cost of not saving dollars is higher than at lower interest rates. Thus, the supply of loanable funds curve is upward sloping.

Loanable funds are needed for investment purposes by businesses and by individuals. Borrowers will pay a price for the funds they borrow.

This price is the **interest rate.** Borrowers want more funds at lower interest rates than they do at higher interest rates. This means that the demand for loanable funds curve is downward sloping. We now have the downward sloping demand for loanable funds curve and the upward sloping supply of loanable funds curve. If we put the two curves together then we have the market equilibrium at the point of intersection of demand and supply. This gives the equilibrium rate of interest that equates the quantity demanded and quantity supplied of loanable funds. Lenders and borrowers who transact at that interest rate are included in the market. Lenders and borrowers who can't or won't transact at that interest rate are excluded from the market. The market interest rate performs an allocative function just as a market price does. The interest rate will adjust to guarantee the equality of quantity demanded and quantity supplied, keeping the market in equilibrium.

Since investment is a component of **Gross Domestic Product** or GDP, the financial markets and their stability is an important part of the economy. Economies need investment funds in order to grow. Economies with higher rates of savings have higher rates of investment and therefore higher growth rates. This is what leads to economic growth. Economies with low rates of savings are economies that don't domestically supply enough funds for investment purposes. These are economies that have lower growth rates. The banking sector with its financial markets is very important for economies. Without a well-developed banking center there is no mechanism for savings. Without savings the economy lacks the investment funds that are required for economic growth. This was the position the former Soviet countries were in after the dissolution of the Soviet Union. The banking system went with the country of Russia and the remainder of the countries had to form their own banking system before they could supply the savings funds needed for investment.

COMPETENCY 5.3 THE RELATIONSHIP BETWEEN POLITICS AND ECONOMICS

Skill 5.3a Analyze the effects of federal, state, and local policies on the distribution of resources and economic decision-making.

Government policies, whether they are federal, state or local, affect economic decision making and in many cases, the distribution of resources. This is the purpose of most economic policies imposed at the federal level. Governments don't implement monetary and fiscal policy at the state or local level, only at the national level. Most state and local laws that affect economic decision making and the distribution of resources have to do with taxation. If taxes are imposed or raised at the state or local level, the effect is less spending. The purpose of these taxes is to raise revenues for the state and local government, not to affect the level of aggregate demand and inflation. At the federal level, the major purpose of these policies is to affect the level of **aggregate demand** and the **inflation rate** or the **unemployment rate**.

Governments at all three levels affect the distribution of resources and economic decision-making through **transfer payments**. This brings about a **redistribution of income** to correct the problem of income inequality. Programs such as Food Stamps, AFDC (welfare), unemployment compensation, and Medicaid all fall into this category. Technically, these government transfer programs result in a rearrangement of private consumption, not a real reallocation of resources. Price support programs in agriculture also result in a redistribution of income and a misallocation of resources. The imposition of artificially high prices results in too many resources going into agriculture and leads to product surpluses.

Laws can be enacted at all three levels to correct for the problem of **externalities**. An externality occurs when uninvolved third parties are affected by some market activity, like pollution. Dumping noxious or poisonous wastes into the air and water means that the air and water are being treated as a free input by the firm. The market does not register all of the costs of production because the firm does not have to pay to use the air or water. The result of free inputs is lower production costs for the firm and an over allocation of resources into the production of the good the firm is producing.

The role for government here is to cause a **redistribution of resources** by somehow shifting all or part of the cost onto the offending firm. Governments can impose fines, taxes, require pollution abatement equipment, sell pollution permits, etc. Whatever method chosen, this raises the costs of production for the firms and forces them to bear some of the cost. Policies can be enacted in order to encourage labor to migrate from one sector of the economy to another. This is primarily done at the national level. The United States economy is so large that it is possible to have unemployment in different areas while the economy is at full employment. The purpose here is to cause unemployed labor in one area to migrate to another area where there are jobs. State unemployment and labor agencies provide the information for these people.

Skill 5.3b   Describe the economic and social effects of government fiscal policies.

Fiscal policy refers to changes in the levels of government spending and taxation. All three levels of government engage in fiscal policy that has economic and social effects. At the state and local levels, the purpose of government spending and taxes is to run the state and local governments. When taxes are raised at the state or local level, the purpose is to provide revenues for the government to function, not to affect the level of aggregate spending in the economy. Even so, these taxes still have economic and social effects on the local population that has less money to spend. Local merchants may see a decrease in their revenues from less spending, in addition to having to pay taxes themselves. When state and local governments spend money through local programs, like repairing or building roads, the effect is to inject money into the local economy even though the purpose is to promote transportation.

Fiscal policy at the national level differs from that at the state and local levels because the purpose of the fiscal policy is to affect the level of aggregate spending in the economy. One of the functions of the federal government is to promote economic stabilization. This means to correct for inflation and unemployment. The way they do this is through changing the level of government spending and/or the level of taxation.

Inflation occurs when there is too high a level of aggregate spending and there is too much spending in the economy. Producers can't keep up with the demand

and the result is rising prices. In this situation, the government implements contractionary fiscal policy which consists of a decrease in government spending and/or an increase in taxes. The purpose is to slow down an economy that expands too quickly by enacting policies that result in people having less money to spend. These policies, depending on how they are implemented, will affect the components of aggregate demand—consumption, investment and government spending. Spending on imports will also decrease. The result of the contractionary fiscal policy will be, hopefully, to end the inflation.

Unemployment is another macroeconomic problem that requires expansionary fiscal policy. Unemployment occurs due to a lack of spending in the economy. There is not enough aggregate demand in the economy to fully employ the labor force. Here the role for government is to stimulate spending. If they can increase spending, producers will increase their output and hire more resources, including labor, thus eliminating the problem of unemployment. Expansionary fiscal policy consists of increasing government spending and/or lowering taxes. The increase in government spending injects money into the economy.

Government programs that build roads mean more jobs. More jobs mean more spending and a higher level of aggregate demand. As producers see an increase in the demand for their product, they increase their output levels. As they expand, they require more resources, including labor. As more of the labor force works, the level of spending increases still further, and so on. Lowering taxes affects the consumption and possibly the investment components of aggregate demand leaving consumers and businesses with more money to spend, thus leading to a higher level of spending and eliminating unemployment.

Skill 5.3c Describe the aims and tools of monetary policy and its economic and social effects.

Nations need a smoothly functioning banking system in order to experience economic growth. **The Federal Reserve** implements monetary policy through the banking system and it is a tool used to promote economic stability at the macro level of the economy. There are three components of monetary policy: the **reserve ratio**, the **discount rate** and **open market operations**. Changes in any of these three components affect the amount of money in the banking system and thus, the level of spending in the economy.

The **reserve ratio** refers to the portion of deposits that banks are required to hold as vault cash or on deposit with the Federal Reserve. The purpose of this reserve ratio is to give the Fed a way to control the money supply. These funds can't be used for any other purpose. When the Federal Reserve changes the reserve ratio, it changes the money creation and lending ability of the banking system. When the Federal Reserve wants to expand the money supply it lowers the reserve ratio, leaving banks with more money to loan. This is one aspect of expansionary monetary policy. When the reserve ratio is increased, this results in banks having less money to make loans with, which is a form of contractionary monetary policy, which leads to a lower level of spending in the economy.

Another way in which monetary policy is implemented is by changing the **discount rate**. When banks have temporary cash shortages, they can borrow from the Federal Reserve. The interest rate on the funds they borrow is called the discount rate. Raising and lowering the discount rate controls the money supply. Lowering the discount rate encourages banks to borrow from the Federal Reserve, instead of restricting their lending to deal with the temporary cash shortage.

By encouraging banks to borrow, their lending ability is increased and this results in a higher level of spending in the economy. Lowering the discount rate is a form of **expansionary monetary policy**. Discouraging bank lending by raising the discount rate, then is a form of **contractionary monetary policy**.

The final tool of monetary policy is called **open market operations**. This consists of the Federal Reserve buying or selling government securities with the public or with the banking system. When the Federal Reserve sells bonds, it takes money out of the banking system. The public and the banks pay for the bonds, thus resulting in fewer dollars in the economy and a lower level of spending. The selling of bonds by the Federal Reserve is a form of contractionary monetary policy that leads to a lower level of spending in the economy. The Federal Reserve is expanding the money supply when it buys bonds from the public or the banking system because it pays for those bonds with dollars that enter the income-expenditures stream. The result of the Federal Reserve buying bonds is to increase the level of spending in the economy.

Skill 5.3d   Assess the tradeoff between efficiency and equality in modern mixed economies, using social policies as examples.

Modern mixed economies do not result in an equal distribution of income for all of their members. Some people are very rich and some people are very poor. The remainder of the population is somewhere in-between. The reason is that not everyone has the same resource skills to supply in the input market from which they derive their income. The fact that they don't supply the same skills means that they don't all receive the same income. Resource owners supplying highly demanded rare skills receive more compensation than those supplying little or no skills: the more abundant the skill or lack of skills, the lower the compensation.

An efficient economy does not result in an equal or equitable distribution of income. This is a fact of capitalism. A role for government then is to implement certain kinds of social policies to correct for the income inequality resulting from a market economy. These policies basically effect a redistribution of income from those in the higher income brackets to those in the lower income brackets. There are different ways to accomplish this income redistribution.

One way of redistributing income is through the federal income tax system. Taxes can be progressive, regressive or proportional. A **progressive tax** is when the tax rate increases as income increases. Those in higher income brackets pay a larger percentage of their income in taxes than those in lower income brackets. The federal income tax is a progressive tax. A **regressive tax** is the opposite, where the tax rate decreases as the level of income increases. Here, the tax rate is higher on lower income brackets than on higher income brackets. The social security tax is in this category. A **proportional tax** is where the tax rate is the same for all income levels. Sales tax is an example of a proportional tax. The progressive tax is based on the idea of equity, that the tax burden should be heavier on people with higher income than on people with lower incomes.

There are many social programs that distribute transfer payments. This is another way of bringing about a redistribution of income to correct for the inequities of a mixed economy. Transfer payment programs are programs such as food stamps, Aid to Families with Dependent Children (AFDC) which people refer to as welfare, Medicaid, etc. All of these programs redistribute tax dollars from the upper income levels to the lower income levels. Most of these programs provide aid to the lower income levels for a specific purpose, whether its food, medical care, support of children, etc. With the exception of AFDC, they are known as in-kind programs because the aid is geared to a specific area and supplies the good or service instead of supplying cash payments.

Agricultural price support programs also bring about a redistribution of income from the population to the agricultural sector by legally mandating prices higher than the market would set. The farmers could not survive without this program and they produce the food for the nation. All of these programs are implemented to try to correct for some of the inequities that result from a market economy.

Skill 5.3e Apply the principles of economic decision-making to a current or historical social problem in America (e.g., land development, resource availability, environmental quality, composition of the economy).

America, like other countries, has experienced the social problem of discrimination. **Discrimination** occurs when one group does not have the same opportunities in spite of having the same qualifications as other members of society. **Opportunities** refer to things like salary, job access, promotion and occupations. **Qualifications** mean things like education, training, abilities and experiences. Equals are not treated equally.

The existence and practice of discrimination are contrary to economic theory. Economics assumes that all economic agents act rationally. The practice of discrimination, especially in labor markets, is not consistent with economic theory because it is not rational because it prevents people from working in their most productive capacity. This results in lower output levels and higher costs.

There are several economic theories that try to explain discrimination. Theorists tried explaining discrimination in terms of market power: a discriminating agent has enough market power to exploit the discriminated against entity. In the output market this would mean charging a higher price to the discriminated against entity and in the input market this means paying a lower wage to the discriminated against entity. Discrimination would have to be industry wide for the practice of wage discrimination to exist or the discriminated against worker would just find employment elsewhere. However, if there is industry-wide wage discrimination, the result is a lower wage bill for the employer. If this is true, then the conclusion is that the market promotes discrimination and it won't be eliminated without some kind of legal action to eliminate the practice. The market power model is not based on prejudice.

If discrimination is based on prejudice of some kind a situation results where the employer is willing to pay to distance himself from the discriminated-against group. Employer prejudice results in the employer paying the discriminated against employee a lower wage than he pays to other workers: the greater the amount of prejudice, the lower the wage, even if the employee is a better worker. In other words, the employer is willing to pay a premium wage to employees who are not a member of the discriminated against group. This explains the existence of wage differentials. Discrimination has to be in some way profitable for the employer or it couldn't last. Discrimination with prejudice can involve non-monetary factors that enter into the situation.

There are other kinds of labor market discrimination. Human capital discrimination refers to individuals not having the same training or educational opportunities. Wage, employment and job discrimination occur in the labor market when individuals don't have the same opportunities in these areas. Employment discrimination refers to the working group that bears the burden of unemployment. Wage and job discrimination mean that a group does not have the same opportunity in terms of salary and occupation.

Economic decision-making can sometimes be linked to social problems, such as resource availability or environmental quality. If it becomes economically feasible to extract more minerals than necessary from the ground, the resource availability will decrease and may become depleted. Environmental quality can be affected when refineries have the goal of producing vast quantities of oil while polluting the air or ground. In cases such as these, economic decision-making is based on the financial **bottom line** rather than on how the production benefits society as a whole.

OMPETENCY 5.4 **ELEMENTS OF THE U.S. LABOR MARKET IN A GLOBAL SETTING**

Skill 5.4a **Describe the circumstances surrounding the establishment of principal American labor unions, procedures that unions use to gain benefits for their members, and the effects of unionization, the minimum wage, and unemployment insurance.**

Labor unions in America arose in response to deplorable working conditions. Employees had no say in their working conditions and began to join forces to try to obtain some input. Viewed in this perspective, the history of the labor movement can be traced back to the colonial period as workers banded together and with other organizations in support of different goals. The workers that engaged in these activities were subject to actions from dismissal to blacklisting. It wasn't until 1881 that the first permanent union structure was founded on the principles of **Samuel Gompers**. This became known as the **American Federation of Labor** and was based on three principles—**practical business unionism**, which is the belief that unions should only concern themselves with the problems of their members: working conditions, hours, wages, job security, etc.; **political neutrality**; and **trade autonomy**, the belief that unions should be organized on the basis of trade. There should be one union for each craft or trade; there should not be unions consisting of members from all trades. The AFL organized only craft or trade workers, and not industrial workers. The large pool of industrial workers was eventually organized by the Congress of Industrial Organization, and in 1955 the two merged to become the AFL-CIO.

The unions have various methods they can use to obtain benefits for their members. They have supported the enactment of various kinds of labor law legislation that eventually regulated both sides of the labor market, union and employer from various unfair labor and union practices such as **yellow-dog contracts, boycotts, featherbedding,** and **hot cargo clauses**. They have also supported legislation that resulted in minimum wage and unemployment insurance.

The most direct way of obtaining benefits has been through the collective bargaining process. **Collective bargaining** refers to the negotiating of a labor agreement or the settling of a grievance under an existing contract. When the union and the employee can't come to terms, the union will strike. During a **strike** the union members withhold their labor services. The purpose is to put financial pressure on the employer. The employer can respond with a lock-out, which puts pressure on the union and the workers. Eventually an agreement is reached, with or without a strike or lock-out.

Minimum wage legislation is a legally mandated wage support. **Unemployment Insurance** is a program that provides income for unemployed workers. The unemployed individual does not have to be a union member to collect unemployment.

Skill 5.4b   **Analyze the current U.S. economy and the global labor market that helps support it, including the types of goods and services produced, the types of skills in demand, the effects of rapid technological change, the inter-and intra-regional shifts in employment, and the impact of international competition.**

The United States is a well-endowed economy with a diversified resource base, yet it is dependent on the global economy to supply goods and labor that it cannot supply itself or to perform tasks that it cannot perform at the same level of costs. The United States can best be characterized as a **capital-technology intensive economy**. This means that its strength is in the production of goods requiring capital and technology, which is why we import so many labor intensive goods that other countries can produce cheaper than we can. This is why there is so much outsourcing with call centers moving to India, Pakistan, and other countries. The United States also needs foreign labor for its agricultural sector. Without low-cost foreign labor, farmers would have to pay much higher wages to attract domestic workers to the agricultural sector. This would result in higher food costs.

Despite its well-diversified resource base, the United States cannot and does not produce all of the goods it consumes, even in agriculture. Coffee and tea as well as other foods are imported. We import a great deal of labor intensive clothing products because they can be produced at a relatively lower cost in other parts of the world, which is also a way of providing employment to workers in other parts of the world. There is little demand for labor intensive workers in the United States. There is more of a demand for capital intensive workers or technology workers or technologically oriented providers of services.

Rapid technological change causes effects throughout the economy as firms, industries and workers try to keep up. Rapidly changing technology costs money to implement. Today's labor force is highly mobile and moves around the country for employment purposes. A new plant opening in a particular region will possibly attract labor from other areas as workers go where the jobs are. So inter- and intra-regional shifts in employment are not uncommon as workers train for new jobs and move to begin new employment. Some of this is also in response to international competition that makes certain job skills obsolete as plants move out of the country to benefit from lower wages.

International competition brings about a restructuring of the labor market as firms leave high-wage countries like the United States and locate their operations in low-wage countries to keep their costs low. The displaced workers must acquire new skills to make them employable in areas where there is a demand for labor.

This may include retraining or acquiring the skills for an entirely different occupation.

Skill 5.4c   Analyze wage differences between jobs and professions.

Wage differentials result because workers and jobs are not all alike. Heterogeneity gives rise to wage differences. Wage differences can exist for a variety of reasons: location, danger, benefits, etc. The greater the differences between the jobs, the larger the wage differentials will be. Heterogeneity among workers also results in wage differences.

People move to acquire education, training and skills that qualify them for the characteristics of a different group. This is called **investing in human capital**. The amount of investment in human capital is a source of wage differences. Workers should be paid based on their skills, education and productivity. More highly skilled workers are paid more than those without skills.

Migration to new jobs geographically also equalizes wages as the supply of labor curves shift in both areas reflecting the changes in quantity of workers.

Skill 5.4d   Analyze the effects of international mobility of capital, labor, and trade on the U.S. economy.

Markets, today, are international in almost all respects. In this age of computers and technology, doing business across international borders is almost as easy as doing business with the firm down the block. The **international mobility** of capital, labor and trade affects all markets and sectors of the economy, except defense. International mobility of factors means that the factors will go where they earn the highest rate of return, whether the factor is capital or labor.

These events are happening today with foreign **outsourcing** and relocating plants overseas in response to lower costs. Call centers are being relocated or established in foreign countries like Pakistan, India, and other countries because of lower labor costs. These lower costs make the company more profitable. Relocating a plant in another country means the differential is great enough to cover shipping costs.

Financial capital also belongs to international markets. Investment funds are truly international, going wherever the highest rate of return is. If interest rates are higher in country A than in country B, funds will flow from country B to country A. This interest rate differential results in an appreciation in country A's currency relative to country B's currency, as units of currency from country B are converted into country A's currency. The flow will continue as long as the interest rate differential exists. Borrowers needing loans will engage in an international search, if necessary, to obtain the best interest rate instead of confining themselves to domestic markets with higher rates. None of these activities is difficult in the era of computers.

All of these factors tie in tightly with international trade. Markets are international. Firms locate plants where labor costs are low in order to increase their profitability. Workers migrate across international borders in response to better employment terms and conditions. Countries specialize in the production of the goods which they can produce at a lower cost than their trading partners. All these factors combine to cause structural changes in the economy as the various sectors adjust to the changes brought about by membership in the international economy. These displaced workers have to find employment and may require retraining. Businesses must diversify and innovate enough to make them competitive in the international economy. This may mean developing new products and services that are demanded in international markets.

COMPETENCY 5.5 AGGREGATE ECONOMIC BEHAVIOR OF THE AMERICAN ECONOMY

Skill 5.5a Describe how measures of economic output are adjusted using indexes.

Most measures of economic output are expressed in terms of dollars. The purchasing power of the dollar can change due to inflation and economic growth. Output figures, such as **Gross Domestic Product**, show fluctuations from year to year. There is no way to know whether these fluctuations are due to actual differences in the level of output or whether they are due to inflation and changes in the price level unless the figures are expressed in terms of constant dollars. This is a way of adjusting for inflation or controlling for the changes in the value of the dollar. **Real GDP** or **constant dollar GDP** is GDP adjusted for inflation. **Nominal, current dollar** or **unadjusted GDP** refers to GDP figures in dollars that have not been adjusted for inflation.

The construction and use of the GDP deflator is rather simple. The first step is to select one year to be the base year and then use that year to construct the price index. It doesn't matter what year is selected as long as the information is stated. The formula is simple.

$$\text{Price Index} = \frac{\text{Price in any year}}{\text{Price in base year}} \times 100$$

This index number then is used to compute the real GDP figure. The formula is given below:

$$\text{Real GDP} = \frac{\text{Nominal GDP}}{\text{Index Number}}$$

This formula takes the GDP figure for any year and expresses it in base-year dollars. GDP figures over any period of time will be expressed in dollars that have the same value as the dollar has in the base year. That's why it doesn't matter which year is used as the base year. Any differences in GDP are the result of real changes in the level of output and are not due to changes in the dollar's value. Therefore, meaningful comparisons can be made between the years. Economists do not want to work with raw unadjusted data because they will not know if the changes are from actual output levels or changes in the dollar.

Skill 5.5b   Define, calculate, and analyze the significance of the changes in rates of unemployment, inflation, and real Gross Domestic Product.

Real GDP, the unemployment rate, and the inflation rate are economic indicators. They reveal what is happening in the economy. **Inflation** refers to a rise in the general level of prices which causes a decrease in the purchasing power of the dollar. This basically means that one dollar does not buy as much as it did before. Policy makers need information on inflation because it calls for contractionary policies in an economy that is expanding too rapidly. The inflation rate is computed from index numbers. The formula is:

$$\text{Price Index} = \frac{\text{Price in any year}}{\text{Price in base year}} \times 100$$

Any year in the series can be selected as the base year and it is then used to compute the index number for the rest of the years, as given in the above formula.

The index numbers are then used to compute the inflation rate using the formula below:

$$\text{Inflation Rate} = \frac{\text{this year's index \# - last year's index \#}}{\text{Last year's index \#}}$$

The unemployment rate refers to the percentage of the labor force that is unemployed, or:

$$\text{Unemployment Rate} = \frac{\text{Number of People Unemployed}}{\text{Number of People in Labor Force}} \times 100$$

The labor force is not one hundred percent of the population. It includes people who are capable of working and are willing to work and are either working or actively seeking employment. Excluded are people who can't work (under the age of sixteen, institutionalized) or who could work but chose not to work, such as stay-at-home parents, full-time students, and retirees. The labor force is roughly one-half of the population.

The Gross Domestic Product is a measure of the economy's current output. It is calculated as the sum of its components: consumption, investment, government spending and net exports.

$$GDP = C + I + G + (X-M)$$

Since GDP is a measure of current output and expressed in current dollars, it must be converted to real terms with the GDP deflator.

This index number then is used to compute the real GDP figure. The formula is given below:

$$Real\ GDP = \frac{Nominal\ GDP}{Index\ Number}$$

Real GDP figures, along with the unemployment figures, tell us the state of the economy. An economy in a recession needs to be stimulated with expansionary monetary and fiscal policy, just as an economy that expands too rapidly needs to be slowed down with contractionary monetary and fiscal policy. Economists and government policy makers can work with the figures and determine the strength of the policy that is needed. They also watch the unemployment, inflation, and GDP figures to ascertain whether the policy is working, and, if not, what else needs to be done.

Skill 5.5c   Distinguish between short and long-term interest rates and explain their relative significance.

The **interest rate** is the price the borrower pays to the lender for the privilege of borrowing funds. Since loans are for different periods of time, there are different rates of interest. This is where the terms short-term and long-term interest rates comes from. What we are talking about here are the debt obligations of the United States government, or **U.S. Treasury securities**. These are T-bills, T-notes and T-bonds and they differ from one another in time to maturity.

A **T-bill** is a short-term instrument that matures in one year or less. A **T-note** has a maturity time from one to ten years. The **T-bond** is the long term instrument that matures in more than ten years. These fixed income securities are a way of lending money to the U.S. government and they carry a specified rate of interest called the coupon. There is an inverse relationship between bond prices and interest rates. This means that when interest rates rise, bond prices fall and vice-versa.

All interest rates are related. Different kinds of bonds of the same time duration that have different coupons, differ in terms of risk. This is called the **risk structure of interest rates** and it is affected by risk, liquidity, and income tax rules. An example of this would be the difference between a T-note and a municipal bond. Risk refers to the chance of default. U.S. government debt obligations are considered to be free of risk. This is not true of other bonds, especially private bonds. Some bonds have a risk premium, which is an additional amount of interest to compensate the holder for the risk of default.

Another factor affecting the risk structure is **liquidity**. Bonds do not have to be held to maturity. They can be sold. Liquidity refers to the ease with which the bond can be sold. The more difficult it is to sell the bond, the greater the amount of interest required to compensate the holder of the bond. The income tax rules treat different kinds of bonds in different ways. This also enters into the interest rate.

The **term structure of interest rates** refers to bonds that differ only in their terms of maturity. These bonds have the same risk, liquidity, and tax treatment so the only difference between them is the amount of time to maturity. Each maturing time period has its own sequence of interest rate bond yields and is referred to as the **term structure**. The difference between any two securities that mature at different times is the expected interest rate. A plot of the yields on these different maturities results in what is called the **yield curve.** This plot describes the term structure of interest rates or the relationship between interest rates during different times to maturity. Longer term interest rates are based on short term interest rate factors and corporate expectations about future interest rates is probably the simplest way of explaining this.

COMPETENCY 5.6 INTERNATIONAL TRADE AND THE AMERICAN ECONOMY

Skill 5.6a Use the concept of comparative advantage to identify the costs of and gains from international trade.

The theory of **comparative advantage** says that trade should be based on the comparative opportunity costs between two nations. The nation that can produce a good more cheaply should specialize in the production of that good and trade for the good in which it has the comparative disadvantage. In this way both nations will experience gains from trade. A basis for trade exists if there are differing comparative costs in each country. Suppose country A can produce ten units of X with thirty units of Y. Country B can produce 30 units of X with thirty units of Y. What are the relative costs in each country? In country A, one X costs three units of Y and in country B one X costs one unit of Y. Good X is cheaper in country B than it is in country A. Country B has the comparative advantage in the production of X. According to trade theory each country should specialize in the production of the good in which it has the comparative advantage. Country B will devote all of its resources to the production of good X and country A will import good X and specialize in another product.

To determine the **gains from trade**, we must first consider the pre-trade production and consumption positions of both countries. Imagine a country whose pre-trade position was where they could have either 10 units of X or 10 units of Y or any combination in between. Let's assume country A chose a combination of 7Y and 3X. In country B, their resources allowed either 30 units of Y or 10 units of X or any combination in between. Let's assume country B chose the combination of 18Y and 4 X. Now let's consider the production and consumption situation before and after trade. Before trade, the total production of good Y was 18 from country B and 7 from country A for a total of 25Y. After trade, total world production is 30Y, with country B specializing in the production of Y. For good X, the pre-trade situation was 3 units of X from country A and 4 units of X from country B, for a total of 7 units of X. After trade, with country A specializing in the production of X, total world production of X is 10 units. Specialization and trade according to comparative advantage results in the world having 30Y rather than 25Y and 10X instead of 7X. This increase is referred to as the gains from trade. Both countries have higher consumption levels of both goods due to specialization. This example refers to free unrestricted trade. Trade barriers introduce distortions.

Skill 5.6b   Compare and contrast the arguments for and against trade restrictions during the Great Depression with those among labor, business, and political leaders today.

Trade theory tells us that free unrestricted trade, without any barriers is best. Free trade leads to the most efficient use of world resources. Any kind of protective measure reduces the volume of world trade and causes higher levels of unemployment and lower levels of income and consumption. Yet nations of the world resort to protective measures when they experience economic difficulties.

During the Great Depression in the 1930s, the U.S. enacted the **Smoot-Hawley Tariff Act** which raised tariffs to their highest level in U.S. history. The result was retaliation from other countries. These actions contributed to the severity and duration of the Depression. These were basically what are called **Beggar Thy Neighbor** policies because the purpose was to protect domestic jobs at the expense of the trading partners.

The arguments heard for protection today are pretty much the same as they were in the 1930s. The job protection argument is still used. The way to protect American jobs is to restrict imports. Americans will buy more domestically produced goods thus leading to an increase in demand for domestic workers. This is the usual argument heard during periods of recession. Beggar Thy Neighbor policies export unemployment to the trading partners.

Another commonly used argument is based on **national security**. This argument says that industries vital to national defense should be protected from foreign competition: that a nation should be self-sufficient in goods it needs for national defense. Fighters and bombers may be essential but what about the inputs used to make them, such as computers and paper clips? Where do you draw the line?

New industries usually ask for protection from the more developed foreign competitors. This is called the **Infant Industry argument** which says give the new industries protection until they can grow and compete in the world market. It makes some economic sense, except the industry will adjust to operating with protection because its removes the pressure from the companies to be competitive.

Another common argument is that the high wage domestic labor should be protected from the low wage country imports. People will buy the lower-priced foreign imports, thus lowering demand for the domestically produced product which could cause unemployment. The problem is that these high wage industries should not try to compete with the comparative advantage of the low wage countries. This kind of behavior isn't consistent with trade theory.

And finally, there is the call for an **anti-dumping tariff** when a nation catches another selling a good at a lower price in the foreign market than in its own domestic market. Dumping is very difficult to prove. Even though the Great Depression occurred many years ago, we still have the same arguments being used for protective trade measures.

Skill 5.6c **Analyze the significance of the changing role of international political borders and territorial sovereignty in a global economy (e.g., General Agreement on Trade and Tariffs (GATT), North American Free Trade Agreement (NAFTA), World Trade Organization (WTO), European Union (EU).**

GATT, NAFTA, WTO and EU are all forms of **trade liberalization. The GATT** or **General Agreements on Tariffs and Trade** was founded in 1947. Today, the organization is known as the **World Trade Organization** or **WTO.** The WTO is the successor to the GATT and came into being in 1995. Its objective is to promote free trade. As such it administers trade agreements, settles disputes, and provides a forum for trade discussions and negotiations. It has close to 150 member nations and is based on three principles. The first is Most Favored National status for all members. This means trade based on comparative advantage without tariffs or trade barriers. The second principle is the elimination of quotas; third, the reduction of trade barriers through multi-lateral trade negotiations.

The **North American Free Trade Agreement** or **NAFTA** and the **EU** are both forms of regional economic integration. Economic integration is a method of trade liberalization on a regional basis. NAFTA represents the lowest form or first step in the regional trade integration process. A **free trade area** consists for two or more countries abolishing tariffs and other trade barriers among themselves but maintaining their own trade barriers against the rest of the world. A free trade area allows for specialization and trade on the basis of comparative advantage within the area. The next stage in the integration process is a **customs union,** which is a free trade area that has common external tariffs against non-members. The third stage is a common market which is a **customs union with free factor mobility** within the area. Factors migrate where they find the best payment within the area. The fourth state is **economic union** where the common market members have common or coordinated economic and social policies. The final stage is **monetary union** where the area has a common currency. This is what defines the European Union. They have a common market and a single currency, the Euro.

The WTO does not change or blur the significance of political borders and territorial sovereignty in the same way that economic integration does. The WTO is a way of settling trade disputes that arise from the different integration agreements. In the advanced stages of economic integration the political borders remain but economic and social policies are common or coordinated and in monetary union, and there is one common currency. Each nation is its own independent entity but each gives up some sovereignty in the interest of a successful union.

Trade agreements proliferate in the world today. The Smoot-Hawley Tariff and the rounds of retaliation in the 1930s laid the basis for what today are the WTO and the European Union (EU). The GATT and the beginnings of the EU came into being as organizations that tried to undo the effects of the Great Depression and World War II. Free trade without trade barriers results in the most efficient use of resources, with higher consumption, employment and income levels for all participants. This is why there are so many free trade agreements being negotiated in today's world.

Skill 5.6d   Describe how international currency exchange rates are determined and their significance.

Nations are free to choose their own form of exchange rate regime. Most major world currencies **float**, with their exchange rate value being determined by supply and demand. This has been the situation since the early 1970s when the regime of fixed exchange rates collapsed. Currency values are relative prices: one currency is expressed in terms of another currency, i.e., U.S. dollars per Euro, Mexican Peso per Venezuelan Bolivar, etc. The term one U.S. dollar has no meaning in world markets without being expressed in terms of another currency. Currency values can be expressed as U.S. dollars per British pound, which is another way of saying how much one British pound costs. They can also be expressed as British pounds per U.S. dollar, or how many British pounds do you get for one U.S. dollar. One is just the reciprocal of the other.

In a **clean float**, supply and demand factors for each currency in terms of another are what determine the equilibrium price or the **exchange rate**. A clean float is a market functioning without any government interference, purely on the basis of demand and supply. Sometimes nations will intervene in the market to affect the value of their currency vis-à-vis the other currency. This situation is referred to as a **managed or dirty float**. A government is not required to intervene to maintain a currency value, as they were under a regime of fixed exchange rates. A government that intervenes in the currency market does so because it wants to, not because it is required to intervene to maintain a certain exchange rate value.

For example, if the U.S. government thinks the dollar is depreciating too much against the Canadian dollar, the U.S. government will buy U.S. dollars in the open market and pay for them with Canadian dollars. This increases the demand for U.S. dollars and increases the supply of Canadian dollars. The U.S. dollar appreciates, or increases in value, and the Canadian dollar depreciates, or decreases in value, in response to the government intervention. A stronger U.S. dollar means Canadian goods are cheaper for Americans, and American goods are more expensive for Canadians.

Not all nations have floating exchange rate regimes. Some nations base the value of their currency on another nation's currency, or they tie or peg their currency value to another currency, usually a trading partner's currency. Then the tied currency moves up or down in the market as the currency it is tied to does. The exchange rate is basically fixed against the currency it is tied to but floats versus the rest of the world.

Fixed exchange rates can lead to various economic problems through the Balance of Payments. The only way that nations could correct for Balance of Payment problems was through the imposition of trade restrictions and trying to bring their exports and imports under control. Since the movement today is toward free trade and specialization according to comparative advantage, floating exchange rates are more suitable goals.

DOMAIN 6   **PRINCIPLES OF GEOGRAPHY**

COMPETENCY 6.1   **TOOLS AND PERSPECTIVES OF GEOGRAPHIC STUDY**

Skill 6.1a   **Describe the criteria for defining regions and identify why places and regions are important.**

The earth's surface is made up of 70% water and 30% land. Physical features of the land surface include mountains, hills, plateaus, valleys, and plains. Other minor landforms include deserts, deltas, canyons, mesas, basins, foothills, marshes and swamps. Earth's water features include oceans, seas, lakes, rivers, and canals.

Mountains are landforms with rather steep slopes at least 2,000 feet or more above sea level. Mountains are found in groups called mountain chains or mountain ranges. At least one range can be found on six of the earth's seven continents. North America has the Appalachian and Rocky Mountains; South America the Andes; Asia the Himalayas; Australia the Great Dividing Range; Europe the Alps; and Africa the Atlas, Ahaggar, and Drakensburg Mountains.

Hills are elevated landforms rising to an elevation of about 500 to 2000 feet. They are found everywhere on earth including Antarctica where they are covered by ice.

Plateaus are elevated landforms usually level on top. Depending on location, they range from being an area that is very cold to one that is cool and healthful. Some plateaus are dry because they are surrounded by mountains that keep out any moisture. Some examples include the Kenya Plateau in East Africa, which is very cool. The plateau extending north from the Himalayas is extremely dry while those in Antarctica and Greenland are covered with ice and snow.

Plains are described as areas of flat or slightly rolling land, usually lower than the landforms next to them. Sometimes called **lowlands** (and sometimes located along **seacoasts)** they support the majority of the world's people. Some are found inland and many have been formed by large rivers. This resulted in extremely fertile soil for successful cultivation of crops and numerous large settlements of people. In North America, the vast plains areas extend from the Gulf of Mexico north to the Arctic Ocean and between the Appalachian and Rocky Mountains. In Europe, rich plains extend east from Great Britain into central Europe on into the Siberian region of Russia. Plains in river valleys are found in China (the Yangtze River valley), India (the Ganges River valley), and Southeast Asia (the Mekong River valley).

Valleys are land areas found between hills and mountains. Some have gentle slopes containing trees and plants; others have steep walls and are referred to as canyons. One example is Arizona's Grand Canyon of the Colorado River.

Deserts are large dry areas of land receiving ten inches or less of rainfall each year. Among the better-known deserts are Africa's large Sahara Desert, the Arabian Desert on the Arabian Peninsula, and the desert Outback covering roughly one third of Australia.

Deltas are areas of lowlands formed by soil and sediment deposited at the mouths of rivers. The soil is generally very fertile and most fertile river deltas are important crop-growing areas. One well-known example is the delta of Egypt's Nile River, known for its production of cotton.

Mesas are the flat tops of hills or mountains usually with steep sides. Sometimes plateaus are also called mesas. **Basins** are considered to be low areas drained by rivers or low spots in mountains. **Foothills** are generally considered a low series of hills found between a plain and a mountain range. **Marshes** and **swamps** are wet lowlands providing growth of such plants as rushes and reeds.

Oceans are the largest bodies of water on the planet. The four oceans of the earth are the **Atlantic Ocean**, one-half the size of the Pacific and separating North and South America from Africa and Europe; the **Pacific Ocean**, covering almost one-third of the entire surface of the earth and separating North and South America from Asia and Australia; the **Indian Ocean**, touching Africa, Asia, and Australia; and the ice-filled **Arctic Ocean**, extending from North America and Europe to the North Pole. The waters of the Atlantic, Pacific, and Indian Oceans also touch the shores of Antarctica.

Seas are smaller than oceans and are surrounded by land. Some examples include the Mediterranean Sea found between Europe, Asia, and Africa; and the Caribbean Sea, touching the West Indies, South and Central America. A lake is a body of water surrounded by land. The Great Lakes in North America are a good example.

Rivers, considered a nation's lifeblood, usually begin as very small streams, formed by melting snow and rainfall, flowing from higher to lower land, emptying into a larger body of water, usually a sea or an ocean. Examples of important rivers for the people and countries affected by and/or dependent on them include the Nile, Niger, and Zaire Rivers of Africa; the Rhine, Danube, and Thames Rivers of Europe; the Yangtze, Ganges, Mekong, Hwang He, and Irrawaddy Rivers of Asia; the Murray-Darling in Australia; and the Orinoco in South America. River systems are made up of large rivers and numerous smaller rivers or tributaries flowing into them. Examples include the vast Amazon Rivers system in South America and the Mississippi River system in the United States.

Canals are man-made water passages constructed to connect two larger bodies of water. Famous examples include the **Panama Canal** across Panama's isthmus connecting the Atlantic and Pacific Oceans and the **Suez Canal** in the Middle East between Africa and the Arabian Peninsula connecting the Red and Mediterranean Seas.

Weather is the condition of the air which surrounds the day-to-day atmospheric conditions including temperature, air pressure, wind and moisture or precipitation which includes rain, snow, hail, or sleet.

Climate is average weather or daily weather conditions for a specific region or location over an extended period of time. Studying the climate of an area includes information gathered on the area's monthly and yearly temperatures and its monthly and yearly amounts of precipitation. In addition, a characteristic of an area's climate is the length of its growing season. Four reasons for the different climate regions on the earth are differences in

- Latitude
- The amount of moisture
- Temperatures in land and water
- The earth's land surface

There are many different climates throughout the earth. It is most unusual if a country contains just one kind of climate. Regions of climates are divided according to latitudes

- 0 - 23 1/2 degrees are the low latitudes
- 23 1/2 - 66 1/2 degrees are the middle latitudes
- 66 1/2 degrees to the Poles are the high latitudes

The **low latitudes** are comprised of the rainforest, savanna, and desert climates. The tropical rainforest climate is found in equatorial lowlands and is hot and wet. There is sun, extreme heat and rain — everyday. Although daily temperatures rarely rise above 90 degrees F, the daily humidity is always high, leaving everything sticky and damp. North and south of the tropical rainforests are the tropical grasslands called savannas, the lands of two seasons: a winter dry season and a summer wet season. Further north and south of the tropical grasslands or savannas are the deserts. These areas are the hottest and driest parts of the earth receiving less than 10 inches of rain a year. These areas have extreme temperatures between night and day. After the sun sets, the land cools quickly dropping the temperature as much as 50 degrees F.

The **middle latitudes** contain the Mediterranean, humid-subtropical, humid-continental, marine, steppe, and desert climates. Lands containing the Mediterranean climate are considered sunny lands found in six areas of the world: lands bordering the Mediterranean Sea, a small portion of southwestern

Africa, areas in southern and southwestern Australia, a small part of the Ukraine near the Black Sea, central Chile, and Southern California. Summers are hot and dry with mild winters. The growing season usually lasts all year and what little rain falls are during the winter months. What is rather unusual is that the Mediterranean climate is located between 30 and 40 degrees north and south latitude on the western coasts of countries.

The humid **subtropical climate** is found north and south of the tropics and is moist. The areas with this type of climate are found on the eastern side of their continents and include Japan, mainland China, Australia, Africa, South America, and the United States. An interesting feature of their locations is that warm ocean currents are found there. The winds that blow across these currents bring in warm moist air all year round. Long, warm summers, short, mild winters and a long growing season allow for different crops to be grown several times a year. All contribute to the productivity of this climate type which supports more people than any of the other climate.

The **marine climate** is found in Western Europe, the British Isles, the U.S. Pacific Northwest, the western coast of Canada and southern Chile, along with southern New Zealand and southeastern Australia. A common characteristic of these lands is that they are either near water or surrounded by it. The ocean winds are wet and warm bringing a mild, rainy climate to these areas. In the summer, the daily temperatures average at or below 70 degrees F. During the winter, because of the warming effect of the ocean waters, the temperatures rarely fall below freezing.

In northern and central United States, northern China, south central and southeastern Canada, and the western and southeastern parts of the former Soviet Union is found the **"climate of four seasons,"** the **humid continental climate**. Cold winters, hot summers, and enough rainfall to grow a variety of crops are the major characteristics of this climate. In areas where the humid continental climate is found are some of the world's best farmlands as well as important activities such as trading and mining. Differences in temperatures throughout the year are determined by the distance a place is from the coasts.

The **steppe or prairie climate** is located in the interiors of large continents like Asia and North America. These dry flatlands are far from ocean breezes and are called prairies or the Great Plains in Canada and the United States and steppes in Asia. Although the summers are hot and the winters are cold, the big difference is rainfall. In the steppe climate, rainfall is light and uncertain, 10 to 20 inches a year mainly in spring and summer is considered normal. Where rain is more plentiful, grass grows; in areas of less, the steppes or prairies gradually become deserts.

These are found in the Gobi Desert of Asia, central and western Australia, southwestern United States, and in the smaller deserts found in Pakistan, Argentina, and Africa south of the Equator.

The two major climates found in the high latitudes are **tundra** and **taiga.** The word tundra is a Russian word that means marshy plain and aptly describes the climate conditions in the northern areas of Russia, Europe, and Canada. Winters are extremely cold and very long. Most of the year the ground is frozen but becomes rather mushy during the very short summer months. Surprisingly, less snow falls in the area of the tundra than in the eastern part of the United States. However, due to the harshness of the extreme cold, very few people live there and no crops can be raised. Despite having a small human population, many plants and animals are found there.

The **taiga** is the northern forest region and is located south of the tundra. In fact, the Russian word taiga means forest. The world's largest forestlands are found here along with vast mineral wealth and furbearing animals. The climate is extreme and very few people live there, not being able to raise crops due to the extremely short growing season. The winter temperatures are colder and the summer temperatures are hotter than those in the tundra because the taiga climate region is farther from the waters of the Arctic Ocean. The taiga is found in the northern parts of Russia, Sweden, Norway, Finland, Canada, and Alaska with most of their lands covered with marshes and swamps.

In certain areas of the earth there exists a type of climate unique to areas with high mountains, usually different from their surroundings. This type of climate is called a **vertical climate** because the temperatures, crops, vegetation, and human activities change and become different as one ascends the levels of elevation. At the foot of the mountain, a hot and rainy climate is found with the cultivation of many lowland crops. As one climbs higher, the air becomes cooler, the climate changes sharply and different economic activities change, such as grazing sheep and growing corn. At the top of many mountains, snow is found year-round.

Skill 6.1b	Explain the nature of map projections and use maps, as well as other geographic representations and technologies (including remote sensing and geographic information systems) to acquire, process, and report information from a spatial perspective.

Although maps have advantages over globes and photographs, they do have a major disadvantage. The major problem of all maps comes about because most maps are flat and the Earth is a sphere. It is impossible to reproduce exactly on a flat surface an object shaped like a sphere. In order to put the earth's features onto a map they must be stretched in some way. This stretching is called **distortion.**

Distortion does not mean that maps are wrong, it simply means that they are not perfect representations of the Earth or its parts. **Cartographers,** or mapmakers, understand the problems of distortion. They try to design them so that there is as little distortion as possible in the maps.

The process of putting the features of the Earth onto a flat surface is called **projection**. All maps are really map projections. There are many different types. Each one deals in a different way with the problem of distortion. Map projections are made in a number of ways. Some are done using complicated mathematics. However, the basic ideas behind map projections can be understood by looking at the three most common types.

(1) **Cylindrical Projections** - These are done by taking a cylinder of paper and wrapping it around a globe. A light is used to project the globe's features onto the paper. Distortion is least where the paper touches the globe. For example, suppose that the paper was wrapped so that it touched the globe at the equator, the map from this projection would have just a little distortion near the equator.

However, in moving north or south of the equator, the distortion would increase as you moved further away from the equator. The best known and most widely used cylindrical projection is the **Mercator Projection.** It was first developed in 1569 by Gerardus Mercator, a Flemish mapmaker. This distortion effect is why Greenland appears to be larger than Africa on a Mercator map.

(2) **Conical Projections** - The name for these maps come from the fact that the projection is made onto a cone of paper. The cone is made so that it touches a globe at the base of the cone only. It can also be made so that it cuts through part of the globe in two different places. Again, there is the least distortion where the paper touches the globe. If the cone touches at two different points, there is some distortion at both of them. Conical projections are most often used to map areas in the **middle latitudes**. Maps of the United States are most often conical projections. This is because most of the country lies within these latitudes.

(3) **Flat-Plane Projections** - These are made with a flat piece of paper. It touches the globe at one point only. Areas near this point show little distortion. Flat-plane projections are often used to show the areas of the north and south poles. One such flat projection is called a **Gnomonic Projection**. On this kind of map all meridians appear as straight lines, Gnomonic projections are useful because any straight line drawn between points on it forms a **Great-Circle Route**.

Great-Circle Routes can best be described by thinking of how on a globe the shortest route between two points can be found by stretching a string from one point to the other. However, if the string were extended in reality, so that it took into effect the globe's curvature, it would then make a great-circle. A great-circle is any circle that cuts a sphere into two equal parts. Because of distortion, most maps do not show great-circle routes as straight lines, Gnomonic projections, however, do show the shortest distance between the two places as a straight line, because of this they are valuable for navigation. They are called Great-Circle Sailing Maps.

To properly analyze a given map one must be familiar with the various parts and symbols that most modern maps use. For the most part, this is standardized, with different maps using similar parts and symbols, these can include:

The Title - All maps should have a title, just like all books should. The title tells you what information is to be found on the map.

The Legend - Most maps have a legend. A legend tells the reader about the various symbols that are used on that particular map and what the symbols represent (also called a **map key**).

The Grid - A grid is a series of lines that are used to find exact places and locations on the map. There are several different kinds of grid systems in use, however, most maps use the longitude and latitude system, known as the **Geographic Grid System**.

Directions - Most maps have some directional system to show which way the map is being presented. Often on a map, a small compass will be present, with arrows showing the four basic directions, north, south, east, and west.

The Scale - This is used to show the relationship between a unit of measurement on the map versus the real-world measure on the Earth. Maps are drawn to many different scales. Some maps show a lot of detail for a small area. Others show a greater span of distance. One should always be aware of just what scale is being used. For instance the scale might be something like 1 inch = 10 miles for a small area or for a map showing the whole world it might have a scale in which 1 inch = 1,000 miles. The point is that one must look at the map key in order to see what units of measurements the map is using.

Maps have four main properties: the **size** of the areas shown on the map, the **shapes** of the areas, consistent **scales,** and **straight line directions**. A map can be drawn so that it is correct in one or more of these properties. No map can be correct in all of them.

Equal areas - One property which maps can have is that of equal areas. In an equal area map, the meridians and parallels are drawn so that the areas shown have the same proportions as they do on the Earth. For example, Greenland is about 118th the size of South America, thus it will appear as 118th the size on an equal area map. The **Mercator projection** is an example of a map that does not have equal areas. In it, Greenland appears to be about the same size of South America. This is because the distortion is very bad at the poles and Greenland lies near the North Pole.

Conformality - A second map property is conformality, or correct shapes. There are no maps which can show very large areas of the earth in their exact shapes. Only globes can really do that, however Conformal Maps are as close as possible to true shapes. The United States is often shown by a Lambert Conformal Conic Projection Map.

Consistent Scales - Many maps attempt to use the same scale on all parts of the map. Generally, this is easier when maps show a relatively small part of the earth's surface. For example, a map of Florida might be a Consistent Scale Map. Generally maps showing large areas are not consistent-scale maps. This is so because of distortion. Often such maps will have two scales noted in the key. One scale, for example, might be accurate to measure distances between points along the Equator. Another might be then used to measure distances between the North Pole and the South Pole.

Maps showing physical features often try to show information about the elevation or **relief** of the land. **Elevation** is the distance above or below the sea level. The elevation is usually shown with colors, for instance, all areas on a map which are at a certain level will be shown in the same color.

Relief Maps - Show the shape of the land surface, flat, rugged, or steep. Relief maps usually give more detail than simply showing the overall elevation of the land's surface. Relief is also sometimes shown with colors, but another way to show relief is with **contour lines**. These lines connect all points of a land surface which are the same height surrounding the particular area of land.

Thematic Maps - These are used to show more specific information, often on a single **theme**, or topic. Thematic maps show the distribution or amount of something over a certain given area such as population density, climate, economic information, cultural, and political information.

In order to obtain information about an object, such as one that is needed in making maps of geographic regions, remote sensing is used. **Remote sensing** means that the information is obtained without making physical contact or on-site investigation. Mountain heights and depths of bodies of water may be measured in this way. Remote sensing is a field of geography.

Geographic information needs to be stored and **geographic information systems** are used for that purpose. The systems can be configured in various ways and are used to store, analyze and display geographic information.

COMPETENCY 6.2   GEOGRAPHIC DIVERSITY OF NATURAL LANDSCAPES AND HUMAN SOCIETIES

Skill 6.2a   Analyze how unique ecologic settings are encouraged by various combinations of natural and social phenomena, including bio-geographic relationships with climate, soil, and terrain.

Ecology is the study of how living organisms interact with the physical aspects of their environment, including soil, water, air, and other living things. **Biogeography** is the study of how the surface features of the earth (form, movement, and climate) affect living things.

Three levels of environmental understanding are critical

1. An **ecosystem** is a community (of any size) consisting of a physical environment and the organisms that live within it.

2. A **biome** is a large area of land with characteristic climate, soil, and mixture of plants and animals. Biomes are made up of groups of ecosystems. Major biomes are: desert, chaparral, savanna, tropical rain forest, temperate grassland, temperate deciduous forest, taiga, and tundra.

3. A **habitat** is the set of surroundings where members of a species normally live. Elements of the habitat include soil, water, predators, and competitors.

Within habitats interactions between members of the species occur. These interactions occur between members of the same species and between members of different species. Interaction tends to be of three types: competition, predation, and symbiosis.

Competition occurs between members of the same species or between members of different species for resources required to continue life, to grow, or to reproduce. For example, competition for acorns can occur between squirrels or it can occur between squirrels and woodpeckers. One species can either push out or cause the demise of another species if it is better adapted to obtain the resource. When a new species is introduced into a habitat, the result can be a loss of the native species and/or significant change to the habitat. For example, the introduction of the Asian plant Kudzu to the American South, has resulted in the destruction of several species because Kudzu grows and spreads very quickly and smothers everything in its path.

Predation occurs when one animal feeds upon another. Predators are organisms that live by hunting and eating other organisms. The species best suited for hunting other species in the habitat will be the species that survives. Larger species that have better hunting skills reduce the amount of prey available for smaller and/or weaker species. This affects both the amount of available prey and the diversity of species that are able to survive in the habitat.

Symbiosis is a condition in which two organisms of different species are able to live in the same environment over an extended period of time without harming one another. In some cases one species may benefit without harming the other. In other cases both species benefit.

Different organisms are by nature best suited for existence in particular environments. When an organism is displaced to a different environment or when the environment changes for some reason, its ability to survive is determined by its ability to adapt to the new environment. **Adaptation** can take the form of structural change, physiological change, or behavior modification.

Biodiversity refers to the variety of species and organisms, as well as the variety of habitats available on the earth. Biodiversity provides the life-support system for the various habitats and species. The greater the degree of biodiversity, the more species and habitats will continue to survive.

When human and other population and migration changes, climate changes, or natural disasters disrupt the delicate balance of a habitat or an ecosystem, species either adapt or become extinct.

Natural changes can occur that alter habitats such as floods, volcanoes, storms, earthquakes. These changes can affect the species that exist within the habitat, either by causing extinction or by changing the environment in a way that will no longer support the life systems. Climate changes can have similar effects. Inhabiting species, however, can also alter habitats, particularly through migration. Human civilization, population growth, and efforts to control the environment can have many negative effects on various habitats. Humans change their environments to suit their particular needs and interests. This can result in changes that result in the extinction of species or changes to the habitat itself. For example, deforestation damages the stability of mountain surfaces. One particularly devastating example is in the removal of the grasses of the Great Plains for agriculture. Tilling the ground and planting crops left the soil unprotected. Sustained drought dried out the soil into dust. When wind storms occurred, the topsoil was stripped away and blown all the way to the Atlantic Ocean.

Skill 6.2b   **Analyze the patterns and networks of economic interdependence across the earth's surface during the agricultural, industrial, and post-industrial revolutions, including the production and processing of raw materials, marketing, consumption, transportation, and other measures of economic development.**

The **Agricultural Revolution**, initiated by the invention of the plow, led to a transformation of human society by making large-scale agricultural production possible. During the period during which the plow was invented, the wheel, numbers, and writing were also invented. Coinciding with the shift from hunting wild game to the domestication of animals, this period was one of dramatic social and economic change.

Numerous changes in lifestyle and thinking accompanied the development of stable agricultural communities. Rather than gathering a wide variety of plants as hunter-gatherers, agricultural communities become dependent on a limited number of plants or crops that are harvested. Subsistence becomes vulnerable to the weather and dependent upon planting and harvesting times.

Agriculture also required a great deal of physical labor and the development of a sense of discipline. Agricultural communities become sedentary or stable in terms of location. This makes the construction of dwellings appropriate. These tend to be built relatively close together, creating villages or towns.

Stable communities free people from the need to carry everything with them. This facilitates the invention of larger, more complex tools. As new tools are envisioned and developed it begins to make sense to have some specialization within the society. Skills begin to have greater value, and people begin to do work on behalf of the community that utilizes their particular skills and abilities. Settled community life also gives rise to the notion of wealth. It is now possible to keep possessions.

In the beginning of the transition to agriculture, the tools that were used for hunting and gathering were adequate to the tasks of agriculture. The initial challenge was in adapting to a new way of life. Once that challenge was met, attention turned to the development of more advanced tools and sources of energy. Six thousand years ago the first plow was invented in Mesopotamia. This plow was pulled by animals. Agriculture was then possible on a much larger scale. Soon tools were developed that make such basic tasks as gathering seeds, planting, and cutting grain faster and easier.

It became necessary to maintain social and political stability to ensure that planting and harvesting times were not interrupted by internal discord or a war with a neighboring community. It also was necessary to develop ways to store the crop and prevent its destruction by the elements, animals, and thieves.

Settled communities that produce the necessities of life are self-supporting. Advances in agricultural technology and the ability to produce a surplus of produce create two opportunities: first, the opportunity to trade the surplus goods for other desired goods, and second, the vulnerability to others who steal to take those goods. Protecting domesticated livestock and surplus, as well as stored, crops become an issue for the community. This, in turn, leads to the construction of walls and other fortifications around the community.

The ability to produce surplus crops creates the opportunity to trade or barter with other communities in exchange for desired goods. Traders begin to develop trade routes between villages and cities. The domestication of animals expands the range of trade and facilitates an exchange of ideas and knowledge.

The **Industrial Revolution** of the eighteenth and nineteenth centuries resulted in changes in human civilization and greater opportunities for trade, increased production, and the exchange of ideas and knowledge.

The first phase of the Industrial Revolution (1750–1830) saw the mechanization of the textile industry, vast improvements in mining, the steam engine, the development and improvement of turnpikes, canals, and the railroad.

The second phase (1830–1910) resulted in vast improvements in a number of industries that had already been mechanized through such inventions as the Bessemer steel process and the invention of steam ships. New industries, such as photography, electricity, and chemical processes, arose as a result of the new technological advances. New sources of power were harnessed and applied, including petroleum and hydroelectric power. Precision instruments were developed and engineering was launched. It was during this second phase that the Industrial Revolution spread to other European countries, Japan, and the United States.

The direct results of the industrial revolution, particularly as they affected industry, commerce, and agriculture, included

- Enormous increases in productivity
- Huge increases in world trade
- Specialization and division of labor
- Standardization of parts and mass production
- Growth of giant business conglomerates and monopolies
- A new revolution in agriculture facilitated by the steam engine, machinery, chemical fertilizers, processing, canning, and refrigeration

The political results included

- Growth of complex government by technical experts
- Centralization of government, including regulatory administrative agencies

- Advantages to democratic development, including extension of franchise to the middle class, and later to all elements of the population, mass education to meet the needs of an industrial society, the development of media of public communication, including radio, television, and cheap newspapers
- Dangers to democracy included the risk of manipulation of the media of mass communication, facilitation of dictatorial centralization and totalitarian control, subordination of the legislative function to administrative directives, efforts to achieve uniformity and conformity, and social impersonalization.

The economic results were numerous

- The conflict between free trade and low tariffs and protectionism
- The issue of free enterprise against government regulation
- Struggles between labor and capital, including the trade-union movement
- The rise of socialism
- The rise of the utopian socialists
- The rise of Marxian or scientific socialism

The social results of the Industrial Revolution include

- Increase of population, especially in industrial centers
- Advances in science applied to agriculture, sanitation and medicine
- Growth of great cities
- Disappearance of the difference between city dwellers and farmers
- Faster tempo of life and increased stress from the monotony of the work routine
- The emancipation of women
- The decline of religion
- Rise of scientific materialism
- Darwin's theory of evolution

Increased mobility produced a rapid diffusion of knowledge and ideas. Increased mobility also resulted in wide-scale immigration to industrialized countries. Cultures clashed and cultures melded.

Skill 6.2c   Describe the processes, patterns, and functions of human settlements from subsistence agriculture to industrial metropolis.

Human communities subsisted initially as **gatherers**—gathering berries, leaves, etc. With the invention of tools it became possible to dig for roots, hunt small animals, and catch fish from rivers and oceans. Humans observed their environments and soon learned to plant seeds and harvest crops. As people migrated to areas in which game and fertile soil were abundant, communities began to develop. When people had the knowledge to grow crops and the skills to hunt game, they began to understand division of labor. Some of the people in the community tended to agricultural needs while others hunted game.

As habitats attracted larger numbers of people, environments became crowded and there was competition. The concept of division of labor and sharing of food soon developed in more heavily populated areas. Groups of people focused on growing crops while others concentrated on hunting. Experience led to the development of skills and of knowledge that made the work easier. Farmers began to develop new plant species and hunters began to protect animal species from other predators for their own use. This ability to manage the environment led people to settle down, guard and manage their resources.

Camps soon became villages. Villages became year-round settlements. Animals were domesticated to meet the needs of the village. **Pottery** was developed for storing and cooking food.

By 8000 BCE, culture began to evolve in these villages. Agriculture was developed for the production of grain crops, which led to a decreased reliance on wild plants. Domesticating animals for various purposes decreased the need to hunt wild game. Life became more settled. It was then possible to turn attention to such matters as managing water supplies, producing tools, making cloth, etc. There were both social interaction and the opportunity to reflect upon existence. Mythologies and religions began.

Two things seem to have come together to produce cultures and civilizations: agriculture and the development of centers of the community with literate social and religious structures. The members of these hierarchies then managed water supply and irrigation, religious life, and exerted their own right to use a portion of the goods produced by the community for their own subsistence in return for their management.

As trade routes developed and travel between cities became easier, trade led to specialization. This, in turn, leads to increased attention to refinements of technique and the sharing of ideas. The knowledge of a new discovery or invention provides knowledge and technology that increases the ability to produce goods for trade.

As each community learns the value of the goods it produces and improves its ability to produce the goods in greater quantity, industry is born.

Skill 6.2d **Analyze the forces of cooperation and conflict among peoples and societies that influence the division and control of the earth's surface (e.g., boundaries and frontiers, the control of resources, centripetal vs. centrifugal forces, spheres of influence).**

Competition for control of areas of the earth's surface is a common trait of human interaction. Societies and groups have sought control for a variety of reasons including religion, economics, politics and administration. Numerous wars have been fought for the control of territory for each of these reasons.

At the same time, groups of people, even societies, have peacefully worked together to establish boundaries around regions or territories that served specific purposes in order to sustain the activities that support life and social organization.

Individuals and societies have divided the earth's surface through conflict for a number of reasons

- The domination of peoples or societies, e.g., colonialism
- The control of valuable resources, e.g., oil
- The control of strategic routes, e.g., the Panama Canal

Conflicts can be spurred by religion, political ideology, national origin, language, or race. Conflicts result from disagreement over how land, ocean or natural resources will be developed, shared, and used and from trade, migration, and settlement rights. They can occur between small groups of people, between cities, between nations, between religious groups, and between multinational alliances.

Today, the world is primarily divided by political/administrative interests into state sovereignties. A particular region is recognized to be controlled by a particular government, including its territory, population and natural resources. The only area of the earth's surface that today is not defined by state or national sovereignty is Antarctica.

Alliances are developed among nations on the basis of political philosophy, economic concerns, cultural similarities, religious interests, or for military defense. Some of the most notable alliances today are

- The United Nations
- The North Atlantic Treaty Organization
- The Caribbean Community
- The Council of Arab Economic Unity
- The European Union

Large companies and multinational corporations also compete for control of natural resources for manufacturing, development, and distribution.

Throughout human history there have been conflicts over the right to divide the Earth according to differing perceptions, needs and values. These conflicts have ranged from tribal conflicts to world wars. While these conflicts have traditionally centered on control of land surfaces, new disputes are beginning to arise over the resources of the oceans and space. Nations will develop **spheres of interest**. Spheres of interest are geographical areas over which a country exerts political or economic influence.

On smaller scales, conflicts have created divisions between rival gangs, use zones in cities, water supply, school districts while economic divisions include franchise areas and trade zones.

COMPETENCY 6.3   CULTURE AND THE PHYSICAL ENVIRONMENT

Skill 6.3a   Describe and analyze ways in which human societies and settlement patterns develop in response to the physical environment, and explain the social, political, economic, and physical processes that have resulted in today's urban and rural landscapes.

By nature, people are essentially social creatures. They generally live in communities or settlements of some kind and of some size. Settlements are the cradles of culture, political structure, education, and the management of resources. The relative placement of these settlements or communities are shaped by the proximity to natural resources, the movement of raw materials, the production of finished products, the availability of a work force, and the delivery of finished products. The composition of communities will, at least to some extent, be determined by shared values, language, culture, religion, and subsistence.

Settlements begin in areas that offer the natural resources to support life—food and water. With the ability to manage the environment one finds a concentration of populations. With the ability to transport raw materials and finished products, comes mobility. With increasing technology and the rise of industrial centers, comes a migration of the workforce.

Cities are the major hubs of human settlement. Almost half of the population of the world now lives in cities. These percentages are much higher in developed regions. Established cities continue to grow. The fastest growth, however, is occurring in developing areas. In some regions there are **metropolitan areas** made up of urban and sub-urban areas. In some places cities and urban areas have become interconnected into **megalopoli** (e.g., Tokyo-Kawasaki-Yokohama).

The concentrations of populations and the divisions of these areas among various groups that constitute the cities can differ significantly. North American cities are different from European cities in terms of shape, size, population density, and modes of transportation. While in North America, the wealthiest economic groups tend to live outside the cities, the opposite is true in Latin American cities.

There are significant differences among the cities of the world in terms of connectedness to other cities. While European and North American cities tend to be well linked both by transportation and communication connections, there are other places in the world in which communication between the cities of the country may be inferior to communication with the rest of the world.

Rural areas tend to be less densely populated due to the needs of agriculture. More land is needed to produce crops or for animal husbandry than for manufacturing, especially in a city in which the buildings tend to be taller. Rural areas, however, must be connected via communication and transportation in order to provide food and raw materials to urban areas.

Skill 6.3b   Recognize the interrelationship of environmental and social policy.

The purpose and aim of social policy is to **improve human welfare** and to **meet basic human** needs within the society. **Social policy** addresses basic human needs for the sustainability of the individual and the society. The concerns of social policy include food, clean water, shelter, clothing, education, health, and social security. Social policy is part of **public policy**, determined by the city, the state, the nation, or the multinational organization responsible for human welfare in a particular region.

Environmental policy is concerned with the sustainability of the earth, the region under the administration of the governing group or individual or a local habitat. The concern of environmental policy is the preservation of the region, habitat or ecosystem.

Because humans, both individually and communally, rely upon the environment to sustain human life, social and environmental policy must be mutually sustainable.

If modern societies act without regard for the sustainability of the earth, it will become impossible for the earth to sustain human existence. Environmental policies must recognize that the planet is the home of humans and other species.

For centuries, social policies, economic policies, and political policies have ignored the impact of human existence and human civilization upon the environment. Human civilization has disrupted the ecological balance, contributed to the extinction of animal and plant species, and destroyed ecosystems through uncontrolled harvesting.

In an age of global warming, unprecedented demand upon natural resources, and a shrinking planet, social and environmental policies must become increasingly interdependent if the planet is to continue to support life and human civilization.

Bibliography

Adams, James Truslow. (2006). "The March of Democracy," Vol 1. "The Rise of the Union". New York: Charles Scribner's Sons, Publisher.

Barbini, John & Warshaw, Steven. (2006). "The World Past and Present." New York: Harcourt, Brace, Jovanovich, Publishers.

Berthon, Simon & Robinson, Andrew. (2006. "The Shape of the World." Chicago: Rand McNally, Publisher.

Bice, David A. (2006). "A Panorama of Florida II". (Second Edition). Marceline, Missouri: Walsworth Publishing Co., Inc.

Bram, Leon (Vice-President and Editorial Director). (2006). "Funk and Wagnalls New Encyclopedia." United States of America.

Burns, Edward McNall & Ralph, Philip Lee. (2006. "World Civilizations Their History and Culture" (5th ed.). New York: W.W. Norton & Company, Inc., Publishers.

Dauben, Joseph W. (2006). "The World Book Encyclopedia." Chicago: World Book Inc. A Scott Fetzer Company, Publisher.

De Blij, H.J. & Muller, Peter O. (2006). "Geography Regions and Concepts" (Sixth Edition). New York: John Wiley & Sons, Inc., Publisher.

Encyclopedia Americana. (2006). Danbury, Connecticut: Grolier Inc, Publisher.

Heigh, Christopher (Editor). (2006). "The Cambridge Historical Encyclopedia of Great Britain and Ireland." Cambridge: Cambridge University Press, Publisher.

Hunkins, Francis P. & Armstrong, David G. (2006). "World Geography People and Places." Columbus, Ohio: Charles E. Merrill Publishing Co. A Bell & Howell Company, Publishers.

Jarolimek, John; Anderson, J. Hubert & Durand, Loyal, Jr. (2006). "World Neighbors." New York: Macmillan Publishing Company. London: Collier Macmillan Publishers.

John Lewis; Archie E. Allen. (1972). "Black Voter Registration Efforts in the South", Notre Dame L. Rev. 105

McConnell, Campbell R. (2006). "Economics-Principles, Problems, and Policies" (Tenth Edition). New York: McGraw-Hill Book Company, Publisher.

Millard, Dr. Anne & Vanags, Patricia. (2006). "The Usborne Book of World History." London: Usborne Publishing Ltd., Publisher.

Novosad, Charles (Executive Editor). (2006). "The Nystrom Desk Atlas." Chicago:
Nystrom Division of Herff Jones, Inc., Publisher.

Patton, Clyde P.; Rengert, Arlene C.; Saveland, Robert N.; Cooper, Kenneth S. & Cam, Patricia T. (2006). "A World View." Morristown, N.J.: Silver Burdette Companion, Publisher.

Schwartz, Melvin & O'Connor, John R. (2006). "Exploring A Changing World." New York: Globe Book Company, Publisher.

"The Annals of America: Selected Readings on Great Issues in American History 1620-1968." (2006). United States of America: William Benton, Publisher.

Tindall, George Brown & Shi, David E. (2006). "America-A Narrative History" (Fourth Edition). New York: W.W. Norton & Company, Publisher.

Todd, Lewis Paul & Curti, Merle. (2006). "Rise of the American Nation" (Third Edition). New York: Harcourt, Brace, Jovanovich, Inc., Publishers.

Tyler, Jenny; Watts, Lisa; Bowyer, Carol; Trundle, Roma & Warrender, Annabelle (2006) 'The Usbome Book of World Geography." London: Usbome Publishing Ltd., Publisher.

United States, Congress. (2017). "America's Wars Fact Sheet." Veteran's Affairs,

Willson, David H. (2006). "A History of England." Hinsdale, Illinois: The Dryder Press,   inc.,   Publisher

Sample Test

1. **The Fertile Crescent was not bounded by:**
(Rigorous) (Skill 1.1b)

   A. Mediterranean Sea
   B. Arabian Desert
   C. Taurus Mountains
   D. Ural Mountains

2. **Which ancient civilization is credited with being the first to develop irrigation techniques through the use of canals, dikes, and devices for raising water?**
(Rigorous) (Skill 1.1c)

   A. The Sumerians
   B. The Egyptians
   C. The Babylonians
   D. The Akkadians

3. **The study of past human cultures based on physical artifacts is:**
(Easy) (Skill 1.1a)

   A. History
   B. Anthropology
   C. Cultural Geography
   D. Archaeology

4. **Development of a solar calendar, invention of the decimal system, and contributions to the development of geometry and astronomy are all the legacy of:**
(Rigorous) (Skill 1.1c)

   A. The Babylonians
   B. The Persians
   C. The Sumerians
   D. The Egyptians

5. **The world religion which includes a caste system is:**
(Average) (Skill 1.1e)

   A. Buddhism
   B. Hinduism
   C. Sikhism
   D. Jainism

6. **An early cultural group was so skillful in navigating on the seas that they were able to sail at night guided by stars. They were the:**
(Rigorous) (Skill 1.1c)

   A. Greeks
   B. Persians
   C. Minoans
   D. Phoenicians

7. **Which of the following is an example of a direct democracy?**
    (Average) (Skill 1.1c)

    A. Elected representatives
    B. Greek city-states
    C. The United States Senate
    D. The United States House of Representative

8. **The Roman Empire gave so much to the world, especially the Western world. Of the legacies below, the most influential, effective and lasting is:**
    (Rigorous) (Skill 1.1c)

    A. The language of Latin
    B. Roman law, justice, and political system
    C. Engineering and building
    D. The writings of its poets an historians

9. **Charlemagne's most important influence on Western civilization is seen today in:**
    (Rigorous) (Skill 1.1f)

    A. Respect for and encouragement of learning
    B. Strong military for defense
    C. The criminal justice system
    D. Cruel dictatorship

10. **The study of a people's culture would be part of all of the following except:**
    (Average) (Skill 1.1a)

    A. Science
    B. Archaeology
    C. History
    D. Anthropology

11. **"Participant observation" is a method of study most closely associated with and used in:**
    (Average) (Skill 1.1a)

    A. Anthropology
    B. Archaeology
    C. Sociology
    D. Political Science

12. **The principle of zero in mathematics is the discovery of the ancient civilization found in:**
    (Rigorous) (Skill 1.1c)

    A. Egypt
    B. Persia
    C. India
    D. Babylon

13. **The early ancient civilizations developed systems of government:** *(Average) (Skill 1.1c)*

A. To provide for defense against attack
B. To regulate trade
C. To regulate and direct the economic activities of the people as they worked together in groups
D. To decide on the boundaries of the different fields during planting seasons

14. **The end to hunting, gathering, and fishing of prehistoric people was due to:** *(Easy) (Skill 1.1b)*

A. Domestication of animals
B. Building crude huts and houses
C. Development of agriculture
D. Organized government in villages

15. **Bathtubs, hot and cold running water, and sewage systems with flush toilets were developed by the:** *(Rigorous) (Skill 1.1c)*

A. Minoans
B. Mycenaeans
C. Phoenicians
D. Greeks

16. **The chemical process of radiocarbon dating would be most useful and beneficial in the field of:** *(Easy) (Skill 1.1a)*

A. Archaeology
B. Geography
C. Sociology
D. Anthropology

17. **The first ancient civilization to introduce and practice monotheism was the:** *(Average) (Skill 1.1d)*

A. Sumerians
B. Minoans
C. Phoenicians
D. Hebrews

18. **Native South American tribes included all of the following except:** *(Easy) (Skill 1.1c)*

A. Aztec
B. Inca
C. Minoans
D. Maya

19. **An ancient Indian civilization known for its worshipping of the dead was the:** *(Rigorous) (Skill 1.2g)*

A. The Mayans
B. The Atacamas
C. The Incas
D. The Tarapacas

20. The belief that man was rationale and capable of creative thought was a philosophy of:
(Rigorous) (Skill 1.2k)

A. Rousseau
B. Immanuel Kant
C. Montesquieu
D. John Locke

21. Which one of the following did not contribute to the early medieval European civilization?
(Rigorous) (Skill 1.2b)

A. The heritage from the classical cultures
B. The Christian religion
C. The influence of the German Barbarians
D. The spread of ideas through trade and commerce

22. All of the following are accomplishments of the Renaissance except:
(Average) (Skill 1.2i)

A. Investment of the printing press
B. A rekindling of interest in the learning of classical Greece and Rome
C. Growth in literature, philosophy and art
D. Better military tactics

23. Who is the most important figure in the spread of Protestantism across Switzerland?
(Average) (Skill 1.2j)

A. Calvin
B. Zwingli
C. Munzer
D. Leyden

24. What was China's last imperial ruling dynasty who made an outstanding impression on Western nations?
(Rigorous) (Skill 1.2h)

A. Min
B. Manchu
C. Han
D. Chou

25. The ideas and innovations of the period of the Renaissance were spread throughout Europe mainly by:
(Average) (Skill 1.2i)

A. Extensive exploration
B. Craft workers and their guilds
C The invention of the printing press
D. Increased travel and trade

26. **India's greatest ruler is considered to be:** *(Rigorous) (Skill 1.2h)*

    A. Akbar
    B. Asoka
    C. Babur
    D. Jahan

27. **The "father of anatomy" is considered to be:** *(Rigorous) (Skill 1.2i)*

    A. Vesalius
    B. Servetus
    C. Galen
    D. Harvey

28. **The changing focus during the Renaissance when artists and scholars were less concerned with religion but centered their efforts on a better understanding of people and the world was called:** *(Average) (Skill 1.2i)*

    A. Realism
    B. Humanism
    C. Individualism
    D. Intellectualism

29. **Which one of the following is not an important legacy of the Byzantine Empire?** *(Rigorous) (Skill 1.2b)*

    A. It protected Western Europe from various attacks from the East by such groups as the Persians, Ottoman Turks, and Barbarians
    B. It played a part in preserving the literature, philosophy, and language of ancient Greece
    C. Its military organization was the foundation for modern armies
    D. It kept the legal traditions of Roman government, collecting and organizing many ancient Roman laws

30. **Studies in astronomy, skills in mapping, and other contributions to geographic knowledge came from:** *(Rigorous) (Skill 1.2i)*

    A. Galileo
    B. Columbus
    C. Eratosthenes
    D. Ptolemy

31. **The major force in eighteenth and nineteenth century politics was:** *(Average) (Skill 1.3e)*

    A. Nationalism
    B. Revolution
    C. War
    D. Diplomacy

32. The Age of Exploration begun in the 1400s was led by: *(Average) (Skill 1.3a)*

  A. The Portuguese
  B. The Spanish
  C. The English
  D. The Dutch

33. The English explorer who gave England its claim to North American was: *(Average) (Skill 1.3a)*

  A. Raleigh
  B. Hawkins
  C. Drake
  D. Cabot

34. Marxism believes which two groups are in continual conflict? *(Rigorous) (Skill 1.3i)*

  A. Farmers and landowners
  B. Kings and the nobility
  C. Workers and owners
  D. Structure and superstructure

35. Which one of the following would not be considered a result of World War II? *(Average) (Skill 1.3j)*

  A. Economic depressions and slow resumption of trade and financial aid
  B. Western Europe was no longer the center of world power
  C. The beginnings of new power struggles not only in Europe but in Asia as well
  D. Territorial and boundary changes for many nations, especially in Europe

36. The first European to see Florida and sail along its coast was: *(Rigorous) (Skill 1.3a)*

  A. Cabot
  B. Columbus
  C. Ponce de Leon
  D. Narvaez

37. A political philosophy favoring or supporting rapid social changes in order to correct social and economic inequalities is called: *(Average) (Skill 1.3e)*

  A. Nationalism
  B. Liberalism
  C. Conservatism
  D. Federalism

38. The results of the Renaissance, Enlightenment, Commercial and Industrial Revolutions were more unfortunate for the people of: *(Average) (Skill 1.3c)*

   A. Asia
   B. Latin America
   C. Africa
   D. Middle East

39. Colonial expansion by Western European powers in the 18th and 19th centuries was due primarily to: *(Average) (Skill 1.3d)*

   A. Building and opening the Suez Canal
   B. The Industrial Revolution
   C. Marked improvements in transportation
   D. Complete independence of all the Americas and loss of European domination and influence

40. Which of the following is not a reason why Europeans came to the New World? *(Average)(Skill 1.3)*

   A. To find resources in order to increase wealth
   B. To establish trade
   C. To increase a ruler's power and importance
   D. To spread Christianity

41. The only colony not founded and settled for religious, political or business reasons was: *(Average) (Skill 2.1c)*

   A. Delaware
   B. Virginia
   C. Georgia
   D. New York

42. What country did not have a colonial stake in America? *(Easy) (Skills 2.1b & 3.1b)*

   A. France
   B. Spain
   C. Mexico
   D. China

43. The year 1619 was a memorable for the colony of Virginia. Three important events occurred resulting in lasting effects on US history. Which one of the following is not one of the events?
(Rigorous) (Skill 2.1c)

A. Twenty African slaves arrived.
B. The London Company granted the colony a charter making it independent.
C. The colonists were given the right by the London Company to govern themselves through representative government in the Virginia House of Burgesses
D. The London Company sent to the colony 60 women who were quickly married, establishing families and stability in the colony.

44. The foundation of modern democracy is embodied in the ideas of:
(Rigorous) (Skill 2.2a)

A. St. Thomas Aquinas
B. Rousseau
C. John Locke
D. Montesquieu

45. France decided in 1777 to help the American colonies in their war against Britain. This decision was based on: (Rigorous) (Skill 2.2a)

A. The naval victory of John Paul Jones over the British ship "Serapis"
B. The survival of the terrible winter at Valley Forge
C. The success of colonial guerilla fighters in the South
D. The defeat of the British at Saratoga

46. The source of authority for national, state, and local governments in the US is:
(Average) (Skill 2.2a)

A. The will of the people
B. The US Constitution
C. Written laws
D. The Bill of Rights

47. Under the brand-new Constitution, the most urgent of the many problems facing the new federal government was that of:
(Easy) (Skills 2.2 a & b)

A. Maintaining a strong army and navy
B. Establishing a strong foreign policy
C. Raising money to pay salaries and war debts
D. Setting up courts, passing federal laws, and providing for law enforcement officers

48. **The principle of "popular sovereignty" allowing people in any territory to make their own decision concerning slavery was stated by;**
(Rigorous) (Skill 2.3h)

A. Henry Clay
B. Daniel Webster
C. John C. Calhoun
D. Stephen A. Douglas

49. **As a result of the Missouri Compromise:**
(Rigorous) (Skill 2.3h)

A. Slavery was not allowed in the Louisiana Purchase
B. The Louisiana Purchase was nullified
C. Louisiana separated from the Union
D. The Embargo Act was repealed

50. **Pre-Civil War American policy did not include:**
(Easy) (Skill 2.3c)

A. Isolationism
B. Imperialism
C. Nationalism
D. No entangling alliances

51. **Leaders in the movement for woman's rights have included all but:**
(Rigorous) (Skill 2.3i)

A. Elizabeth Cady Stanton
B. Lucretia Borgia
C. Susan B. Anthony
D. Lucretia Mott

52. **The Federalists:**
(Rigorous) (Skill 2.3a)

A. Favored state's rights
B. Favored a weak central government
C. Favored a strong federal government
D. Supported the British

53. **The belief that the United States should control all of North America was called:**
(Easy) (Skill 2.3c)

A. Westward Expansion
B. Pan Americanism
C. Manifest Destiny
D. Nationalism

54. **The three-day Battle of Gettysburg was the turning point of the Civil War for the North leading to ultimate victory. The winning commander was:**
(Average) (Skill 2.4c)

A. McDowell
B. Lee
C. Jackson
D. McClellan

55. **The Radical Republicans who pushed the harsh Reconstruction measures through Congress after Lincoln's death lost public and moderate Republican support when they went too far:** *(Rigorous) (Skill 2.4d)*

A. In their efforts to impeach the President
B. By dividing ten southern states into military-controlled districts
C. By making the ten southern states give freed African Americans the right to vote
D. Sending carpetbaggers into the South to build up support for Congressional legislation

56. **Jim Crow refers to:** *(Average) (Skill 2.4f)*

A. Equality
B. Labor Movement
C. Racism
D. Free trade

57. **The Union had many strengths over the Confederacy. Which was not a strength?** *(Easy) (Skill 2.4b)*

A. Railroads
B. Industry
C. Slaves
D. Manpower

58. **It can be reasonably stated that the change in the United States from primarily an agricultural country into an industrial power was due to all of the following except:** *(Rigorous) (Skill 2.4d)*

A. Tariffs on foreign imports
B. Millions of hardworking immigrants
C. An increase in technological developments
D. The change from steam to electricity for powering industrial machinery

59. **The post-Civil War years were a time of low public morality, a time of greed, graft, and dishonesty. Which one of the reasons listed would not be accurate?** *(Rigorous) (Skill 2.5a)*

A. The war itself because of the money and materials needed to carry on the War
B. The very rapid growth of industry and big business after the War
C. The personal example set by President Grant
D. Unscrupulous heads of large impersonal corporations

60. **What was the impact of industrialization on the United States?** *(Easy) (Skill 2.5e)*

A. Decrease in population
B. Fewer jobs
C. Better transportation system
D. Decline in Infrastructure

61. **In the United States, federal investigations into deceptive business activities are handled by the:** *(Average) (Skill 2.5c)*

A. Department of Treasury
B. Security & Exchange Commission
C. Government Accounting Office
D. Federal Trade Commission

62. **After the Civil War, the US adapted an attitude of isolation from foreign affairs. But the turning point marking the beginning of the US becoming a world power was:** *(Rigorous) (Skill 2.6a)*

A. World War I
B. Expansion of business and trade overseas
C. The Spanish-American War
D. The building and financial of the Panama Canal

63. **During the 1920s, the United States almost completely stopped all immigration. One of the reasons was:** *(Rigorous) (Skill 2.7c)*

A. Plentiful cheap unskilled labor was no longer needed by industrialists
B. War debts from World War I made it difficult to render financial assistance
C. European nations were reluctant to allow people to leave since there was a need to rebuild populations and economic stability
D. The United States did not become a member of the League of Nations

64. **The term Red Scare refers to:** *(Average) (Skill 2.7a)*

A. The Halloween holiday
B. The fear of communists
C. Sun Spots
D. Labor strikes

65. **Drought is a problem in Africa and other places because:** *(Average) (Skill 2.8b)*

A. There is flooding
B. The rivers change course
C. People flock to see the drought
D. The dried-out soil turns to dust and cannot grow food

66. **Which of the following contributed to the severity of the Great Depression in California?**
(Rigorous) (Skill 2.8b)

A. An influx of Chinese immigrants
B. The dust bowl drove People out of the cities.
C. An influx of Mexican immigrants.
D. An influx of Oakies.

67. **The international organization established to work for world peace at the end of the Second World War is the:**
(Average) (Skill 2.9d)

A. League of Nations
B. United Federation of Nations
C. United Nations
D. United World League

68. **Which country was not a part of the Axis in World War II?** *(Easy) (Skill 2.9b)*

A. Germany
B. Italy
C. Japan
D. United States

69. **Of all the major causes of both World Wars I and II, the most significant one is considered to be:**
(Average) (Skill 2.9a)

A. Extreme nationalism
B. Military buildup and aggression
C. Political unrest
D. Agreements and alliances

70. **After World War II, the United States:**
(Average) (Skill 2.10b)

A. Limited its involvement in European affairs
B. Shifted foreign policy emphasis from Europe to Asia
C. Passed significant legislation pertaining to aid to farmers and tariffs on imports
D. Entered the greatest period of economic growth in its history

71. **A significant change in immigration policy occurred after World War II when the United States:**
(Average) (Skill 2.10a)

A. Eliminated restrictions
B. Prevented Japanese immigration
C. Imposed policies based on ethnicity and country of origin
D. Banned immigration

72. **Which country was a Cold War foe?** *(Easy) (Skill 2.11a)*

    A. Russia
    B. Brazil
    C. Canada
    D. Argentina

73. **Which one of the following was not a post-World War II organization?** *(Easy) (Skill 2.11b)*

    A. Monroe Doctrine
    B. Marshall Plan
    C. Warsaw Pact
    D. North Atlantic Treaty Organization

74. **Which of the following is not a name associated with the Civil Rights movement?** *(Rigorous) (Skill 2.12a)*

    A. Rosa Parks
    B. Emmett Till
    C. Tom Dewey
    D. Martin Luther King, Jr.

75. **During the period of Spanish colonialism, which of the following was not a key to the goal of exploiting, transforming and including the native people?** *(Rigorous) (Skill 3.1b)*

    A. Missions
    B. Ranchos
    C. Presidios
    D. Pueblos

76. **Native communities in early California are commonly divided into several cultural areas. How many cultural areas?** *(Rigorous) (Skill 3.1a)*

    A. 4
    B. 5
    C. 6
    D. 7

77. **From about 1870 to 1900 the settlement of America's "last frontier", the West, was completed. One attraction for settlers was free land but it would have been to no avail without:** *(Easy) (Skill 3.2b)*

    A. Better farming methods and technology
    B. Surveying to set boundaries
    C. Immigrants and others to seek new land
    D. The railroad to get them there

78. Historians state that the West helped to speed up the Industrial Revolution. Which one of the following statements was not a reason for this?
(Rigorous) (Skill 3.2a)

A. Food supplies for the ever increasing urban populations came from farms in the West
B. A tremendous supply of gold and silver from western mines provided the capital needed to build industries
C. Descendants of western settlers, educated as engineers, geologists, and metallurgists in the East, returned to the West to mine the mineral resources needed for industry
D. Iron, copper, and other minerals from western mines were important resources in manufacturing products

79. What event sparked a great migration of people from all over the world to California?
(Rigorous) (Skill 3.2a)

A. The birth of Labor Unions
B. California statehood
C. The invention of the automobile
D. The gold rush

80. Which of the following shows a difference between the California and U.S. Constitutions?
(Rigorous) (Skill 3.2c)

A. The governor of California has the pocket veto
B. In California representation in both houses of the legislature is based on population
C. The Governor and Lt. Governor are elected separately
D. The equivalent of cabinet positions are elected rather than appointed.

81. The United States legislature is bi-cameral, this means:
(Average) (Skill 3.2c)

A. It consists of several houses
B. It consists of two houses
C. The Vice-President is in charge of the legislature when in session
D. It has an upper and lower house

82. Who applied Locke's principles to the American situation?
(Rigorous) (Skill 4.1a)

A. Thomas Paine
B. Samuel Adams
C. Benjamin Franklin
D. Thomas Jefferson

83. **There is no doubt of the vast improvement of the US Constitution over the weak Articles of Confederation. Which one of the four accurate statements below is a unique yet eloquent description of the Constitution?**
(Rigorous) (Skill 4.1c)

A. The establishment of a strong central government in no way lessened or weakened the individual states.
B. Individual rights were protected and secured.
C. The Constitution is the best representation of the results of the American genius for compromise.
D. Its flexibility and adaptation to change gives it a sense of timelessness.

84. **Of the thirteen English colonies, the greatest degree of religious toleration was found in:**
(Easy) (Skill 4.2a)

A. Maryland
B. Rhode Island
C. Pennsylvania
D. Delaware

85. **The Pilgrims came to America to:**
(Average) (Skill 4.2a)

A. To drill for oil
B. To be the official representatives of the king
C. To take over the East India Company
D. To flee religious persecution

86. **The Constitution can:**
(Easy) (Skill 4.3d)

A. Never be changed
B. Be rewritten
C. Be discarded
D. Be amended

87. **In the United States, power or control over public education, marriage, and divorce is:**
(Average) (Skill 4.3e)

A. Implied or suggested
B. Concurrent or shared
C. Delegated or expressed
D. Reserved

88. **In the U.S., the power of coining money is:**
(Rigorous) (Skill 4.3a)

A. Implied or suggested
B. Concurrent or shared
C. Delegated or expressed
D. Reserved

89. **Which is not a branch of the federal government?**
(Easy) (Skill 4.3a)

A. Popular
B. Legislative
C. Executive
D. Judicial

90. **In the United States government, the power of taxation and borrowing is:**
(Average) (Skill 4.3a)

A. Implied or suggested
B. Concurrent or shared
C. Delegated or expressed
D. Reserved

91. **The term that best describes how the Supreme Court can block laws that may be unconstitutional from being enacted is:**
(Average) (Skill 4.4b)

A. Jurisprudence
B. Judicial Review
C. Exclusionary Rule
D. Right of Petition

92. **What Supreme Court ruling dealt with the issue of civil rights?**
(Rigorous) (Skill 4.4c)

A. Jefferson v. Madison
B. Lincoln v. Douglas
C. Dred Scott v. Sanford
D. Marbury v. Madison

93. **"Marbury v. Madison (1803)" was an important Supreme Court case which set the precedent for:**
(Average) (Skill 4.4b)

A. The elastic clause
B. Judicial review
C. The supreme law of the land
D. Popular sovereignty in the territories

94. **The Electoral College:**
(Average) (Skill 4.5c)

A. Elects the Senate but not the House
B. Elects the House but not the Senate
C. Elects both the House and Senate
D. Elects the President

95. **Which one of the following is not a function or responsibility of the U.S. political parties?**
(Easy) (Skill 4.5a)

A. Conducting elections or the voting process
B. Obtaining funds needed for election campaigns
C. Choosing candidates to run for public office
D. Making voters aware of issues and other public affairs information

96. On the spectrum of American politics, the label that most accurately describes voters to the "right of center" is: *(Average) (Skill 4.5d)*

   A. Moderates
   B. Liberals
   C. Conservatives
   D. Socialists

97. The study of the exercise of power and political behavior in human society today would be conducted by experts in: *(Easy) (Skill 4.6b)*

   A. History
   B. Sociology
   C. Political Science
   D. Anthropology

98. When referring to government, who said: "the good of the many outweighs the good of the few and also of the one"? *(Rigorous) (Skill 4.6b)*

   A. Plato
   B. Aristotle
   C. Cicero
   D. Gaius

99. The function of government is to provide for the welfare of the people is the philosophy of: *(Rigorous) (Skill 4.6B)*

   A. Aristotle
   B. John Locke
   C. Plato
   D. Thomas Hobbes

100. The significance of a free press does not include which of the following: *(Average) (Skill 4.7a)*

   A. Providing information
   B. Reporting illegal actions
   C. Libel
   D. Reporting in a responsible and civic-minded manner

101. A political system in which there is a one-party state, centralized control, and a repressive police system with private ownership is called: *(Average) (Skill 4.8a)*

   A. Communism
   B. Fascism
   C. Socialism
   D. Constitutional Monarchy

102. The "wall of separation between church and state' came from: *(Rigorous) (Skill 4.9a)*

   A. Aristotle
   B. Alexander Hamilton
   C. Thomas Jefferson
   D. Thomas Paine

103. The study of the ways in which different societies around the world deal with the problems of limited resources and unlimited needs and wants is in the area of: *(Easy) (Skill 5.1a)*

   A. Economics
   B. Sociology
   C. Anthropology
   D. Political Science

104. **A planned economy functions on the basis of:** *(Rigorous) (Skill 5.1d)*

A. Public ownership
B. Private ownership
C. Stockholder control
D. An elected management board

105. **Potential customers for any product or service are not only called consumers but can also be called:** *(Easy) (Skill 5.2a)*

A. Resources
B. Bases
C. Commodities
D. Markets

106. **In a market economy, markets function on the basis of:** *(Rigorous) (Skill 5.2a)*

A. Government control
B. Manipulation
C. Demand and Supply
D. Planning

107. **Competition leads to:** *(Rigorous) (Skill 5.2c)*

A. Fights
B. Waste
C. Overproduction
D. Efficient use of resources

108. **The economic system promoting individual ownership of land, capital, and businesses with minimal governmental regulations is called:** *(Average) (Skill 5.2h)*

A. Macro-economy
B. Micro-economy
C. Laissez-faire
D. Free enterprise & market economy

109. **Which of the following is not a tool of monetary policy?** *(Average) (Skill 5.3c)*

A. Open market operations
B. Changing the discount rate
C. Changing the exchange rate
D. Changing the reserve ratio

110. **The idea that increasing government spending would end depressions was:** *(Average) (Skill 5.3a)*

A. The basis of modern economics
B. Called Classical economics
C. Known as federalism
D. Called isolationism

111. **The programs such as Medicaid and Food Stamps are the responsibility of:** *(Easy) (Skill 5.3a)*

A. Federal government
B. Local government
C. State government
D. Communal government

112. **Unions were founded on the basis of the beliefs of:**
(Average) (Skill 5.4a)

   A. Thomas Robert Malthus
   B. John Stuart Mill
   C. Samuel Gompers
   D. John Maynard Keynes

113. **The American labor union movement started gaining new momentum:**
(Average) (Skill 5.4a)

   A. During the building of the railroads
   B. After 1865 with the growth of cities
   C. With the rise of industrial giants such as Carnegie and Vanderbilt
   D. During the war years of 1861-1865

114. **Gross Domestic Product is:**
(Average) (Skill 5.5a)

   A. A measure of well being
   B. A well-known social indicator
   C. A measure of a nation's output
   D. A measure of a nation's trade

115. **One method of trade restriction used by some nations is:**
(Average) (Skill 5.6b)

   A. Limited treaties
   B. Floating exchange rate
   C. Bill of exchange
   D. Import quotas

116. **The doctrine of comparative advantage explains:**
(Average) (Skill 5.6a)

   A. Why nations trade
   B. How to fight a war
   C. Time zones
   D. Political divisions

117. **Which one of the following does not affect climate?**
(Rigorous) (Skill 6.1a)

   A. Elevation or altitude
   B. Ocean currents
   C. Latitude
   D. Longitude

118. **Geography was first studied in an organized manner by:**
(Rigorous) (Skill 6.1)

   A. The Egyptians
   B. The Greeks
   C. The Romans
   D. The Arabs

119. **Meridians, or lines of longitude, not only help in pinpointing locations but are also used for:**
(Average) (Skill 6.1b)

   A. Measuring distance from the Poles
   B. Determining direction of ocean currents
   C. Determining the time around the world
   D. Measuring distance on the equator

120. **A famous canal is the:**
(Easy) (Skill 6.1a)

A. Pacific Canal
B. Arctic Canal
C. Panama Canal
D. Atlantic Canal

121. **In which of the following disciplines would the study of physical mapping, modern or ancient, and the plotting of points and boundaries be least useful?**
(Easy) (Skill 6.1a)

A. Sociology
B. Geography
C. Archaeology
D. History

122. **The study of "spatial relationships and interaction" would be done by people in the field of:**
(Easy) (Skill 6.1)

A. Political Science
B. Anthropology
C. Geography

D. Sociology

123. **The study of how living organisms interact is called:** *(Average) (Skill 6.2a)*

A. Ecology
B. Sociology
C. Anthropology
D. Political Science

124. **Which of the following is an organization or alliance for defense purposes?**
(Average) (Skill 6.2d)

A. North Atlantic Treaty Organization
B. The Common Market
C. The European Union
D. North American Free Trade Association

125. **What term does not describe a settlement in the physical and cultural sense?**
(Average) (Skill 6.3A)

A. Climate
B. Religion
C. Shared values
D. Shared language

Answer Key

1. D	41. C	81. B	121. A
2. A	42. D	82. D	122. C
3. D	43. B	83. C	123. A
4. D	44. C	84. B	124. A
5. B	45. D	85. D	125. A
6. D	46. A	86. D	
7. B	47. C	87. D	
8. B	48. D	88. C	
9. A	49. A	89. A	
10. A	50. B	90. B	
11. A	51. B	91. B	
12. C	52. C	92. C	
13. C	53. C	93. B	
14. C	54. B	94. D	
15. A	55. A	95. A	
16. A	56. C	96. C	
17. D	57. C	97. C	
18. C	58. A	98. B	
19. C	59. C	99. A	
20. B	60. C	100. C	
21. D	61. D	101. B	
22. D	62. C	102. C	
23. A	63. A	103. A	
24. B	64. B	104. A	
25. C	65. D	105. D	
26. A	66. D	106. C	
27. A	67. C	107. D	
28. B	68. D	108. D	
29. C	69. A	109. C	
30. D	70. D	110. A	
31. A	71. C	111. C	
32. A	72. A	112. C	
33. D	73. A	113. B	
34. C	74. C	114. A	
35. A	75. B	115. D	
36. C	76. C	116. A	
37. B	77. D	117. D	
38. C	78. C	118. B	
39. B	79. D	119. C	
40. B	80. A	120. C	

Rigor Table

	Easy %20	Average Rigor %40	Rigorous %40
Question	3, 14, 16, 18, 42, 47, 50, 53, 57, 60, 68, 72, 73, 77, 84, 86, 89, 95, 97, 103, 105, 111, 120, 121, 122	5, 7, 10, 11, 13, 17, 22, 23, 25, 28, 31, 32, 33, 35, 37, 38, 39, 40, 41, 46, 54, 56, 61, 64, 65, 67, 69, 70, 71, 81, 85, 87, 90, 91, 93, 94, 96, 100, 101, 108, 109, 110, 112, 113, 114, 115, 116, 119, 123, 124, 125	1, 2, 4, 6, 8, 9, 12, 15, 19, 20, 21, 24, 26, 27, 29, 30, 34, 36, 43, 44, 45, 48, 49, 51, 52, 55, 58, 59, 62, 63, 66, 74, 75, 76, 78, 79, 80, 82, 83, 88, 92, 98, 99, 102, 104, 106, 107, 117, 118

Rationales with Sample Questions

1. **The Fertile Crescent is not bound by:** *(Rigorous) (Skill 1.1b)*

    A. Mediterranean Sea
    B. Arabian Desert
    C. Taurus Mountains
    D. Ural Mountains

The correct answer is D. Ural Mountains
(A) Mediterranean Sea forms the Western border of the Fertile Crescent (B) the Arabian Desert is the Southern boundary and (C) the Taurus Mountains form the Northern boundary. (D) The Ural Mountains are farther north in Russia and form the border between Russia and Europe.

2. **Which ancient civilization is credited with being the first to develop irrigation techniques such as the use of canals, dikes, and devices for raising water?** *(Rigorous) (Skill 1.1c)*

    A. The Sumerians
    B. The Egyptians
    C. The Babylonians
    D. The Akkadians

The correct answer is A. The Sumerians
The ancient (A) Sumerians of the Fertile Crescent of Mesopotamia were the first to develop irrigation techniques. The (B) Egyptians practiced controlled irrigation but that was through the use of the Nile's predictable flooding schedule. The (C) Babylonians were noted more for their revolutionary systems of law than their irrigation systems.

3. **The study of past human cultures based on physical artifacts is:** *(Easy) (Skill 1.1a)*

    A. History
    B. Anthropology
    C. Cultural Geography
    D. Archaeology

The correct answer is D. Archaeology
Archaeology is the study of past human cultures based on physical artifacts such as fossils, carvings, paintings, and engraved writings.

4. **Development of a solar calendar, invention of the decimal system, and contributions to the development of geometry and astronomy are all legacies:** *(Rigorous) (Skill 1.1c)*

A. The Babylonians
B. The Persians
C. The Sumerians
D. The Egyptians

The correct answer is D. The Egyptians
The (A) Babylonians of ancient Mesopotamia flourished for a time under their great contribution of organized law and code, called Hammurabi's Code (1750 BCE), after the ruler Hammurabi. The fall of the Babylonians to the Persians in 539 BCE made way for the warrior-driver Persian Empire to expand from Pakistan to the Mediterranean Sea. The Sumerians of ancient Mesopotamia were most noted for their early advancements as one of the first civilizations and their contributions towards written language known as cuneiform. It was the (D) Egyptians who were the first true developers of a solar calendar, the decimal system, and made significant contributions to the development of geometry and astronomy.

5. **A world religion, which includes a caste system, is:** *(Average) (Skill 1.1e)*

A. Buddhism
B. Hinduism
C. Sikhism
D. Jainism

The correct answer is B. Hinduism
Buddhism, Sikhism, and Jainism all rose out of protest against Hinduism and its practices of sacrifice and the caste system. The caste system, in which people were born into castes, would determine their class for life including who they could marry, what jobs they could perform, and their overall quality of life.

6.   **An early cultural group was so skillful in navigating the sea that they were able to sail at night guided by stars. They were the:** *(Rigorous) (Skill 1.1c)*

    A. Greeks
    B. Persians
    C. Minoans
    D. Phoenicians

The correct answer is D. Phoenicians
Although the Greeks were quite able sailors, it was the Eastern Mediterranean culture of the Phoenicians that had first developed the astronomical skill of sailing at night with the stars as their guide. The Minoans were an advanced early civilization off the Greek coast on Crete more noted for their innovations in terms of sewage systems, toilets, and running water.

7.   **Which of the following is an example of a direct democracy?** *(Average) (Skill 1.1c)*

    A. Elected representatives
    B. Greek city-states
    C. The Constitution
    D. The Confederate States

The correct answer is B. Greek city-states
The Greek city-states are an example of a direct democracy because the citizens themselves were given voice in government. (A) Elected representatives in the United States represent the citizens. The United States Congress, the Senate, and the House of Representatives are examples of indirect democracy as they represent the citizens in the legislature as opposed to citizens who represent themselves.

8.   **The Roman Empire gave so much to the Western world. Of the legacies below, the most influential, effective and lasting is: (Rigorous) (Skill 1.1c)**

A. The language of Latin
B. Roman law, justice, and political system
C. Engineering and building
D. The writings of its poets and historians

The correct answer is B. Roman law, justice, and political system
Of the lasting legacies of the Roman Empire, it is their law, justice, and political system that has been the most effective and influential on our Western world. Their legal justice system is also the foundation of our own. We still use many Latin words in our justice system, terms such as *habeas corpus* and *voir dire*. The Roman language, Latin itself has died out. Roman engineering and building and their writings and poetry have been influential but not nearly to the degree that their government and justice systems have been.

9.   **Charlemagne's most important influence on Western civilization is seen today in: (Rigorous) (Skill 1.1f)**

A. Respect for and encouragement of learning
B. Strong military for defense
C. The criminal justice system
D. Cruel dictatorship

The correct answer is A. Respect for and encouragement of learning
Charlemagne was the leader of the Germanic Franks who became head of the Holy Roman Empire. Although he unified governments and aided the Pope, he re-crowned himself in 802 A.D. to demonstrate that his power and right to rule was not a grant from the Pope, but rather a secular achievement. The Pope used Charlemagne to take the Church to new heights. Thus, Charlemagne had an influence on the issues between Church and state and was well-known for his respect of learning.

10.   **The study of a people's culture is not a part of all of:** *(Average) (Skill 1.1a)*

A. Science
B. Archaeology
C. History
D. Anthropology

The correct answer is A. Science
The study of a people's culture would be a part of studies in the disciplines of archaeology, (study of ancient artifacts including written works), history (the study of the past) and anthropology, the study of the relationship between man and his culture. Culture would be less important in science that is based on hard facts.

11.   **"Participant observation" is a method of study most closely associated with:** *(Average) (Skill 1.1a)*

A. Anthropology
B. Archaeology
C. Sociology
D. Political science

The correct answer is A. Anthropology
"Participant observation" is a method of study most closely associated with and used in (A) anthropology or the study of current human cultures. (B) Archaeologists typically the study of the remains of people, animals or other physical things. (C) Sociology is the study of human society and usually consists of surveys, controlled experiments, and field studies. (D) Political science is the study of political life including justice, freedom, power and equality in a variety of methods.

12.   **The principle of zero in mathematics is the discovery of the ancient civilization found in:** *(Rigorous) (Skill 1.1c)*

A. Egypt
B. Persia
C. India
D. Babylon

The correct answer is C. India
Although the Egyptians practiced algebra and geometry, the Persians developed an alphabet and the Babylonians developed Hammurabi's Code, which would come to be considered among the most important contributions of the Mesopotamian civilization. It was the Indians who created the idea of zero in mathematics changing drastically our ideas about numbers.

13. **The early ancient civilizations developed systems of government:** *(Average) (Skill 1.1c)*

   A. To provide for defense against attack
   B. To regulate trade
   C. To regulate and direct the economic activities of the people as they worked together in groups
   D. To decide on the boundaries of the different fields during planting seasons

The correct answer is C. To regulate and direct the economic activities of the people as they worked together in groups
Although ancient civilizations were concerned with defense, trade regulation, and the maintenance of boundaries in their fields, they could not have done any of them without first regulating and directing the economic activities of the people as they worked in groups. This provided for a stable economic base from which they could trade and actually had something worth defending.

14. **The end of hunting, gathering, and fishing by prehistoric people was due to:** *(Easy) (Skill 1.1b)*

   A. Domestication of animals
   B. Building crude huts and houses
   C. Development of agriculture
   D. Organized government in villages

The correct answer is C. Development of agriculture
Although the domestication of animals, the building of huts and houses and the first organized governments were all very important steps made by early civilizations, it was the development of agriculture that ended the once dominant practices of hunting, gathering, and fishing among prehistoric people. The development of agriculture provided a more efficient use of time and for the first time a surplus of food. This greatly improved the quality of life and contributed to early population growth.

15. **Bathtubs, hot and cold running water, and sewage systems with flush toilets were developed by the:** *(Rigorous) (Skill 1.1c)*

    A. Minoans
    B. Mycenaeans
    C. Phoenicians
    D. Greeks

The correct answer is A. Minoans
The (A) Minoans were one of the earliest Greek cultures and existed on the island of Crete and flourished from about 1600 BCE to about 1400 BCE. During this time, the (B) Mycenaean were flourishing on the mainland of what is now Greece. However, it was the Minoans on Crete who are best known for their advanced ancient civilization in which such advances as bathtubs, hot and cold running water, sewage systems and flush toilets were developed. The (C) Phoenicians also flourished around 1250 BCE but their primary development was in language and arts. The Phoenicians created an alphabet that has considerable influence in the world today. The great developments of the (D) Greeks were primarily in the fields of philosophy, political science, and early ideas of democracy.

16. **The chemical process of radiocarbon dating would be most useful to the field of:** *(Easy) (Skill 1.1a)*

    A. Archeology
    B. Geography
    C. Sociology
    D. Anthropology

The correct answer is A. Archeology
Radiocarbon dating is a chemical process that helps generate a more accurate method for dating artifacts and remains by measuring the radioactive materials present in them today and calculating how long it takes for certain materials to decay. Since geographers mainly study locations and special properties of earth's living things and physical features, sociologists mostly study human society and social conditions and anthropologists generally study human culture and humanity, the answer is archeology because archeologists study past human cultures by studying their remains.

17. **The first ancient civilization to introduce and practice monotheism was the:** *(Average) (Skill 1.1d)*

   A. Sumerians
   B. Minoans
   C. Phoenicians
   D. Hebrews

The correct answer is D. Hebrews
The (A) Sumerians and (C) Phoenicians both practiced religions in which many gods and goddesses were worshipped. Often these gods/goddesses were based on a feature of nature such as a sun, moon, weather, rocks, water, etc. The (B) Minoan culture shared many religious practices with the Ancient Egyptians. The king was somewhat of a god figure and the queen, a goddess. Much of the Minoan art points to worship of multiple gods. Therefore, only the (D) Hebrews introduced and fully practiced monotheism, or the belief in one God.

18. **Native South American tribes included all of the following except:** *(Easy) (Skill 1.1c)*

   A. Aztec
   B. Inca
   C. Minoans
   D. Maya

The correct answer is C. Minoans
The (A) Aztec and (D) Mayans were tribes in Mexico and Central America. (B) The Inca were South American. The Minoans were an early civilization but not from the Americas.

19. **An ancient Indian civilization known for its worship of the dead was the:** *(Rigorous) (Skill 1.2g)*

   A. Mayans
   B. Atacamas
   C. Incas
   D. Tarapacas

The correct answer is C. Incas
The Incas of Peru were an ancient civilization that practiced the worship of the dead.

20. **The belief that man was rationale and capable of creative thought was a philosophy of:** *(Rigorous) (Skill 1.2k)*

    A. Rousseau
    B. Immanuel Kant
    C. Montesquieu
    D. John Locke

The correct answer is B. Immanuel Kant
Immanuel Kant (1724–1804) was the German metaphysician and philosopher, who believed in the rationality of man and believed that man was capable of creative thought.

21. **Which one of the following did not contribute to the early medieval European civilization?** *(Rigorous) (Skill 1.2b)*

    A. The heritage from the classical cultures
    B. The Christian religion
    C. The influence of the German Barbarians
    D. The spread of ideas through trade and commerce

The correct answer is D. The spread of ideas through trade and commerce
The heritage of the classical cultures such as Greece, the Christian religion which became dominant, and the influence of the Germanic Barbarians (Visigoths, Saxons, Ostrogoths, Vandals and Franks) were all contributions to early medieval Europe and its plunge into feudalism. During this period, lives were often difficult and lived out on one single manor, with very little travel or spread of ideas through trade or commerce. Civilization seems to have halted progress during these years.

22. **All of the following are accomplishments of the Renaissance except:** *(Average) (Skill 1.2i)*

    A. Invention of the printing press
    B. A rekindling of interest in the learning of classical Greece & Rome
    C. Growth in literature, philosophy, and art
    D. Better military tactics

The correct answer is D. Better military tactics
The Renaissance in Western Europe produced many important achievements that helped push immense progress among European civilization. Some of the most important developments during the Renaissance were Gutenberg's invention of the printing press in Germany and a reexamination of the ideas and philosophies of classical Greece and Rome that helped Renaissance thinkers to approach more modern ideas. Also important during the Renaissance was the growth in literature (Petrarch, Boccaccio, Erasmus), philosophy (Machiavelli, More, Bacon) and art (Van Eyck, Giotto, da Vinci). Therefore, improved military tactics is the only possible answer as it was clearly not a characteristic of the Renaissance in Western Europe.

23. **Who is the most important figure in the spread of Protestantism across Switzerland?** *(Average) (Skill 1.2j)*

    A. Calvin
    B. Zwingli
    C. Munzer
    D. Leyden

The correct answer is A. Calvin
Huldreich Zwingli (1484–1531) was the first to spread the Protestant Reformation in Switzerland around 1519, but it was John Calvin (1509–1564), whose less radical approach to Protestantism who really made the most impact in Switzerland. Calvin's ideas separated from the Lutherans over the "Lord's Supper" debate over the sacrament, and his branch of Protestantism became Calvinism. Thomas Munzer (1489–1525) was a German Protestant reformer whose radical and revolutionary ideas about God's will to overthrow the ruling classes and his siding with the peasantry got him beheaded. Munzer has since been studied and admired by Marxists for his views on class. Leyden (or Leiden) was a founder of the University of Leyden, a Protestant place for study in the Netherlands.

24. **What was China's last imperial ruling dynasty who made an outstanding impression on Western nations?**
(Rigorous) (Skill 1.2h)

  A. Ming
  B. Manchu
  C. Han
  D. Chou

The correct answer is B. Manchu
The (A) Ming Dynasty lasted from 1368 to1644 and was among the more successful dynasties but focused attention towards foreign trade and encouraged growth in the arts. Therefore, it was the (B) Manchu Dynasty, the last imperial ruling dynasty, which came to power in the 1600s and expanded China's power in Asia greatly that was and still is considered to be among the most important, most stable, and most successful of the Chinese dynasties. The (C) Han and (D) Chou Dynasties were part of the "ancient" dynasties of China and while important in Chinese history, their influence was not as great as the Manchu.

25. **The ideas and innovations of the period of the Renaissance were spread throughout Europe mainly by:** *(Average) (Skill 1.2i)*

  A. Extensive exploration
  B. Craft workers and their guilds
  C. The invention of the printing press
  D. Increased travel and trade

The correct answer is C. The invention of the printing press
The ideas and innovations of the Renaissance were spread throughout Europe for a number of reasons. While exploration, increased travel, and spread of craft may have aided the spread of the Renaissance to small degrees, nothing was as important to the spread of ideas as Gutenberg's invention of the printing press in Germany.

26.   India's greatest ruler is considered to be: *(Rigorous) (Skill 1.2h)*

  A. Akbar
  B. Asoka
  C. Babur
  D. Jahan

The correct answer is A. Akbar
Akbar (1556–1605) is considered to be India's greatest ruler. He combined a drive for conquest with a magnetic personality and went so far as to invent his own religion, Dinillahi, a combination of Islam, Christianity, Zoroastrianism, and Hinduism. Asoka (273 BCE–232 BCE) was also an important ruler as he was the first to bring together a fully united India. Babur (1483–1540) was both considered to be a failure as he struggled to maintain any power early in his reign, but later to be somewhat successful in his quest to reunite Northern India. Jahan's (1592–1666) rule of India is considered to be the golden age of art and literature in the region.

27.   Who is the "father of anatomy"? *(Rigorous) (Skill 1.2i)*

  A. Vesalius
  B. Servetus
  C. Galen
  D. Harvey

The correct answer is A. Vesalius
Andreas Vesalius (1514–1564) is considered to be the "father of anatomy" as a result of his revolutionary work on the human anatomy based on dissections of human cadavers. Prior to Vesalius, men such as Galen had done work in the field of anatomy, but they had based the majority of their work on animal studies.

28.   The changing focus during the Renaissance when artists and scholars were less concerned with religion but centered their efforts on a better understanding of people and the world was called: *(Average) (Skill 1.2i)*

    A. Realism
    B. Humanism
    C. Individualism
    D. Intellectualism

The correct answer is B. Humanism
Realism is a medieval philosophy that contemplated independence of existence of the body, the mind, and God. The idea of individualism is usually either a reference to an economic or political theory. Intellectualism is the placing of great importance and devotion to the exploring of the intellect. Therefore, the changing focus during the Renaissance when artists and scholars were less concerned with religion but centered their efforts on a better understanding of people and the world was called humanism.

29.   Which of the following is not an important legacy of the Byzantine Empire? *(Rigorous) (Skill 1.2b)*

    A. It protected Western Europe from various attacks from the East by such groups as the Persians, Ottoman Turks, and Barbarians
    B. It played a part in preserving the literature, philosophy, and language of ancient Greece
    C. Its military organization was the foundation for modern armies
    D. It kept the legal traditions of Roman government, collecting and organizing many ancient Roman laws.

The correct answer is C. Its military organization was the foundation for modern armies
Although regarded as having a strong infantry, cavalry, and engineering corps along with excellent morale amongst its soldiers, the Byzantine Empire is not particularly considered a foundation for modern armies.

30.   **Studies in astronomy, skills in mapping, and other contributions to geographic knowledge came from:** *(Rigorous) (Skill 1.2i)*

      A. Galileo
      B. Columbus
      C. Eratosthenes
      D. Ptolemy

The correct answer is D. Ptolemy
Ptolemy (2nd century AD) was important in the fields of astronomy and geography. His theory stated that the earth was the center of the universe and all the other planets rotated around it, a theory that was later proven false. Ptolemy, however, was important for his contributions to the fields of mapping, mathematics, and geography. Galileo (1564–1642) was also important in the field of astronomy but did not make the mapping and geographic contributions of Ptolemy. He invented and used the world's first telescope and advanced Copernicus' theory that the earth revolved around the sun, much to the dismay of the Church.

31.   **The major force in eighteenth and nineteenth century politics was:** *(Average) (Skill 1.3e)*

      A. Nationalism
      B. Revolution
      C. War
      D. Diplomacy

The correct answer is A. Nationalism
Nationalism was the driving force in politics in the eighteenth and nineteenth century. Groups of people that shared common traits and characteristics wanted their own government and countries. This led to some revolution, war and the failure of diplomacy.

32.   **The Age of Exploration begun in the 1400s was led by:** *(Average) (Skill 1.3a)*

      A. The Portuguese
      B. The Spanish
      C. The English
      D. The Dutch

The correct answer is A. The Portuguese
Although the Age of Exploration had many important players among them, it was the Portuguese who sent the first explorers to around the Cape of Good Hope and to Asia.

33. **The English explorer who gave England its claim to North America was:** *(Average) (Skill 1.3a)*

    A. Raleigh
    B. Hawkins
    C. Drake
    D. Cabot

The correct answer is D. Cabot

Sir Walter Raleigh (1554–1618) was an English explorer and navigator, who was sent to the New World in search of riches. He founded the lost colony at Roanoke, Virginia. Sir John Hawkins (1532–1595) and Sir Francis Drake (1540–1596) were both navigators who worked in the slave trade and commanded ships against the Spanish Armada in 1588. John Cabot (1450–1498) was the English explorer who gave England claim to North America.

34. **Marxism believes which two groups are in continual conflict:** *(Rigorous) (Skill 1.3i)*

    A. Farmers and landowners
    B. Kings and the nobility
    C. Workers and owners
    D. Structure and superstructure

The correct answer is C. Workers and owners

Marxism believes that the workers and owners are in continual conflict. Marxists refer to these two groups as the proletariat and the bourgeoisie. The proletariat is exploited by the bourgeoisie and will, according to Marxism, rise up over the bourgeoisie in class warfare in an effort to end private control over the means of production.

35.   **Which of the following would is not a result of World War II?** *(Average) (Skill 1.3j)*

    A. Economic depressions and slow resumption of trade and financial aid
    B. Western Europe was no longer the center of world power
    C. The beginnings of new power struggles not only in Europe but in Asia, as well
    D. Territorial and boundary changes for many nations, especially in Europe

The correct answer is A. Economic depressions and slow resumption of trade and financial aid
Following World War II, the economy was vibrant and flourished from the stimulant of war and an increased dependence of the world on United States industries. Answers B, C and D are events that did happen as a result of World War II.

36.   **The first European to see Florida and sail along its coast was:** *(Rigorous) (Skill 1.3a)*

    A. Cabot
    B. Columbus
    C. Ponce de Leon
    D. Narvaez

The correct answer is C. Ponce de Leon
(A) John Cabot (1450–1498) was the English explorer who gave England claim to North America and the first European to see Florida and sail along its coast. (B) Columbus (1451–1506) was sent by the Spanish to the New World and has received false credit for "discovering America" in 1492, although he did open up the New World to European expansion, exploitation, and Christianity. (C) Ponce de Leon (1460–1521), the Spanish explorer, was the first European to actually land on Florida. (D) Panfilo de Narvaez (1470–1528) was also a Spanish conquistador, but he was sent to Mexico to force Cortes into submission. He failed and was captured.

37. **A political philosophy supporting rapid social changes in order to correct social and economic inequalities is called:** *(Average) (Skill 1.3e)*

    A. Nationalism
    B. Liberalism
    C. Conservatism
    D. Federalism

The correct answer is B. Liberalism
A political philosophy favoring rapid social changes in order to correct social and economic inequalities is called Liberalism. Liberalism was a theory that could be said to have started with the great French philosophers Montesquieu (1689–1755) and Rousseau (1712–1778).

38. **The results of the Renaissance, Enlightenment, Commercial and the Industrial Revolutions were more unfortunate for the people of:** *(Average) (Skill 1.3c)*

    A. Asia
    B. Latin America
    C. Africa
    D. Middle East

The correct answer is C. Africa
The results of the Renaissance, Enlightenment, Commercial and Industrial Revolutions quite beneficial for many people. New ideas of humanism, religious tolerance, and secularism were spread. Increased trade and manufacturing were surging economies in much of the world. The people of Africa, however, suffered during these times as they were largely left out of the developments. Also, the people of Africa were stolen, traded, and sold into slavery to provide a cheap labor force for the growing industries of Europe and the New World.

39.   **Colonial expansion by Western European powers in the 18th and 19th centuries was due primarily to:** *(Average) (Skill 1.3d)*

    A. Building and opening the Suez Canal
    B. The Industrial Revolution
    C. Marked improvements in transportation
    D. Complete independence of all the Americas and loss of   European domination and influence

The correct answer is B. The Industrial Revolution
Colonial expansion by Western European powers in the late eighteenth and nineteenth centuries was due primarily to the Industrial Revolution in Great Britain that spread across Europe and needed new natural resources and therefore, new locations from which to extract the raw materials needed to feed the new industries.

40.   **Which of the following is not a reason why Europeans came to the New World?** *(Average) (Skill 1.3)*

    A. To find resources in order to increase wealth
    B. To establish trade
    C. To increase a ruler's power and importance
    D. To spread Christianity

The correct answer is B. To establish trade
The Europeans came to the New World for a number of reasons; often they came to find new natural resources to extract for manufacturing. The Portuguese, Spanish and English were sent over to increase the monarch's power and spread influences such as religion (Christianity) and culture. Therefore, the only reason given that Europeans didn't come to the New World was to establish trade.

41.   **The only colony not founded and settled for religious, political, or business reasons was:** *(Average) (Skill 2.1c)*

    A. Delaware
    B. Virginia
    C. Georgia
    D. New York

The correct answer is C. Georgia
Georgia was started as a place for debtors from English prisons.

42. **What country did not have a colonial stake in America?**
     (Easy) (Skills 2.1b & 3.1b)

     A. France
     B. Spain
     C. Mexico
     D. China

The correct answer is D. China
(A) France, (B) Spain and (C) Mexico all had colonies in America. The country that didn't was (D) China.

43. **The year 1619 was memorable for the colony of Virginia. Three important events occurred. Which of the following was not one of the events?**
     (Rigorous) (Skill 2.1c)

     A. Twenty African slaves arrived.
     B. The London Company granted the colony a charter making it independent.
     C. The colonists were given the right by the London Company to govern themselves through representative government in the Virginia House of Burgesses.
     D. The London Company sent to the colony 60 women who quickly established families in the colony.

The correct answer is B. The London Company granted the colony a charter making it independent.
In the year 1619, the Southern colony of Virginia had an eventful year including the first arrival of twenty African slaves, the right to self-governance through representative government in the Virginia House of Burgesses (their own legislative body), and the arrival of sixty women sent to marry and establish families in the colony. The London Company did not, however, grant the colony a charter in 1619.

44.   The foundation of modern democracy is embodied in the ideas of:
       (Rigorous) (Skill 2.2a)

       A. St. Thomas Aquinas
       B. Rousseau
       C. John Locke
       D. Montesquieu

The correct answer is C. John Locke
(A) It was St. Thomas Aquinas (1225–1274) who merged Aristotelian ideas with Christianity, who helped lay the ideas of modern constitutionalism and the limiting of government by law. (B) Rousseau (1712–1778) and (D) Montesquieu (1689–1755) were political philosophers who explored the idea of what has come to be known as liberalism. They believed the interconnectedness of economics, geography, climate and psychology could be made to improve life. (C) John Locke (1632–1704), whose book *Two Treatises of Government* has long been considered a founding document on the rights of people to rebel against an unjust government, was an important figure in the founding of the U.S. Constitution and on general politics of the American colonies. Locke is the one who laid the basis for modern democracy.

45.   France decided in 1777 to help the American colonies in their war against Britain. This decision was based on:
       (Rigorous) (Skill 2.2a)

       A. The naval victory of John Paul Jones over the British ship "Serapis"
       B. The survival of the terrible winter at Valley Forge
       C. The success of colonial guerilla fighters in the South
       D. The defeat of the British at Saratoga

The correct answer is D. The defeat of the British at Saratoga
The defeat of the British at Saratoga was the overwhelming factor in the Franco-American alliance of 1777 that helped the American colonies defeat the British. Some historians believe that without the Franco-American alliance, the American Colonies would not have been able to defeat the British and American would have remained a British colony.

46. **The source of authority for national, state, and local governments in the United States is:** *(Average) (Skill 2.2a)*

   A. The will of the people
   B. The United States Constitution
   C. Written laws
   D. The Bill of Rights

The correct answer is A. The will of the people
The source of authority for national, state, and local governments in the United States is the will of the people. Although the United States Constitution, the Bill of Rights, and the other written laws of the land are important guidelines for authority, they may ultimately be altered or changed by the will of the people.

47. **Under the Constitution, the most urgent of the many problems facing the new federal government was:** *(Easy) (Skills 2.2 a & b)*

   A. Maintaining a strong army and navy
   B. Establishing a strong foreign policy
   C. Raising money to pay salaries and war debts
   D. Setting up courts, passing federal laws, and providing for law enforcement officers

The correct answer is C. Raising money to pay salaries and war debts
However, the most important and pressing issue was how to raise money to pay salaries and war debts from the Revolutionary War. Alexander Hamilton (1755–1804), Secretary of the Treasury, proposed increased tariffs and taxes on products such as liquor. This money would be used to pay off war debts and to pay for internal programs.

48. **The principle of popular sovereignty, allowing people in any territory to make their own decision concerning slavery, was stated by:** *(Rigorous) (Skill 2.3h)*

   A. Henry Clay
   B. Daniel Webster
   C. John C. Calhoun
   D. Stephen A. Douglas

The correct answer is D. Stephen A. Douglas
(A) Henry Clay and (B) Daniel Webster were prominent Whigs whose main concern was keeping the United States one nation. They opposed Andrew Jackson and his Democratic party around the 1830s in favor of promoting what Clay called "the American System". (C) John C. Calhoun served as Vice-President under John Quincy Adams and Andrew Jackson, and then as a Senator from South Carolina. He was pro-slavery and a champion of states' rights. The principle of popular sovereignty, in which people in each territory could make their own decisions concerning slavery, was the doctrine of (D) Stephen A. Douglas. Douglas was looking for a middle ground between the abolitionists of the North and the pro-slavery Democrats of the South. However, as the polarization of pro- and anti-slavery sentiments grew, he lost the presidential election to Republican Abraham Lincoln, who later abolished slavery.

49. **As a result of the Missouri Compromise:** *(Rigorous) (Skill 2.3h)*

   A. Slavery was not allowed in the Louisiana Purchase
   B. The Louisiana Purchase was nullified
   C. Louisiana separated from the Union
   D. The Embargo Act was repealed

The correct answer is A. Slavery was not allowed in the Louisiana Purchase
The Missouri Compromise was the agreement that eventually allowed Missouri to enter the Union. It did not nullify (B) the Louisiana Purchase or repeal (D) the Embargo Act and did not (C) separate Louisiana from the Union. (A) As a result of the Missouri Compromise slavery was specifically banned north of the boundary 36° 30'.

50. **Pre-Civil War American policy did not include:** *(Easy) (Skill 2.3c)*

   A. Isolationism
   B. Imperialism
   C. Nationalism
   D. No entangling alliances

The correct answer is B. Imperialism

(A) Isolationism, (C) nationalism and (D) a practice of no entangling alliances characterized pre-Civil War practices. (B) Imperialism, or the establishment of colonies, was not a policy of the United States.

51. **Leaders in the movement for woman's rights have included all but:** *(Rigorous) (Skill 2.3i)*

   A. Elizabeth Cady Stanton
   B. Lucretia Borgia
   C. Susan B. Anthony
   D. Lucretia Mott

The correct answer is B. Lucretia Borgia

The only name not associated with the woman's rights movement is Lucretia Borgia. The others were all pioneers in the movement with Susan B. Anthony and Elizabeth Cady Stanton being the founders of the National Woman Suffrage Association in 1869.

52. **The Federalists:** *(Rigorous) (Skill 2.3a)*

   A. Favored state's rights
   B. Favored a weak central government
   C. Favored a strong federal government
   D. Supported the British

The correct answer is C. Favored a strong federal government

The Federalists were opposed to (A) state's rights and a (B) weak federal government. (D) Most of them opposed the British. (C) The Federalists favored a strong federal government.

53.   **The belief that the United States should control all of North America is called:** *(Easy) (Skill 2.3c)*

    A. Westward Expansion
    B. Pan Americanism
    C. Manifest Destiny
    D. Nationalism

The correct answer is C. Manifest Destiny
The belief that the United States should control all of North America was called (B) Manifest Destiny. This idea fueled much of the violence and aggression towards those already occupying the lands such as the Native Americans. Manifest Destiny was driven by sentiments of (D) nationalism and gave rise to (A) westward expansion.

54.   **The battle in the West that sealed the South's defeat was the day after Gettysburg at:** *(Average) (Skill 2.4c)*

    A. Perryville
    B. Vicksburg
    C. Stones River
    D. Shiloh

The correct answer is B. Vicksburg
The Battle of Vicksburg was crucial in reinforcing the North's victory and sealing the South's defeat for a couple of reasons. First, the Battle of Vicksburg gave the Union full control of the Mississippi River. More importantly, the battle split the Confederate Army and allowed General Grant to reach his goal of restoring commerce to the important northwest area.

55. **The Radical Republicans who pushed harsh Reconstruction measures through Congress after Lincoln's death lost public and moderate Republican support when they went too far:** *(Rigorous) (Skill 2.4d)*

   A. In their efforts to impeach the President
   B. By dividing ten southern states into military-controlled districts
   C. By making the ten southern states give freed African-Americans the right to vote
   D. Sending carpetbaggers into the South to build up support for Congressional legislation

The correct answer is A. In their efforts to impeach the President
Public support was drawn towards the more radical end of the Republican spectrum following Lincoln's death. Because many felt as though Andrew Johnson's policies towards the South were too soft and ran the risk of rebuilding the old system of white power and slavery. Even moderate Republicans in the North felt it essential to rebuild the South but with the understanding that they must abide by the Fourteenth and Fifteenth Amendment assuring Blacks freedom and the right to vote. The radical Republicans were so frustrated that the President would make concessions to the old Southerners that they attempted to convict him after they impeached him. This turned back the support that they had received from the public and from moderates.

56. **Jim Crow refers to:** *(Average) (Skill 2.4f)*

   A. Equality
   B. Labor Movement
   C. Racism
   D. Free trade

The correct answer is C. Racism
(C) Jim Crow is a term used to describe the policies of racism and discrimination. It has nothing to do with the (B) labor movement or (D) free trade and is the opposite of (A) the concept of equality.

57. **The Union had many strengths over the Confederacy. Which was not a strength?** *(Easy) (Skill 2.4b)*

   A. Railroads
   B. Industry
   C. Slaves
   D. Manpower

The correct answer is C. Slaves
At the time of the Civil War, the South was mostly a plantation economy based on using slaves. The industry, railroads and manpower were located in the North, which made transportation and weapons easier for the North to obtain and use than the South.

58. **It can be reasonably stated that the change in the United States from primarily an agricultural country to an industrial power was due to all of the following except:** *(Rigorous) (Skill 2.4d)*

   A. Tariffs on foreign imports
   B. Millions of hardworking immigrants
   C. An increase in technological developments
   D. The change from steam to electricity for powering industrial machinery

The correct answer is A. Tariffs on foreign imports
The only reason given that really had little effect was the tariffs on foreign imports.

59. **The post-Civil War years were a time of low public morality, graft, and dishonesty. Which one of the reasons listed would not be accurate?** *(Rigorous) (Skill 2.5a)*

   A. The war itself because of the money and materials needed to carry on war
   B. The very rapid growth of industry and big business after the war
   C. The personal example set by President Grant
   D. Unscrupulous heads of large impersonal corporations

The correct answer is C. The personal example set by President Grant
The post-Civil War years were a particularly difficult time for the nation and public morale was especially low. The war had plunged the country into debt and ultimately into a recession by the 1890s. Racism was rampant throughout the South and the North where freed Blacks were taking jobs for low wages. The rapid growth of industry and big business caused a polarization of rich and poor, workers and owners. Many people moved into the urban centers to find work in the new industrial sector, jobs were typically low-wage, long hours, with poor working conditions. The heads of large impersonal corporations were arrogant in treating their workers inhumanely and letting morale drop to a record low. The heads of corporations showed their greed and malice towards the workingman by trying to prevent and disband labor unions.

60. **What was the impact of industrialization on the United States?** *(Easy) (Skill 2.5e)*

   A. Decrease in population
   B. Fewer jobs
   C. Better transportation system
   D. Decline in Infrastructure

The correct answer is C. Better transportation system
(A) Industrial resulted in more jobs which actually resulted in an increase in the population and people moved to where the jobs were. (B) Industrialization created jobs and more output. The income earned from the jobs gave people the money to purchase the increased output which in turn created more jobs. (D) Industrialization represented an increase in the infrastructure as new factories were built. (C) One of the aspects of industrialization was a better transportation system as railroads came into being.

61.   In the United States, federal investigations into deceptive business activities are handled by the: *(Average) (Skill 2.5c)*

    A. Department of Treasury
    B. Security and Exchange Commission
    C. Government Accounting Office
    D. Federal Trade Commission

The correct answer is D. Federal Trade Commission
The Department of Treasury (A), established in 1789, is an executive government agency that is responsible for advising the president on fiscal policy. There is no Government Accounting Office. The Federal Trade Commission (FTC) handles federal investigations into business activities. The establishment of the FTC in 1915 as an independent government agency was done to assure fair and free competition among businesses.

62.   What was the turning point that led to the U.S. becoming a world power?
    (Rigorous) (Skill 2.6a)

    A. World War I
    B. Expansion of business and trade overseas
    C. The Spanish-American War
    D. The construction of the Panama Canal

The correct answer is C. The Spanish-American War
The turning point marking the beginning of the United States becoming a super power was the Spanish-American War. This was seen as an extension of the Monroe doctrine, calling for United States dominance in the Western Hemisphere and removal of European powers in the region. The United States' relatively easy defeat of Spain marked the beginning of a continuing era of dominance for the United States. Spain's easy defeat at the hands of the United States in Cuba, the Philippines, and elsewhere showed the strength of the United States across the globe.

63.   **During the 1920s, the United States almost stopped all immigration. One of the reasons was:** *(Rigorous) (Skill 2.7c)*

A. Plentiful cheap, unskilled labor was no longer needed by industrialists
B. War debts from World War I made it difficult to render financial assistance
C. European nations were reluctant to allow people to leave since there was a need to rebuild populations and economic stability
D. The United States did not become a member of the League of Nations

The correct answer is A. Plentiful cheap, unskilled labor was no longer needed by industrialists
The primary reason that the United States almost stopped all immigration during the 1920s was because the much needed, cheap, unskilled labor were no longer needed. This has much to do with the increased use of machines to do the work once done by cheap, unskilled laborers.

64.   **The term Red Scare refers to:** *(Average) (Skill 2.7a)*

A. The Halloween holiday
B. The fear of communists
C. Sun Spots
D. Labor strikes

The correct answer is B. The fear of communists
(B) Communists were known as Reds so the term Red Scare referred to a fear of Communists in the government.

65.   **Drought is a problem in Africa and other places because:** *(Average) (Skill 2.8b)*

A. There is flooding
B. The rivers change course
C. People flock to see the drought
D. The dried-out soil turns to dust and cannot grow food

The correct answer is D. The dried-out soil turns to dust and cannot grow food
Since a drought is a period of dryness and a lack of rain, there (A) is no flooding and (B) the rivers do not change course especially since most of them are dry. (C) People may go to the drought but that does not cause the drought. (D) drought is accompanied by famine since the soil cannot grow food.

66. **Which of the following contributed to the severity of the Great Depression in California?** *(Rigorous) (Skill 2.8b)*

   A. An influx of Chinese immigrants.
   B. The dust bowl drove people out of the cities.
   C. An influx of Mexican immigrants.
   D. An influx of Oakies.

The correct answer is D. An influx of Oakies

The answer is "An influx of Oakies" (D). The Dust Bowl of the Great Plains destroyed agriculture in the area. People living in the plains areas lost their livelihood and many lost their homes in the great dust storms that resulted from a period of extended drought. People from all of the states affected by the Dust Bowl made their way to California in search of a better life. Because the majority of the people were from Oklahoma, they were all referred to as "Oakies." These migrants brought with them their distinctive plains culture. The great influx of people seeking jobs exacerbated the effects of the Great Depression in California.

67. **The international organization established to work for world peace at the end of the Second World War is the:** *(Average) (Skill 2.9d)*

   A. League of Nations
   B. United Federation of Nations
   C. United Nations
   D. United World League

The correct answer is C. United Nations

The international organization established to work for world peace at the end of the Second World War was the United Nations. The United Nations continues to be a major player in world affairs today.

68. **Which country was not a part of the Axis in World War II?** *(Easy) (Skill 2.9b)*

   A. Germany
   B. Italy
   C. Japan
   D. United States

The correct answer is D. United States

(A) Germany, (B) Italy and (C) Japan were the member of the Axis in World War II. (D) The United States was a member of the Allies which opposed the Axis.

69. **What was the major cause of both World Wars?** *(Average) (Skill 2.9a)*

    A. Extreme nationalism
    B. Military buildup and aggression
    C. Political unrest
    D. Agreements and alliances

The correct answer is A. Extreme nationalism
Although military buildup and aggression, political unrest, and agreements and alliances were all characteristic of the world climate before and during World War I and World War II, the most significant cause of both wars was extreme nationalism. Nationalism is the idea that the interests and needs of a particular nation are of the utmost importance. The nationalism that sparked WWI included a rejection of German, Austro-Hungarian, and Ottoman imperialism by Serbs, Slavs and others culminating in the assassination of Archduke Ferdinand by a Serb nationalist in 1914. Following WWI and the Treaty of Versailles, many Germans and others in the Central Alliance Nations, were disaffected by the concessions and reparations of the treaty started a new form of nationalism. Adolf Hitler and the Nazi regime led this extreme nationalism. Hitler's ideas were an example of extreme, oppressive nationalism combined with political, social and economic scapegoating and was the primary cause of WWII.

70. **After World War II, the United States:** *(Average) (Skill 2.10b)*

    A. Limited its involvement in European affairs
    B. Shifted foreign policy emphasis from Europe to Asia
    C. Passed significant legislation pertaining to aid to farmers and tariffs on imports
    D. Entered the greatest period of economic growth in its history

The correct answer is D. Entered the greatest period of economic growth in its history
After World War II, the United States did not limit or shift its involvement in European affairs. In fact, it escalated the Cold War with the Soviet Union at a swift pace and attempted to contain Communism to prevent its spread across Europe. There was no significant legislation pertaining to aid to farmers and tariffs on imports. In fact, since World War II, trade has become more liberal than ever. After World War II the United States was the only major economy left standing. This allowed for decades of economic superiority for the United States.

71. **A significant change in immigration policy occurred after World War II when the United States:** *(Average) (Skill 2.10a)*

A. Eliminated restrictions
B. Prevented Japanese immigration
C. Imposed policies based on ethnicity and country of origin
D. Banned immigration

The correct answer is C. Imposed policies based on ethnicity and country of origin
(A) The policies that changed after the war did not include the elimination of restrictions. (B) Japanese immigration was not prevented and (D) immigration itself was not banned. (C) Policies were aimed at allowable limits based on ethnicity and country of origin.

72. **Which country was a Cold War foe?** *(Easy) (Skill 2.11a)*

A. Russia
B. Brazil
C. Canada
D. Argentina

The correct answer is A. Russia
(B) Brazil and (D) Argentina are in South America and (C) Canada is in North America. (A) Russia is the country that was a Cold War superpower and foe of the United States.

73. **Which of the following did not occur after World War II?** *(Easy) (Skill 2.11b)*

A. Monroe Doctrine
B. Marshall Plan
C. Warsaw Pact
D. North Atlantic Treaty Organization

The correct answer is A. Monroe Doctrine
(B) The Marshall Plan provided funds for the reconstruction of Europe after World War II. (C) The Warsaw Pact and (D) NATO were both organizations that came into being for defense purposes. The Warsaw Pact was for the defense of Eastern Europe and NATO was for the defense of Western Europe. (A) The Monroe Doctrine was a nineteenth century theory in which the United States was committed to defend all countries in the hemisphere.

74. **Which of the following is not a name associated with the Civil Rights movement?** *(Rigorous) (Skill 2.12a)*

A. Rosa Parks
B. Emmett Till
C. Tom Dewey
D. Martin Luther King, Jr.

The correct answer is C. Tom Dewey
(A) Rosa Parks was a black lady who wouldn't move to the back of the bus. (B) Emmett Till was the civil rights worked who was killed. (C) Martin Luther King, Jr. was a Civil Rights leader. (C) Tom Dewey was never involved in the Civil Rights movement but was a candidate for President.

75. **During the period of Spanish colonialism in California, which of the following was not a key to the goal of exploiting the native people?** *(Rigorous) (Skill 3.1b)*

A. Missions
B. Ranchos
C. Presidios
D. Pueblos

The correct answer is B. Ranchos
The answer is "Ranchos" (b). The goal of Spanish colonialism was to exploit, transform and include the native people of California. The Spanish empire gathered the native people into communities where they could both be taught Spanish culture and be converted to Roman Catholicism. The social institution by which this was accomplished was the encouragement of the Mission System, which established a number of Catholic missions a day's journey apart. Once the native people were brought to the missions, they were incorporated into a mission society and indoctrinated in the teachings of Catholicism. The Presidios were fortresses that were constructed to protect Spanish interests from invaders. The Pueblos were small civilian communities that attracted settlers with the gift of land, seed, and farming equipment. The function of the Pueblos was to produce food for the missions and for the presidios.

76. **Native communities in early California are commonly divided into several cultural areas. How many cultural areas?**
   (Rigorous) (Skill 3.1a)

   A. 4
   B. 5
   C. 6
   D. 7

The correct answer is C. 6
The answer is 6 (C). Due to the great diversity of the native communities, the state is generally divided into six culture areas. The culture areas are (1) the Southern Culture Area, (2) the Central Culture Area, (3) the Northwestern Culture Area, (4) the Northeastern Culture Area, (5) the Great Basin Culture Area, and (6) the Colorado River Culture Area. These areas are geographically distinct and supported different sorts of cultures.

77. **From about 1870 to 1900, the last settlement of the American the West was completed. One attraction for settlers was free land but it would have been to no avail without:**
   (Easy) (Skill 3.2b)

   A. Better farming methods and technology
   B. Surveying to set boundaries
   C. Immigrants and others to see new lands
   D. The railroad to get them there

The correct answer is D. The railroad to get them there
From about 1870 to 1900, the settlement of the American West was made possible by the building of the railroad. Without the railroad, the settlers never could have traveled such distances in an efficient manner.

78.   Historians state that the West helped to speed up the Industrial Revolution. Which of the following statements was not a reason for this? *(Rigorous) (Skill 3.2a)*

   A. Food supplies for the ever-increasing urban populations came from farms in the West.
   B. A tremendous supply of gold and silver from western mines provided the capital needed to build industries.
   C. Descendants of western settlers, educated as engineers, geologists, and metallurgists in the East, returned to the West to mine the mineral resources needed for industry.
   D. Iron, copper, and other minerals from western mines were important resources in manufacturing products.

The correct answer is C. Descendants of western settlers, educated as engineers, geologists, and metallurgists in the East, returned to the West to mine the mineral resources needed for industry.
The West helped to speed up the Industrial Revolution in a number of important and significant ways. First, the land yielded crops for the growing urban populations. Second, the gold and silver supplies coming out of the Western mines provided the capital needed to build industries. Also, resources such as iron and copper were extracted from the mines in the West and provided natural resources for manufacturing. The descendants of western settlers typically didn't become educated and then returned to the West as miners. The miners were typically working class with little or no education.

79.   What event sparked a great migration of people from all over the world to California? *(Rigorous) (Skill 3.2a)*

   A. The birth of Labor Unions
   B. California statehood
   C. The invention of the automobile
   D. The gold rush

The correct answer is D. The gold rush
The discovery of gold in California created a lust for gold that quickly brought immigrants from the eastern United States and many parts of the world. To be sure, there were struggles and conflicts, as well as the rise of nativism. Yet this vast migration of people from all parts of the world began the process that has created California's uniquely diverse culture.

80. **Which of the following shows a difference between the California and U.S. Constitutions?** *(Rigorous) (Skill 3.2c)*

   A. The governor of California has the line-item veto
   B. In California representation in both houses of the legislature is based on population
   C. The Governor and Lt. Governor are elected jointly
   D. The equivalent of cabinet positions are elected rather than appointed.

The correct answer is A. The governor of California has the line-item veto.
The line-item veto is a policy that permits the governor to veto individual items that are part of a piece of legislation without nullifying the entire piece of legislation. Congress approved a line-item veto for the president, but the Supreme Court ruled that unconstitutional.

81. **The United States legislature is bi-cameral, this means:** *(Average) (Skill 3.2c)*

   A. It consists of several houses
   B. It consists of two houses
   C. The Vice-President is in charge of the legislature when in session
   D. It has an upper house and a lower house

The correct answer is B. It consists of two houses
The bi-cameral nature of the United States legislature means that it has two houses, the Senate and the House of Representatives that make up the Congress. The Vice-President is part of the Executive branch of government but presides over the Senate and may act as a tiebreaker. An upper and lower house would also be parts of a Parliamentary system of government such as the governments of Great Britain and Israel.

82. **Who applied Locke's principles to the American situation?**
(Rigorous) (Skill 4.1a)

A. Thomas Paine
B. Samuel Adams
C. Benjamin Franklin
D. Thomas Jefferson

The correct answer is D. Thomas Jefferson It was Thomas Jefferson who took the ideals and principles of John Locke and applied them to the writing of the Declaration of Independence.

83. **Which of the four statements below is not a description of the Constitution?**
(Rigorous) (Skill 4.1c)

A. The establishment of a strong central government in no way lessened or weakened the individual states
B. Individual rights were protected and secured
C. The Constitution demands unquestioned respect and subservience to the federal government by all states and citizens
D. Its flexibility and adaptation to change gives it a sense of timelessness

The correct answer is C. The Constitution demands unquestioned respect and subservience to the federal government by all states and citizens. (A) The authors of the Constitution clearly stated that the establishment of a strong central government in no way lessened or weakened the individual states. (B) The Bill of Rights protects individual citizens. (D) Possibly the most important feature of the Constitution is the amendment process that allows us to change the Constitution when necessary.

Therefore, the only statement made that doesn't describe some facet of the Constitution is "The Constitution demands unquestioned respect and subservience to the federal government by all states and citizens." On the contrary, the Constitution made sure that citizens could critique and make changes to their government and encourages such critiques and changes as necessary for the preservation of democracy.

84. **Of the thirteen English colonies, the greatest degree of religious freedom was found in:** *(Easy) (Skill 4.2a)*

   A. Maryland
   B. Rhode Island
   C. Pennsylvania
   D. Delaware

The correct answer is B. Rhode Island
Roger Williams, founder of Providence and Rhode Island, had objected to the Massachusetts colonial seizure of Indian lands and settlements and the relationship between these seizures and the Church of England. Williams was banished from Massachusetts and set up Rhode Island as the first colony with a true separation of church and state.

85. **The Pilgrims came to America to:** *(Average) (Skill 4.2a)*

   A. Drill for oil
   B. Be the official representatives of the king
   C. Take over the East India Company
   D. Flee religious persecution

The correct answer is D. Flee religious persecution
The Pilgrims and others suffered religious persecution and because of this came to America.

86. **The Constitution can:** *(Easy) (Skill 4.3d)*

   A. Never be changed
   B. Be rewritten
   C. Be discarded
   D. Be amended

The correct answer is D. Be amended
The Constitution is the law of the land. As such, it cannot be discarded. It can be changed officially through the amendment process.

87.   In the United States, power or control over public education, marriage, and divorce is: *(Average) (Skill 4.3e)*

    A. Implied or suggested
    B. Concurrent or shared
    C. Delegated or expressed
    D. Reserved to the states

The correct answer is D. Reserved to the states
In the United States government, power or control over public education, marriage, and divorce is reserved to the states.

88.   In the United States, the power of coining money is: *(Rigorous) (Skill 4.3a)*

    A. Implied or suggested
    B. Concurrent or shared
    C. Delegated or expressed
    D. Reserved to the states

The correct answer is C. Delegated or expressed
In the United States, the power of coining money is delegated or expressed. Therefore, only the United States government may coin money. The states may not coin money for themselves.

89.   Which is not a branch of the federal government? *(Easy) (Skill 4.3a)*

    A. Popular
    B. Legislative
    C. Executive
    D. Judicial

The correct answer is A. Popular
The three branches of government are the (B) legislative, (C) executive and (D) judicial branches. Each has its own distinct functions and duties. There is no such branch as the (A) popular.

90. **In the United States government, the power of taxation and borrowing is:** *(Average) (Skill 4.3a)*

   A. Implied or suggested
   B. Concurrent or shared
   C. Delegated or expressed
   D. Reserved to the states

The correct answer is B. Concurrent or shared

In the United States government, the power of taxation is concurrent or shared with the states. An example of this is the separation of state and federal income tax and the separate filings of tax returns for each.

91. **The term that best describes how the Supreme Court can block unconstitutional laws is:**
   (Average) (Skill 4.4b)

   A. Jurisprudence
   B. Judicial Review
   C. Exclusionary Rule
   D. Right of Petition

The correct answer is B. Judicial Review

(A) Jurisprudence is the study of the development and origin of law. (B) Judicial review is the term that best describes how the Supreme Court can block laws that they deem as unconstitutional as set forth in *Marbury vs Madison*. The (C) exclusionary rule is a reference to the Fourth Amendment of the Constitution and says that evidence gathered in an illegal manner or search must be thrown out and excluded from evidence. There is nothing called the (D) Right of Petition, however the Petition of Right is a reference to a statement of civil liberties sent by the English Parliament to Charles I in 1628.

92. **What Supreme Court ruling dealt with the issue of civil rights?**
    (Rigorous) (Skill 4.4c)

    A. Jefferson v. Madison
    B. Lincoln v. Douglas
    C. Dred Scott v. Sanford
    D. Marbury vs Madison

The correct answer is C. Dred Scott v. Sanford
Marbury v. Madison established the principal of judicial review. The Supreme Court ruled that it held no authority in making the decision (regarding Marbury's commission as Justice of the Peace in District of Columbia) as the Supreme Court's jurisdiction (or lack thereof) in the case, was conflicted with Article III of the Constitution. (C) The Dred Scot case is the well-known civil rights case that had to do with the rights of the slave.

93. **Marbury v. Madison (1803) is an important Supreme Court case which set the precedent for:** ***(Average) (Skill 4.4b)***

    A. The elastic clause
    B. Judicial review
    C. The supreme law of the land
    D. Popular sovereignty in the territories

The correct answer is B. Judicial review
Marbury v. Madison (1803) is an important case for the Supreme Court as it established judicial review (B). In that case, the Supreme Court set precedence to declare laws passed by Congress as unconstitutional. Popular sovereignty (D) in the territories was a failed plan pushed by Stephen Davis to allow states to decide the slavery question for themselves. The supreme law of the land (C) is the Constitution. (A) The elastic clause refers to the "necessary and proper" clause of the U.S. Constitution that permits Congress to pass laws that are "necessary and proper" even though the specific type of law may not be listed in the Constitution.

94. **The Electoral College:** ***(Average) (Skill 4.5c)***

    A. Elects the Senate but not the House
    B. Elects the House but not the Senate
    C. Elects both the House and Senate
    D. Elects the President

The correct answer is D. Elects the President
The Electoral College only exists to cast votes for the President of the United States. Senators or Representatives are elected by majority vote of the people from the respective states.

95. **Which one of the following is not a responsibility of political parties?** *(Easy) (Skill 4.5a)*

    A. Conducting elections or the voting process
    B. Obtaining funds needed for election campaigns
    C. Choosing candidates to run for public office
    D. Making voters aware of issues and other public affairs information

The correct answer is A. Conducting elections or the voting process
The U.S. political parties have numerous functions and responsibilities. Among them are obtaining funds needed for election campaigns, choosing the candidates to run for office, and making voters aware of the issues. The political parties, however, do not conduct elections or the voting process, as that would be an obvious conflict of interest.

96. **On the spectrum of American politics the label that most accurately describes voters to the "right of center" is:** *(Average) (Skill 4.5d)*

    A. Moderates
    B. Liberals
    C. Conservatives
    D. Socialists

The correct answer is C. Conservatives
(A) Moderates are considered voters who teeter on the line of political centrality or drift slightly to the left or right. (B) Liberals are voters who stand on the left of center. (C) Conservative voters are those who are "right of center." (D) Socialists would land far to the left on the political spectrum of America.

97. **The study of the exercise of power and political behavior in human society today would be conducted by experts in:** *(Easy) (Skill 4.6b)*

    A. History
    B. Sociology
    C. Political Science
    D. Anthropology

The correct answer is C. Political Science
Experts in the field of political science today would likely conduct the study of exercise of power and political behavior in human society.

98. **When referring to government, who said: "the good of the many outweighs the good of the few and also of the one"?** *(Rigorous) (Skill 4.6b)*

   A. Plato
   B. Aristotle
   C. Cicero
   D. Gaius

The correct answer is B. Aristotle
Aristotle is the one who wrote the quote. It showed his true insight as one of the great political and social commentators and philosophers of all time.

99. **Whose philosophy describes the function of government as to provide for the people's welfare?** *(Rigorous) (Skill 4.6B)*

   A. Aristotle
   B. John Locke
   C. Plato
   D. Thomas Hobbes

The correct answer is A. Aristotle
(D) Thomas Hobbes (1588–1679) wrote the important work *Leviathan* in which he pointed out that people are by all means selfish, individualistic animals that will always look out for themselves and therefore, the state must combat this nature desire. (B) John Locke (1632–1704) whose book *Two Treatises of Government* has long been considered a founding document on the rights of people to rebel against an unjust government was an important figure in the founding of the U.S. Constitution and on general politics of the American Colonies. Aristotle's (384–322 BCE) contribution to theories of government included the idea that government exists to benefit the populace.

100. **The significance of a free press does not include which of the following:** *(Average) (Skill 4.7a)*

   A. Providing information
   B. Reporting illegal actions
   C. Libel
   D. Reporting in a responsible and civic-minded manner

The correct answer is C. Libel
(A) Providing information is definitely one of the functions of a free press as well as (B) reporting on illegal actions of others and (D) acting in a professional and responsible civic-minded manner. (C) Libel, or the publication of false and damaging information is not one of those functions.

101. **A political system in which there is a one-party state, centralized control, and a repressive police system with private ownership is called:** *(Average) (Skill 4.8a)*

   A. Communism
   B. Fascism
   C. Socialism
   D. Constitutional Monarchy

The correct answer is B. Fascism
(A) Communism and (C) Socialism both are based on the public ownership of the means of production. (D) A constitutional monarchy would have private ownership. (B) Fascism is the only form of government that has all of the characteristics mentioned in the statement.

102. **The "wall of separation between church and state' came from:** *(Rigorous) (Skill 4.9a)*

   A. Aristotle
   B. Alexander Hamilton
   C. Thomas Jefferson
   D. Thomas Paine

The correct answer is C. Thomas Jefferson
Thomas Jefferson is the author of the above quote which expresses one of the founding beliefs of America.

103. **The study of ways in which different societies deal with the problems of limited resources and unlimited needs is in the area of:** *(Easy) (Skill 5.1a)*

   A. Economics
   B. Sociology
   C. Anthropology
   D. Political Science

The correct answer is A. Economics
The study of the ways in which different societies deal with the problems of limited resources and unlimited needs is a study of Economics. Economists consider the law of supply and demand as fundamental to the study of the economy.

104. **A planned economy functions on the basis of:** *(Rigorous) (Skill 5.1d)*

   A. Public ownership
   B. Private ownership
   C. Stockholder control
   D. An elected management board

The correct answer is A. Public ownership
(B) Private owner ship is a facet of capitalism and (C) stockholder control and (D) elected management board are parts of private ownership. (A) Public ownership is a part of a planned economy.

105. **Potential customers for any product or service are not only called consumers but can also be called:** *(Easy) (Skill 5.2a)*

   A. Resources
   B. Bases
   C. Commodities
   D. Markets

The correct answer is D. Markets
Potential customers for any product or service are not only customers but can also be called markets. A resource is a source of wealth; natural resources are the basis for manufacturing goods and services. A commodity is anything that is bought or sold, any product.

106. **In a market economy, markets function on the basis of:** *(Rigorous) (Skill 5.2a)*

   A. Government control
   B. Manipulation
   C. Supply and demand
   D. Planning

The correct answer is C. Supply and Demand
(A) Government control is not a manifestation of the functioning of free markets since government interferes with the operating mechanism of the market. (B) Manipulation refers to the interfering with the price-quantity adjustment mechanism that prevents markets from operating efficiently. (D) Planning is a mechanism that replaces the market. (C) Supply and demand describes the basis for the adjustment mechanism which is how free markets function.

107.   Competition leads to: *(Rigorous) (Skill 5.2c)*

   A. Fights
   B. Waste
   C. Overproduction
   D. Efficient use of resources

The correct answer is D. Efficient use of resources
Competition is the basis for the functioning of markets. It may cause disagreements among market participants but it does not lead to (B) waste or (C) overproduction since competition results in (D) the efficient use of resources.

108.   The economic system promoting individual ownership of land, capital, and businesses with minimal governmental regulations is called: *(Average) (Skill 5.2h)*

   A. Macro-economy
   B. Micro-economy
   C. Laissez-faire
   D. Free enterprise or market economy

The correct answer is D. Free Enterprise or market economy
(D) Free enterprise, market economy, is the economic system that promotes private ownership of land, capital, and business with minimal government interference. (C) Laissez-faire is the idea that an "invisible hand" (therefore no regulations) will guide the free enterprise system to the maximum potential efficiency.

109.   Which of the following is not a tool of monetary policy? *(Average) (Skill 5.3c)*

   A. Open market operations
   B. Changing the discount rate
   C. Changing the exchange rate
   D. Changing the reserve ratio

The correct answer is C. Changing the exchange rate
(A) Open Market Operations is the buying and selling of government securities and is a way of increasing or decreasing bank reserves. (B) The discount rate is the rate of interest banks pay to borrow from the Federal Reserve System. (D) The reserve ratio is the percentage of deposits that the bank must hold and can't make available for loans. (C) The exchange rate is determined in foreign exchange markets and is not a tool of monetary policy.

110. **The idea that increasing government spending will end depressions is:** *(Average) (Skill 5.3a)*

    A. The basis of modern economics
    B. Called Classical economics
    C. Known as federalism
    D. Called isolationism

The correct answer is A. The basis of modern economics
John Maynard Keynes (1883–1946) advocated an economic system in which government regulations and spending on public works would stimulate the economy and lead to full employment. This broke from the classical idea that free markets would lead to full employment and prosperity. Keynes was a firm believer in capitalism, but in a less classical sense than Adam Smith (1723–1790), whose *Wealth of Nations* advocated for little or no government interference in the economy.

111. **Programs such as Medicaid and Food Stamps are administered by:** *(Easy) (Skill 5.3a)*

    A. Federal government
    B. Local government
    C. State government
    D. Communal government

The correct answer is C. State Government
Assistance programs, such as Medicaid and Food Stamps are funded by the federal government but are administered by the state governments.

112. **Unions were founded on the basis of the beliefs of:** *(Average) (Skill 5.4a)*

    A. Thomas Robert Malthus
    B. John Stuart Mill
    C. Samuel Gompers
    D. John Maynard Keynes

The correct answer is C. Samuel Gompers
(A) Thomas Malthus was a British economist who introduced the study of population and early on considered famine, war, and disease to be the primary checks on world population. (B) John Stuart Mill was a progressive British philosopher and economist. Mill advocated for political and social reforms, including emancipation for women, labor organizations, and farming cooperatives. (D) John Maynard Keynes was also an important economist. He advocated an economic system in which government regulations and spending on public works would stimulate the economy and lead to full employment. (C) Samuel Gompers was a labor leader whose beliefs of practical business unionism formed the basis for the modern labor union.

113. **The American labor union movement started gaining new momentum:** *(Average) (Skill 5.4a)*

    A. During the building of the railroads
    B. After 1865, with the growth of cities
    C. With the rise of industrial giants such as Carnegie and Vanderbilt
    D. During the war years of 1861–1865

The correct answer is B. After 1865, with the growth of cities
The American Labor Union movement began in the late eighteenth and early nineteenth centuries. The Labor movement began to first experience persecution by employers in the early 1800s. The American Labor Movement remained relatively ineffective until after the Civil War. In 1866, the National Labor Union was formed, pushing such issues as the eight-hour workday and new policies of immigration. This gave rise to the Knights of Labor and eventually the American Federation of Labor (AFL) in the 1890s and the Industrial Workers of the World (1905). Therefore, it was the period following the Civil War that empowered the labor movement in terms of numbers, militancy, and effectiveness.

114. **Gross Domestic Product is:** *(Average) (Skill 5.5a)*

    A. A measure of nation's output
    B. A well-known social indicator
    C. A measure of well being
    D. A measure of a nation's trade

The correct answer is A. A measure of nation's output
The Gross Domestic Product cannot be used as a (B) social indicator or a (C) measure of well-being. (D) It contains information about trade but goes much further in that it is (A) a measure of a nation's output. Since it doesn't say anything about hours worked or hours of leisure, it can't be used as a measure of well-being.

115. **One method of trade restriction used by some nations is:** *(Average) (Skill 5.6b)*

    A. Limited treaties
    B. Floating exchange rate
    C. Bill of exchange
    D. Import quotas

The correct answer is D. Import quotas
An import quota regulates the amount of imported goods in an effort to protect domestic enterprise and limit foreign competition. The United States imposes import quotas to protect domestic industries.

116. **The doctrine of comparative advantage explains:** *(Average) (Skill 5.6a)*

    A. Why nations trade
    B. How to fight a war
    C. Time zones
    D. Political divisions

The correct answer is A. Why nations trade
The principle of comparative advantage is the basis for the theory of international trade and says that nations engage in trade with other nations when they can produce the good at a comparatively lower price than the other nation can.

117.   **Which one of the following does not affect climate?**
        (Rigorous) (Skill 6.1a)

        A. Elevation and altitude
        B. Ocean currents
        C. Latitude
        D. Longitude

The correct answer is D. Longitude
Latitude is the primary influence of earth's climate as it determines the climatic region in which an area lies. Elevation or altitude and ocean currents are considered to be secondary influences on climate. Longitude is considered to have no important influence over climate.

118.   **Geography was first studied in an organized manner by the:**
        (Rigorous) (Skill 6.1)

        A. Egyptians
        B. Greeks
        C. Romans
        D. Arabs

The correct answer is B. Greeks
The Greeks were the first to study geography, possibly because of the difficulties they faced as a result of geographic conditions. Greece had difficulty as their steep, treacherous, mountainous terrain made it difficult for the city-states to unite. As the Greeks studied their geography, it became possible to defeat more powerful armies on their home turf, such as the great victory over the Persians at Marathon.

119.   **Meridians, or lines of longitude, not only help in pinpointing locations, but are also used for:** *(Average) (Skill 6.1b)*

        A. Measuring distance from the Poles
        B. Determining direction of ocean currents
        C. Determining the time around the world
        D. Measuring distance from the Equator

The correct answer is C. Determining the time around the world
Meridians, or lines of longitude, are the determining factor in separating time zones around the world.

120. A famous canal is the: *(Easy) (Skill 6.1a)*

A. Pacific Canal
B. Arctic Canal
C. Panama Canal
D. Atlantic Canal

The correct answer is C. Panama Canal
(C) The only canal is the selection of answers is the Panama Canal. The Pacific, Artic and Atlantic are oceans, not canals.

121. In which of the following disciplines would the study of physical mapping, modern or ancient, and the plotting of points and boundaries be least useful? *(Easy) (Skill 6.1a)*

A. Sociology
B. Geography
C. Archaeology
D. History

The correct answer is A. Sociology
In geography, archaeology, and history, the study of maps and plotting of points and boundaries is very important as all three of these disciplines hold value in understanding the spatial relations and regional characteristics of people and places. Sociology, however, mostly focuses on the social interactions of people and while location is important, the physical location is not as important as the social location such as the differences between studying people in groups or as individuals.

122. The Study of "spatial relationships and interaction" would be done by people in the field of: *(Easy) (Skill 6.1)*

A. Political Science
B. Anthropology
C. Geography
D. Sociology

The correct answer is C. Geography
Geography is the discipline within Social Science that most concerns itself with the study of "spatial relationships and interaction."

123. **The study of how living organisms interact is called:** *(Average) (Skill 6.2a)*

    A. Ecology
    B. Sociology
    C. Anthropology
    D. Political Science

The correct answer is A. Ecology
(B) Sociology is the study of human society and usually consists of surveys, controlled experiments, and field studies. (C) Anthropology is the study of human culture. (D) Political science is the study of political life including justice, freedom, power and equality in a variety of methods. (A) Ecology is a study of the interaction of living organisms.

124. **Which of the following is an organization or alliance for defense purposes?** *(Average) (Skill 6.2d)*

    A. North Atlantic Treaty Organization
    B. The Common Market
    C. The European Union
    D. North American Free Trade Association

The correct answer is A. North Atlantic Treaty Organization
(B) The Common Market, (C) The European Union and (D) the North American Free Trade Organization are all forms of economic integration and are in place to promote free trade and factor mobility. (D) The North Atlantic Treaty Organization, NATO, is the organization that provides for the defense of Europe.

125. **What term does not describe a settlement in the physical and cultural sense?** *(Average) (Skill 6.3A)*

    A. Climate
    B. Religion
    C. Shared values
    D. Shared language

The correct answer is A. Climate
(B) Religion, (C) shared values and (D) shared language are common factors of a settlement. People settle where they have something in common with the other people. (A) Climate is a part of the environment and science and not a shared trait of a settlement.

CPSIA information can be obtained
at www.ICGtesting.com
Printed in the USA
BVHW010911160419
545655BV00014B/589/P